Cultural Revolutions

Cultural Revolutions

Everyday Life and Politics in Britain, North America, and France

Leora Auslander

University of California Press
Berkeley   Los Angeles

University of California Press, one of the most distinguished university presses in the United States, enriches lives around the world by advancing scholarship in the humanities, social sciences, and natural sciences. Its activities are supported by the UC Press Foundation and by philanthropic contributions from individuals and institutions. For more information, visit www.ucpress.edu.

University of California Press
Berkeley and Los Angeles, California

First published in the United Kingdom in 2009 by Berg, an imprint of Oxford International Publishers Ltd. Please visit www.bergpublishers.com

Auslander, Leora.
 Cultural revolutions : everyday life and politics in Britain, North America, and France / Leora Auslander.
  p.   cm.
 Includes bibliographical references and index.
 ISBN 978-0-520-25920-1 (cloth : alk. paper)
 ISBN 978-0-520-25921-8 (pbk. : alk. paper)
 1. Politics and culture—Great Britain—History—17th century.   2. Politics and culture—United States—History—18th century.   3. Politics and culture—France—History—18th century.   4. Revolutions—Great Britain—History—17th century.   5. Great Britain—Politics and government—1603–1714.
6. Revolutions—United States—18th century.   7. United States—Politics and government—1775–1783.   8. Revolutions—France—History—18th century.
9. France—Politics and government—1789–1799.   I. Title.

DA435.A87   2009
306.209'033—dc22   2008040721

Manufactured in the United Kingdom

18   17   16   15   14   13   12   11   10   09
10   9   8   7   6   5   4   3   2   1

For Tom

Contents

Illustrations

Acknowledgements

This book has been long in the making and I have accumulated many debts along the way. I'd like, first of all, to thank a number of colleagues who assisted in this project long ago, when they were still graduate students at Chicago. Without the research assistance of Robert Beachy, Elisa Camiscioli, Matthew Lindsay, Stephanie Whitlock and, particularly, Elizabeth Heath, this book would never have seen the light of day. Mike Wakeford did a spectacular job as a teaching assistant in a course I did on the topic. Both he and the students in that course provided vital enthusiasm and insights. Emily Lord Fransee greatly assisted the last push towards publication. I am deeply grateful to all of them.

Julia Coyne Allen's work as administrative assistant in the Center for Gender Studies, where I wrote the first draft of this book, made that writing possible.

Lynn Hunt, Sheryl Kroen, Eric Slauter and Marty Ward have all commented on parts of the manuscript or related work. Their comments were most helpful. I am equally grateful to Katie Scott and Dror Wahrman for commissioning articles that advanced my thinking on material culture. And, although I have not much discussed this book in particular with him, Alf Lüdtke has been a consistent source of support and inspiration in thinking about the politics of the everyday. Colleagues in the History Department and elsewhere at the University of Chicago have created an atmosphere in which projects, like this one, that break out of disciplinary moulds are accepted; I am very grateful for that. Finally, I would like to express my profound gratitude to Linda Kerber and the anonymous reader for the University of California Press, both of whom provided crucially helpful comments.

Presentations at conferences at Indiana University, Northwestern University, the University of Virginia, and the American Antiquarian Society provided terrific contexts to refine and test some of the ideas in this book, while a Burkhardt fellowship from the ACLS and support from the Social Sciences Division at the University of Chicago provided vital time. Several editors at Berg have patiently awaited the long-delayed delivery of the manuscript; I'm grateful for their continued confidence.

Much of the book was written in the village of Villerville on the Norman coast, where, thanks to Jacqueline Feldman, I have now finished one book and written the bulk of another. Françoise Basch's apartment in Paris provided a home for the work at another crucial stage, and for that I also offer thanks. Michelle Zancarini-Fournel has pressed me to strengthen the gender argument, has been resourceful and absolutely determined in her quest for the book to come out in French, and has simply encouraged its getting done. My debt to her is very great.

My daughter Shoshana has been patient and accepting of the time spent on this and other work, but it is for her impatience and her zing and joy in life that I most particularly give thanks. My mother is a mathematician but also a very gifted needlewoman; many of the thoughts here about women's creativity and political engagement come from her.

Finally, this book is dedicated to Tom Holt. Tom has read this manuscript more times than he cares to remember, and supplied the appropriate doses of critique and encouragement. He has been extraordinarily generous with his historical wisdom and time.

–1–

The First Cultural Revolutions

For most readers, no doubt, "cultural revolution" evokes the Chinese Communists' moment of brutal and radical experiment in political and social transformation. The phrase is likely therefore to bring to mind images of revolutionary excess, totalitarianism, and a regressive rupture in the foundational modern divide between public and private life. Such images are unfortunate, for they obscure the centrality of the problem of culture to the three revolutions – the English, American and French – often credited with ushering the Western world into modernity, particularly into liberal, republican, and democratic forms of governance.[1] In each, radical cultural transformations emerged as instruments of political revolution, and together they challenge us to rethink the place of culture and emotion in the political.[2] Notwithstanding some superb historical research on the mobilization of culture during the French and Russian revolutions as well as on political culture and the politics of culture in the early modern world, the concept of "cultural revolution" itself – which implies a complex relation between such political transformations, culture, and emotions – has attracted little attention.[3]

Such a rethinking is necessary, I would argue, if we are to recognize that political commitment is not simply a matter of rational calculation or even disinterested thought. Ernest Renan articulated as much in his famous essay suggesting that *sentiment*, "feelings," play a crucial role in creating national attachment.[4] One might extend that argument to citizens' allegiances to particular forms of governance. Certainly many of those engaged in these revolutions recognized that the political transformations they sought required not simply a change of mind but of heart. Citizens of these new national formations must be made to "feel" that republicanism, rather than monarchism, was the "right" political system. The solutions they arrived at varied with each historical context, but they all thought it necessary to address the problem. All also worried about the possible infringement on individual freedom and rights such a program might entail.[5]

The last decade has seen a resurgence in scholarly interest in the history of emotion, and in the relation between emotion and politics.[6] That interest has been spurred not only by an intellectual dissatisfaction with our current explanations for political mobilization and change but also by a sense of an urgent need to grasp better how our contemporaries arrive at their political judgments. That such political action and positioning is not only a matter of reason, but also of feeling, seems evident; *how* emotions matter, however, is still far from clear. It is a good moment, then, to return to the place of the mind and the heart, and particularly the latter, since it has been far less examined, in those founding revolutions.

As inhabitants of modern nation-states, we take for granted the presence and power of rituals, of monuments, of national celebrations. Everyone has had the conscious experience of being awed, moved, alienated, angered, or intimidated by state symbols and manifestations of state power: flags, military uniforms, parades, government buildings, national anthems. We may, however, be less aware of the influence of the quotidian incarnations of the state – coins, stamps, and street signs – on our sense of national belonging. Finally, we are most often virtually unconscious of the capacity of the nationally-inflected trivial objects and small gestures that shape our everyday lives – of proper names, of conventions for greeting and parting, of melodies of popular songs, of the organization and appearance of our dwellings and cities, of the food we eat, even how we dress, hold our bodies and walk – to make us feel at home in our polity and be comfortable with those with whom we share that space. Indeed, the semiotics of such cultural practices often only reveal themselves when one is *not* at home. Most of those who have traveled abroad have had the experience of being recognized as a foreigner or as a fellow national, all on the basis of gait, shoes, clothes or hairstyle.

Everyday rituals, holidays, material culture, and embodied practices not only serve to create loyalty to the state and a sense of national community but also cause us to identify with, or feel distant from, others with whom we share a national, but not a social or political, space. The work of scholars as diverse as Pierre Bourdieu, Mihaly Csikszentmihalyi, and Serge Tisseron has demonstrated that we tend to be drawn to those whose practices and tastes echo our own, and many of us have had the experience of pleasure (and perhaps reassurance) when we discover affinities for certain styles, certain food, or certain music in a new acquaintance whom we would like to know better, or, alternatively have our heart sink at the realization that someone whom we absolutely do not want to resemble shares our own taste in movies or furniture.[7] Quotidian habits and aesthetics are associated not only with social and national milieux, but also with politics. All but those living in the most homogeneous of worlds have, therefore, experienced the sensation of hopeless out-of-placeness when the manners learned in one social world or in one national context suddenly no longer work in a situation made foreign by class, by place, or by political position. That sentiment is sharpened by the knowledge that the error is most often beyond conscious repair.

Our recollections of such moments are more likely to produce a sense of uneasiness than intellectual insight, however. The idea that symbols, commodities, accents, and manners – the aesthetics of everyday life – could be crucially important in the constitution of national identities, or personal affinities or group consciousness may well run counter to our sense of what *really* matters. Many of us are taught in childhood to judge people not by their taste, not by their beauty, nor certainly by their clothes, but rather by what is inside them. We might say that taste, like beauty, is only on the surface, a coating over the real person. We might believe that we are tolerant of difference in everyday manners and of variations in taste, although our actions often belie that claim. In parallel, most of us act and speak as if we believed that the power of polities rests on armies and on Gross National Products, rather than on language policies, national monuments, or museums, or on the consumer goods their economies produce and their inhabitants purchase.

This commonplace contradiction is even more manifest in the conventions of historical analysis. Many people, despite the historical profession's at least half-century-long acceptance of the salience of other topics, think that what the past most fundamentally has to teach us lies in the history of battles, of political structures, or of great men and women, whether they be politicians, philosophers or painters. Some, persuaded by the work of social historians, might define History's domain somewhat differently, arguing for the salience of economic and social transformations like industrialization, demographic change, and the trade-union or women's movements; but their commitment to texts, events, and organizations is no less evident. Few think that the histories of clothing, of furniture, of song, of architecture, or of manners are of much weight.

Cultural Revolutions argues otherwise. I will demonstrate that the first three modern revolutions – the English, American, and French – also helped give the big and small symbols of state, the goods that furnish our everyday lives, the clothes that cover our bodies, the food we eat, as well as the songs and plays to which we turn for insight and distraction – the elements of our "culture" in other words – the particular importance they came to possess in nineteenth- and twentieth-century nation-states and societies.[8] "Culture" here is understood both in its humanistic sense and as it is often used in the discipline of anthropology. Conventionally, culture denotes aesthetics, embracing the decorative and fine arts, literature, architecture, music, and theater. For many anthropologists the term refers to the creation of meaning, and contains all of the ways members of a particular community (however defined) give sense and order to their individual lives and collective existences.[9] Thus, in this usage, modes of keeping time, measuring distance and weight, bodily comportment, foodways, and ritual practices are all part of culture.

In the early modern period, the nature of culture and the nature of politics, as well as the ways in which culture could be politicized, were transformed by expanding economies and challenges to the principles of divine right and absolute monarchy. Each moment of political turmoil also, therefore, brought with it a moment of rethinking of the relation between culture and politics. The question was first opened in the context of the mid-seventeenth-century English Civil War, and grew in intensity of reflection and action over the century that followed during the conflicts that led to the American War of Independence. Debate culminates in the French Revolution, when the necessity, possibility, and dangers of cultural revolution for modern nation-states became manifest. This book will demonstrate further that these revolutionary efforts to change material, visual, theatrical and musical culture, and in some cases, foodways, coinage, language and measurements as well, were not simply imposed by revolutionary thinkers and leaders, but generated by those who lived their politics more quietly.

Although these revolutions have not heretofore been analyzed together as "cultural revolutions," they have all, in one way or another, at one time or another, been considered to share another attribute – that of being "bourgeois."[10] Those who initially proposed the "bourgeois revolution" thesis argued it from the revolutionaries' relation to the means of production. They claimed to demonstrate that each revolution was led by men who had become wealthy through new industries, commerce, or the professions, and who sought political power commensurate with their wealth as well as a political regime that would serve their interests. The English and French revolutions were thus understood to be bourgeois in a double sense, first, of having been led by the bourgeoisie and, second, of having laid the foundations for a form of governance favorable to that class. Subsequent empirical research invalidated the finding that revolutionary leaders always shared a relation to the means of production – the traditional definition of class.[11] Both the nobility and the professional and commercial classes were internally divided and, as often as not, shared political positions across "class" lines. In the last two decades, however, the "bourgeois revolution" thesis has been revived in the French case by some scholars who now see a class created through *consumption and culture* rather than through *relation to the means of production*. They have argued that the development of a commercial culture and a non-courtly public sphere in the second half of the eighteenth century formed a group of people who read the same books, saw the same plays, wore the same clothes, and initiated the same fashions in interior decoration, thereby coming to constitute a self-conscious class capable of collective political action.[12] That claim has, in turn, been effectively countered by the historian Sarah Maza, who has shown that there is little evidence that those who purchased similar goods, who established similar lifestyles, and who frequented the same salons, coffee-houses and concerts either called themselves or *perceived themselves* to be bourgeois.[13] She has demonstrated, in other words, that there was not a pre-revolutionary self-conscious bourgeoisie constructed through shared consumption patterns, any more than there was a self-conscious bourgeoisie constructed through a shared relation to the means of production. The cumulated scholarship on the French eighteenth century has, however, definitively demonstrated the reality of economic and conceptual transformations and a political critique that enabled the coming into being of a lively and heterogeneous commercial and cultural public sphere beyond the court, a domain in which political contestation could be, and was, fostered.[14] It was not a space in which *one* vision of an alternative politics or culture emerged, but rather one whose power and limits lay precisely in its imaginative range and complex relation to the social and economic changes of the period.

The historiography of eighteenth-century North America has gone through a parallel series of re-interpretations, although given that the American Revolution was primarily a war of colonial independence, the focus here has been on national, rather than class, identity. Thus the historian T. H. Breen has argued that the American Revolution should be understood as a "consumer revolution," that is, that during the middle decades of the eighteenth century the colonists had come to share an identity through the goods they consumed.[15] The conflict was an expression of a pre-existing national identity constructed through a world of things and of cultural practices. This position, too, assumes rather than argues that people come to conscious group identification as a result of shared consumption patterns. Even were one to accept that assumption, a close study at the local and regional level demonstrates that people, despite the widespread availability of a range of imported British goods, experienced highly differentiated access to, and taste in, much of the stuff of everyday life.

In the chapters to follow I will argue that although consumer society had not developed in eighteenth-century colonial America or France to the point where firm self-identifications were generally rooted there, the accessibility of consumer goods, and the increasingly sophisticated advertising used to sell them, provided a new way of thinking about the place of objects in the production of social meaning and of the self. Those new notions – that *ordinary* people's possessions could carry symbolic and affective meaning and that people could be connected through shared style and taste – would provide essential grounding for revolutionary reflections on the place of material culture in political transformation. It is, in other words, evident that transformations in eighteenth-century commercial culture *were* crucial to the shape of the American and French revolutions, creating some of the conditions of possibility for what I have called "cultural revolution." To these economic and cultural changes must be added the influence of sensationalism, the philosophical school born in England in the late seventeenth century, elaborated in Scotland in the eighteenth, from whence it traveled to America and France.[16] Sensationalism convinced some of the power of the material, the embodied and the experiential to change people's minds and hearts. My underscoring of the importance of commercialization and sensationalist philosophy should not, of course, be read to diminish the crucial role of the more explicitly political visions that had emerged from Enlightened salons, coffeehouses and the press in this period. It is, rather, intended to remind readers of a less familiar, but equally crucial, set of eighteenth-century transformations.

Given that commercialism was less developed, the Enlightenment only nascent, and sensationalism not yet conceptualized, the role of material culture and the everyday were quite different in early- to mid-seventeenth-century England. No historian has attempted to revive the "bourgeois revolution" thesis for England, despite the fact that there is ample evidence for both new economic forms and an expansion in the quality and quantity of consumer goods (particularly food, semi-durables, and small durables) available on the market, as well as a lively commercial urban culture – particularly, but not only, in London.[17] The availability of new products – including starch, cheaper fabrics, tobacco, and coffee – and new and more elaborate sites of public entertainment, in conjunction with ubiquitous and heated debate on their faults and virtues, no doubt added to the challenges facing monarchical authority and the culture of the court. There is, however, little evidence that they created a self-conscious bourgeoisie. While some historians have claimed that seventeenth-century England was a consumer society, no one has claimed that consumption had political consequences at this early date.[18] The central and complex role of religion in the century's political upheaval further complicates any efforts at both class and economic analysis.

Although both the original and more recent arguments for the bourgeois revolution thesis on the grounds of shared consciousness derived either from relations to the means of production or shared consumption patterns and culture seem problematic, there is no doubt that the economies in the three polities experienced substantial transformations – with corresponding challenges to existing social and political systems – in the periods preceding each revolution. Those decades also saw a dramatic range of challenges to established intellectual, cultural and religious norms. In this context the fiscal crises that each government suffered would prove cataclysmic. The Crown's shortage of funds required, in the English and French cases, recourse to Parliament and the Estates General, respectively, each of which were called in the hopes that they would endorse a variety of moneymaking strategies. In each instance, the calling of these ostensibly representational bodies, in a matrix of social, economic, political, intellectual, cultural and religious change, had unforeseen consequences. Members of the English Parliament and of the French Third Estate used the occasion of their assemblage to protest both the irregularity of their political participation and other issues of concern to those who had previously been marginal to political power. In the case of the American Revolution – triggered by Parliament's imposition of new tax burdens – debate also focused on political representation, but in this case on the right of the colonies either to be represented in the British Parliament or not to be taxed by that body. In all three instances, the issue of political representation, and with it the question of who, in fact, constituted the political nation came quickly to center stage. And in each case non-royal, non-aristocratic actors claimed a new kind of political voice, claimed, in fact, to *be* the nation.

Those involved in all three revolutions inherited social and political systems in which culture played a fundamental and essential role in constituting and reproducing the political order. Kings, queens and the nobility commissioned musical compositions, had portraits painted, palaces built, furniture cast of solid silver, jewels crafted, and furs fashioned for reasons of state. These luxurious goods demonstrated the wealth of the Crown and the capital in the skill and talent of the artists and artisans at the court's disposition. The festivals, concerts, masques, operas and plays to which the nobility (and some gentry) as well as ambassadors sent by foreign rulers were invited, were both payment to those upon whom the

Crown ultimately depended for their loyalty and support, and displays of royal power. Monarchs tried, furthermore, through sumptuary legislation, to limit access to certain fabrics and furs to their dependants and clients, thereby granting those courtiers desired distinction and prestige. The Crown largely relied on this chain of patronage, from royalty to aristocracy, from aristocracy to notables, from notables to gentry and so on, but did also occasionally make its divine and paternal presence felt to a broader public through processions, fireworks displays, mass celebrations of coronations, royal birthdays, and other occasions, as well as through proclamations, printed portraiture, and in some cases coinage and other manifestations of the monarch's power.

Although the apogee of this system in France came during the second half of the seventeenth century under the reign of Louis XIV, the precocity of the English economy in combination with the Puritan critique of luxury brought potent challenges to it decades earlier in England. Sectors of commerce escaped from the Crown's control, sumptuary laws were not enforced, and the theatrical productions licensed by the Crown often took the freedom to criticize the very court that had given them the right to perform. In France, as well, the patronage system had intrinsic frailties; the granting of privileges, like the selling of offices (vastly increased under Louis XIV), momentarily increased the Crown's income, but ultimately undermined its power. By the time Louis XVI took office, the Crown had lost its monopoly on style and its control of the economy, while the British Crown's presence in its North American colonies had been diluted by the sheer distance from England, by the varied charters granted them upon their founding, and by the diversity of their populations. On the eve of revolution in all three nations, commercial expansion, increased availability of goods, and religious and economic critiques of luxury exposed the weaknesses and limits of this system of the royal cultivation of power through ostentatious display and symbolic performance. It remained, however, the normative form.

English, American and French revolutionaries had grown up within and were therefore familiar with this world in which culture and politics were deeply imbricated in ways appropriate to a monarchical regime, just as they were familiar with cultural productions that escaped or critiqued it. It is therefore not surprising that they all engaged, at different moments and in different ways, with the question of how to use culture in the making of radical political change. In all three revolutions discussed here, it was understood that not only was it necessary to transform the rules of governance, the structure of institutions, and the definition of the citizenry, but that the habits, routines, and décor – the culture in other words – of the new citizens' everyday lives had to be remade. Revolutionaries were convinced that in order to change their nation's form of political regime (and in the American case, create a nation) changes were also necessary in the appearance of furniture, clothing, and buildings, in the food one ate, in what holidays one celebrated and how they were fêted. In their efforts to make a culture appropriate to their vision of the polity, they melded repertoires they inherited from the world they were trying to leave with their new visions of that which they hoped to create. The inherited repertoires varied greatly with each of the three cases, but in all three it is to those broad cultural repertoires that one should look first to understand the revolutionary process.

Given the destruction of familiar vertical ties of loyalty and obligation, the revolutions' task, ultimately, was to forge new horizontal ties that could connect the citizenry and create a sense of national identity. The trajectory from the early efforts in that direction in the English Civil War to the more thorough projects of the American and French revolutions reflects, in part at least, how fully that task was understood and embraced. Making a shared culture was understood to enable the recognition among strangers essential for republican brotherhood (or for the Puritans, for a religious commonwealth).

It follows, then, that this is also a deeply gendered story. The scholarship of the last thirty years has established that a fundamental characteristic of modernity was the radical reconfiguration of the relation between state and family.[19] It was also a period characterized by the making of new kinds of divisions between the public and the private, between polity and society, between reason and emotion, between the universal and the particular, and between constraint in the interests of the public good and individual freedom. Much of the explanation for modernity's difficulty with women's participation in politics (banning them from even the vote in the otherwise most participatory polities for at least a century and often far more) is that women belonged to the second element in each of those binaries. The notion that women were emotional rather than rational, particular rather than universal, and belonged in the social and private realm rather than the political and public did not mean that they were irrelevant to the polity, however. Quite the contrary. Those involved in these three revolutionary moments argued forcefully that modern forms of governance and modern nation-states required "women's" qualities as much as "men's." Although women's supposedly essentially emotional character made them dangerous to the state, they made them essential to the nation. For transforming the heart as well as the mind, the home as well as the legislature, were as necessary to the difficult task of turning monarchists into republicans and subjects into citizens, as was creating new systems of governance and taxation. There was emotional as well as intellectual political work to be done, in other words, and that work was understood to fall within women's domain. Thus each revolution saw a moment when women's demand for full political participation had limited acceptance and as the politicization of the everyday intensified, each subsequently created a newly rigid division of labor in which men constructed the abstractness of the institutional state and women the concreteness of the cultural nation.

As will be shown in detail in later chapters, these revolutions that sought to replace the filial with the fraternal relation, divided the state from the nation, and the public from the private. In the process the gendering of the binaries of state/public and nation/private were reinforced. Rather than a hermaphroditic monarch, embodying both the state and the nation, the father and the mother (in which in England women could reign as queen, and in France wield tremendous power as regents) the state now consisted of a regicidal/patricidal band of brothers. That fraternity resolved both their struggle for control over women and the need for new affective ties to bind the state's inhabitants, now that the old filial ties were no more, by the allocation of the emotional labor of national identification to women, in the private, domestic sphere. As the political theorist Michael Walzer put it in his study of Puritanism and the English Civil War, "The activity of the Calvinist saints ... required recognition that ... the government was not a household, the state not an extended family, and the king not a loving father."[20] Again, this refiguring and gendering of the public and the private, and of the importance of women's emotional labor in creating national culture took its distinct course in each of the three revolutionary moments, but was common to all.

The shared vision, however, of a nation based on cultural likeness posed profound challenges to revolutionary ideals of individual freedom. There was, therefore, intense debate, especially in the American and French revolutions, about balancing individual liberty and collective solidarity, as well as private rights and public duties. The English Interregnum also saw fierce struggles over freedom, but in this case centered on religious freedom. These tensions sometimes resulted in rapid changes in policy, sometimes in incoherencies in practice, sometimes in unexpected spaces of creativity. The new governments tried to resolve these dilemmas through institutional means, and would eventually – although it took until nearly the end of the nineteenth century for these institutions to become firmly established – create museums, schools, and libraries designed to teach taste. They would simultaneously reinforce the critical role of wives and mothers as "nationals" who would instill national taste in their children from infancy as well as help sustain their husbands' loyalty to the nation and the polity.[21]

While thus far I have introduced the parallels in the three revolutionary moments as if they were each on independent trajectories, that image is, of course, over-simplified. Occupying crucial points in the Atlantic world, the three polities had extensive commercial, political, cultural, and intellectual interaction before, during and after their revolutionary moments. Thus, all three efforts to come to terms with the place of culture in revolutionary change were interconnected. Had the British Crown not been in intense rivalry with the French, monarchical culture in both realms would have looked very different. Had the British not been attempting to establish colonies in North America, the seventeenth century in the archipelago would have looked very different. Had American intellectuals not been actively engaged in the Enlightenment (both Scots and French), the terms in which the conflict between North America and Britain were debated and played out would have been very different. Had the Americans not declared themselves independent, French history, in turn, might have taken a different course. It is also interconnected at a more human level. Enslaved Africans traversed the Atlantic to work in North

America and through that labor influenced that society's cultural forms. Settlers from Britain, France, the German lands, and the Netherlands made new lives in North America, but retained ties on the other shore. Books, tea, china, fabric, mirrors and musical scores also moved across that body of water. This is fundamentally an "Atlantic" history, in the sense that it is a history made possible by the movement and interconnection of people, goods and ideas that that body of water enabled. It is also an Atlantic history in the sense that I have sought to grasp how those engaged in all three revolutions faced similar challenges, each from their own particular location, yet all acutely conscious of each other's.[22]

Cultural Revolutions is, however, as much a story of differences as it is of inter-actions, influences and of the making of "the" modern nation-state. Seventeenth-century England, mid-to-late eighteenth-century colonial North America, and late-eighteenth-century France were characterized by different economic, social, political and religious forms, and each of their revolutions had correspondingly different dynamics. The "English Revolution" is more usually called a Civil War, and the place of religion, the dynamics of the war, the Commonwealth, and the Protectorate, as well as the limited elaboration of consumer culture in mid-seventeenth-century England, all made its revolution of culture more a limited renunciation than a new creation. While rejecting many of the Stuarts' courtly forms, Parliament and the Protectorate invented few new ones. Masques, dancing, and many musical forms were banned, but no novel revolutionary styles replaced them. Clothing and food, and to some extent architecture, were radically simplified, but not reinvented.

The American Revolution was, first of all, a war of colonial independence, ultim-ately involving thirteen separate, highly individuated, colonies. In 1776 the North American colonies were united in their refusal of English rule, but they embraced populations of different national origin and religious belief and substantially different economic and political systems. The revolutionaries had, however, unlike the seventeenth-century English, the cultural vocabulary provided both by the diversity of the colonies' inhabitants and by the lively market in consumer goods of the late eighteenth century. The revolutionary period thus saw the simultaneous elaboration of a republican political form and a national cultural imaginary. American patriots rejected, for a time, English culture, rituals, and practices, but they also started the long and complicated process of creating and disseminating viable new ones.

The French Revolution, although destined to end with a return to an authoritarian form of governance, most vigorously assumed the task of revolutionary transformation and achieved the most elaborated version of a new republican culture. French revolutionaries built on the centralized state and conceptions of the relation of culture and politics they had inherited from the Old Regime, as well as Enlightened and other critiques and the emerging commercial culture, to develop a very complex and rich set of new cultural forms. Those included units of time, weights and measures, administrative boundaries within the nation, and architectural, theatrical and musical styles.

Ultimately, therefore, *Cultural Revolutions* is a story of changes over time and of mutual influences, rather than simply a series of case studies. Chapter 2 of this book will sketch how culture worked to constitute political power and to fashion identity in pre-revolutionary England and France and colonial America. The comparison will demonstrate that both political form and economic development crucially shaped people's relation to goods and other aspects of culture. Thus, although there was a powerful critique of luxury in both seventeenth-century England and eighteenth-century France, both the discourses and the practices of consumption were quite different in the English Civil War and Revolution than they would be in the French. In the American case, we see the use of goods and rituals both to differentiate and to unite the very diverse inhabitants of North America in the seventeenth and the early-to-mid eighteenth centuries. Chapter 3 explicates how the term "cultural revolution" may be usefully applied in an analysis of the English Civil War and Interregnum. This was a usage of culture saturated by radical Protestantism and constrained by a society in which goods had been extensively mobilized in the interests of monarchical power, but, although certainly present in the lives of those beyond the court, not yet imagined as a means of group identification. In Chapter 4 we turn to how culture was used by the soon-to-be-ex-colonists, and by the nascent Americans, in the war against England as well as in the early national period to forge a new nation. The next chapter focuses on the French Revolution, the revolution whose participants most thoroughly elaborated a new world of goods and everyday life to match their vision of a new polity. The combination of a rich semiotics of power from the Old Regime, the nature of the critique of existing forms of rule, and the expansion of the market, as well as the unfolding of the revolutionary process itself, powerfully shaped the possibilities for utopian visions. *Cultural Revolutions* concludes with an analysis of the legacies of these efforts to re-imagine the relation between culture and politics in nineteenth- and twentieth-century nation-states.

Narrating the English, American and French stories will help explain not only the different constructions of culture in these polities but also the very different conceptions of political representation they later adopted. Many of the similarities *and* differences among these three nation-states in their post-revolutionary modern forms are a result of how each reconfigured the relation of politics and culture in their revolutionary moments. In each case there was a substantial reworking of the boundaries between public and private, the political and the cultural, and a reshaping of the meaning of "representation"; but each took a quite different form. The results may still be observed. In France, to this day, the division between public and private is the most fiercely defended, and women's access to that most public of domains – formal politics – remains deeply problematic. The United States, by contrast, continues to be shaped by the revolutionary heritage of the politics of homespun in which domesticity and women played a key role. Perhaps as a result, there is a continuous history in that country of women's organizational and political work, a history more closely shared by Britain than France. Differences in the definition of representation also endure from the moment of revolutionary rupture. In France, politicians are elected to represent the nation as a whole, while in England, and even more dramatically in the United States, they are elected primarily to serve the interests of their local constituents in a national forum. The French Revolution correspondingly ushered in a politics of assimilation of all individuals and groups into a universal and homogeneous nation. The French were to share interests and share taste. Here, the English story again lies, in some sense, between the two extremes of the French vision of homogeneity and the American of unity through diversity. Finally, the American story sheds light on the particularly complex and contemporary task of constructing the symbolism of a national identity in a period following an independence won by force of arms from a colonizing power.

In writing such a book-length essay, intended to provoke further research on the relation of politics and emotion, on material culture, and on the concept of cultural revolution, I have relied upon, and am infinitely indebted to, the very rich scholarship on culture and politics in early modern Britain, North America and France. All authors dream that their books will be more than the sum of their parts; this is particularly true in this case. I have not scoured archives to find new documents, nor attics and flea-markets to bring forgotten material traces of these moments to light. I trust, instead, that my narrative accounts of the individual topics to follow will be familiar to scholars upon whose work I have relied, but that the *juxtaposition* of these three modern revolutions, a thinking-together by a non-specialist, may render the familiar strange, and the strange familiar. From that juxtaposition I hope the contribution of this book will emerge.[23]

Cultural Revolutions seeks to make a historical argument about the place of material culture, embodied practices and ritual in political transformation and political attachments. By focusing on these three revolutionary moments, I intend not only to illuminate new aspects of those historic events but also to offer a privileged space from which to examine the importance of material culture and everyday life to historical explanation. Revolutionary periods are by definition moments of radical critique of the political and social order. More conscious decisions are made, not just about objects, but about all aspects of the usually taken-for-granted practices and rituals of everyday life, during revolutions than at any other time. As we will see below, units of measurement, norms of musical composition, theatrical performances, place-names, calendars, mealtimes and festivals can suddenly assume new meanings, or at least have their old meanings questioned. These matters take on particular importance because politically active people are always a minority of the population. Revolutionaries are, therefore, inevitably faced with the problem of how to persuade, in the deepest sense of that word, their fellow inhabitants of the evils of the old order and the legitimacy of the new. Once the old order is toppled, they are faced with how to prevent backsliding and how to lodge new definitions of the polity and of the social order not only in people's minds, but in their hearts. These moments of radical critique of political form, located in periods of massive economic change, sparked rich discourses on taste and everyday life as well as on how material culture and ritual could be mobilized in service of revolution, of republicanism, and of the nation.

This book will, in other words, demonstrate that history can be made by objects, rituals and practices; that changes in culture are not just the unintended consequences of historical change that happens elsewhere, but rather can be a motor of change. It does this from a phenomenological standpoint that argues for the centrality of embodiedness – particularly the qualities of three-dimensionality, possession of five senses, and mortality – in human existence. As I have argued at greater length elsewhere, each of the five senses contributes its own form of knowledge and feeling.[24] The methodological implication of that observation for historical analysis is that material culture and ritual should be used as evidence, not simply as illustration of points established on the basis of written documents. It is worth remembering that most people for most of human history have not used written language as their major form of expression. They have communicated meaning through textiles, wood, metal, dance and music. What if we think about cultural objects and their attributed meanings as active agents in history? Both the printing press and the printed books it made possible, for example, did not just *reflect* a change in the world; by their capacity to transmit uniform knowledge relatively cheaply and durably throughout the world they *changed* that world. Likewise, the cotton gin and the calicoes it made possible, by changing people's relation to covering their bodies, by ultimately making variation in clothing, play in clothing – fashion in other words – available to large numbers of people, rather than to only a small elite, also changed the world. Small innovations in goods, their design or their aesthetic, also structure people's perceptions of the world and thereby change that world. The relations of colors in a rug, the detail of a design on the arm of a chair, the ways in which windows are dressed, because we use them day after day and because we cease to think about them consciously or even perhaps to perceive them, can change our imaginaries. Objects take on meaning within patterns of use, practices of everyday life, and ritual celebration. Like matters of taste, everyday life, and norms of musical composition or of theatrical performance are often invisible, yet they shape our sense of time, our conceptions of order and disorder, our understanding of space. Whether the music we listen to is polyphonous or has a single line, whether it relies mostly on the chorus or on soloists, may shape how we think about the relation between parts and the whole or individuals and the collective, or about the relation between dissonance and harmony. Whether actors inform the audience that they know and that they know the audience knows that this is *only* a play, or whether suspension of disbelief is maintained, may tell us something about how the relation between surface and inner being, between appearance and reality are understood. Street names, and decisions to keep or change them, the routes people follow as they traverse a city, the hours at which they eat their meals and what they eat, all can, because they shape people's lives, be profoundly informative.

The ultimate task of this book is to show *how* taste, social and cultural practices, and everyday life make history. Our problem is determining how these goods and practices mattered, because they did not always matter in the same way. Indeed, it is not objects alone that are the focus of discussion here. Objects take on meanings, and their capacity to effect historical change, through social relations. Objects are dreamed of, invented, produced, sold, bought, used, and destroyed by people. People are both free and constrained in their intervention into the lives of these objects. This approach enables us to grasp how and why objects do certain kinds of "work" at certain historical moments; that is, how people use objects. Revolutions offer especially clear windows on to that work.

Given the centrality of objects to this argument, and the obvious impossibility of bringing three-dimensional things into the reader's hands, the figures in this book are particularly important. They serve not merely as an illustration of a point resting on textual substantiation but are themselves crucial evidence. Consistent with the position that viewing an actual object even behind glass yields a very different kind of knowledge than does even the best two-dimensional representation, I have included many references to objects held in public museum collections. Flat, small images, generally either too matt or too glossy, often with the color wiped out or altered, convey only a very partial sense of an embroidery (which can be as small as a hand or as large as a wall). Reproductions make it difficult to imagine the weight of a coin and the feel of its embossed image on the palm or the heft of a teapot (even if viewing objects in display cases still, of course, poses challenges to the imagination). Figures in books also obscure the movement between the tiny stitches and the smooth fabric of a quilt, or the mark of the cabinetmaker's chisel on a drawer. Since those museums are, however, scattered across three continents, I have also provided references to the web-sites on which vivid color images of a vast array of material may easily be seen. In an age when paper is ever more expensive, it is to be hoped that the reader will find satisfying this combination of verbal description, two-dimensional representation, and a map to where the objects' virtual presence on the web may be found as well as to where the three-dimensional objects may be experienced in all their "thingness."

–2–

Ermine and Buckskins

Culture and Politics in Early Modern Courtly and Colonial Society

The Civil War that broke out in 1642 in Britain and the American and French revolutions of the late eighteenth century each brought a radical rupture in the political order and initiated a moment of questioning of the definition of the nation and of appropriate forms of rule. All three brought, at least briefly, the vision of vastly expanded participation in the political process. Re-imagining the boundaries of the political nation and the form of governance also involved reassessing the mechanisms of the consolidation and reproduction of legitimate power and collective identification. Consequently, the starting point for all revolutionaries was the existing power structures and their respective repertoires of political process and representation. This chapter describes those structures, networks, and repertoires in pre-revolutionary Britain, metropolitan France, and the thirteen North American colonies.

Although historians of both English and French Old Regime politics have debated the relative weights of patronage and bureaucracy in the two polities, it is clear that in both countries, monarchs *understood* their power to require systems of patronage, in which ostentatious display and demonstrations of cultural power were central.[1] To borrow the historian Roger Chartier's elegant formulation: "In a monarchy the sumptuousness of the court is a kind of rhetoric, intended to make a point, to persuade others of the king's power: first the court, then subjects. Monuments and rituals are emblems of public power – images that can be manipulated."[2] The situation of the North American colonies, despite being under monarchical rule, was quite different. While the contiguity in time and mutual influence between the American and French revolutions brought significant parallels, the distance between metropolitan and colonial regimes also brought many divergences between the English and French experiences, on the one hand, and the American, on the other. Both the differences and the similarities necessarily shaped the dynamics of the cultural politics of revolution.

The political cultures of seventeenth-century metropolitan England and eighteenth-century metropolitan France concerned contiguous territories inhabited by people most of whose parents and grandparents had also been born within the kingdom.[3] France's boundaries did shift (particularly in the Eastern part of the realm) in the seventeenth and early eighteenth centuries, but unification of the great bulk of the territory under the French Crown had occurred long before. The population of North America in the eighteenth century, and its relationship to the British Crown and government, present a stark contrast. The colonies were the product of an imperial project motivated by the goals of establishing a protected market for English manufactured goods, a reliable and cheap source of raw materials, an outlet for "surplus" population, and a pawn in the struggle for European power; all goals oriented toward the well-being of a metropole understood as distinct from those of the colonial possessions. This project involved, furthermore, the seizure and occupation of already occupied land and interaction with indigenous peoples. English possession of the North American continent was also far from uncontested within Europe; all of the major powers sought to acquire it. The American colonies were not analogous to provincial England or France, therefore, nor were they simply overseas extensions of the mother country. Rather, the colonies were both highly heterogeneous – in terms of climate, settlement, polity and economy – and highly distinctive, made so by the cohabitation of Europeans with Native Americans and enslaved Africans as well as their colonial status. Many of the rituals of rule and representations of power understood to be possible and necessary within contiguous kingdoms were neither possible nor viable in an imperial context, although there were some shared practices. In each of the three, efforts were made – through celebrations, holidays, portraiture, and proclamations – to incarnate the monarch in the everyday lives of his or her subjects. In the American case such efforts were greatly diluted by the distance from the British court, the diverse national origins of the settlers, and the patchwork of political forms. Explaining the political culture inherited by North American revolutionaries, therefore, requires a different focus than that needed to elucidate the political culture of metropolitan England or France. The emphasis in the section on the American colonies will, therefore, be less on patronage, monumental architecture, and court life, and more on elaborating how the heterogeneity of the American colonies and their distance – in all senses of the word – from England structured the nature of the national and political imaginary there.

Royal politicizing of culture and substantial investment in the rituals of rule would be critically evaluated by those contesting the monarchical order in both England and France, although they would make quite different use of their inherited repertoires. Some of those differences had to do with divergences in the nature of the two revolutions and will be the subject of later chapters. Some differences were the result of variation in how each polity was administered and representation understood under the early Stuarts on the one hand and the Bourbons on the other. Yet other differences were the result of the changes in the availability and meaning of goods, as well as the elaboration of sensationalist philosophy, in the almost century-and-a-half separating the English Civil War and the American and French revolutions. An expansion in the quantity and accessibility of consumer goods available in the eighteenth century in conjunction with new understandings of the role of the senses in the making of the self enabled new ways of thinking the politics of material culture, an imaginary inconceivable in the mid-seventeenth century. This chapter will, therefore, also provide a sketch of the material culture and interpretative grids available for political interpolation by the revolutionaries of the seventeenth and eighteenth centuries on either side of the Atlantic.

Courtly Culture and Rituals of Rule

> No one understood better than Louis XIV the art of enhancing the value of a favour by his manner of bestowing it... He loved splendour, magnificence, and profusion in all things, and encouraged similar tastes in his Court; to spend money freely on equipages and buildings, on feasting and at cards, was a sure way to gain his favour, perhaps to obtain the honour of a word from him. Motives of policy had something to do with this; by making expensive habits the fashion, and, for people in a certain position, a necessity, he compelled his courtiers to live beyond their income, and gradually reduced them to depend on his bounty for the means of subsistence.
>
> *Memoirs of the Duc de Saint-Simon*[4]

English and French rulers in the early modern period constructed their power not only on the basis of the military forces they could mobilize, nor only on the wealth they controlled directly, nor on the resources to which they could obtain access, nor on the diplomatic relations they could cultivate, but also on their ability to generate and maintain the loyalty of the nobility, the notables, and the newly important commercial and professional men.[5] That loyalty was needed in part for political, and in part for financial, reasons. The aristocracies of both countries were powerful, controlling their own resources and their own people, and had long histories of independence. They could pose, and had in the recent past in fact posed, real threats to the Crown. But the Crown also depended upon them economically; finding adequate resources was a permanent challenge for all early modern monarchs. Recourse to new forms of revenue or the revival of old, including innovative taxation programs, borrowing, the sale of offices, and the granting of monopolies and privileges, and, ultimately, to Parliament, in the English case, or the Estates General, in the French, was required to meet their ever-growing financial needs.[6] They could not go to war, or even pay to maintain their own households, without the support of the nobility and the notables who both themselves cooperated and encouraged the king's "lesser" subjects to cooperate, in royal money-raising strategies. It was, therefore, in the monarch's interest to make the Crown's power manifest at all moments as well as to provide patronage, pensions, gifts, power and access to power, and entertainment to those upon whom the monarch depended.[7]

In the British case, the monarchy that governed the kingdoms of England, Ireland, Scotland and Wales was both "personal" and "mixed." It was personal in that the Crown had important discretionary powers, as well as the capacity to name a substantial portion of the government, judiciary, and administration that operated in its name; personal, too, in that the court remained a center of power. As crucial was the monarch's power to wage war, enact emergency measures, and call and dismiss Parliament.[8] It was not, however, an absolute monarchy.[9] The divinely anointed monarch was seconded by, among others, the Privy Council and the Parliament. The Parliament, divided into a House of Lords and one of Commons, was called only at the Crown's will – a move that was often precipitated by a revenue crisis. The frequency with which Parliament met in the first third of the seventeenth century is testimony to the Crown's dependence upon it. The proportion of the population participating *actively* in the political life of the realm was very small, although the House of Commons expanded somewhat under the Stuarts (from 464 members at the beginning of James I's reign to 507 at the close of his son's reign). Unlike the size of the House, however, neither the class of electors, nor the qualifications for running for office were broadened. All women and minors were excluded from suffrage, and property qualifications eliminated approximately three-quarters of adult men. Reducing the real scope of the political nation further was the nature of the elections: few seats were actually contested, but rather local notables rotated membership among themselves, or a single member was systematically returned. Members, furthermore, often also served as Justices of the Peace and held other offices. Given the absence of a civil service, police force or standing army, the members of Parliament tended to be the dominant conduit between the nation's subjects and its rulers.

While opportunities for political participation for those beyond the highest echelons of the elite were few in England before the mid-seventeenth century, those available to their analogues across the Channel were even fewer. Historians have demonstrated in great detail the limits of the power of the theoretically "absolute" French monarchs, but those limits were imposed very largely by the long history of a very powerful, provincially based nobility, the patch-work quality of the French administrative and juridical state, and the Crown's enormous need of funds, not by the popular classes (despite their capacity for riot and armed insurrection).[10] The only national level governmental body in which those of lesser rank than the nobility (whether that rank was inherited or purchased) were present was the Estates General. The Estates General were made up of representatives of the nobility, the Clergy and the Third Estate, and were therefore, theoretically, an institution in which non-aristocrats could be heard. That body was, however, not convened for over 150 years (between 1614 and 1789). The French monarch in fact ruled with the advice of his Ministers and Councils, and with assistance of the provincial governers, *Intendants*, and *Parlements*. The governors – who were supposed to be the king's representatives in the provinces – had traditionally come from the most powerful and wealthiest families, but since they had played a key role in the civil wars of the sixteenth and seventeenth centuries, the Crown chose to limit their power by creating the parallel office of *Intendant*. *Intendants* had responsibility for finances, justice and policing in the *généralité* (region) to which they were attached. In addition to these administrators, the king's will was to be made manifest in the provinces through the local *Parlements*, which had the task of enacting royal edicts or conveying complaints concerning those edicts, or even refusals to implement them, to the king. In the case of a refusal, the Crown could have recourse to a *lit de justice* to force compliance.[11] The *Parlements* could also pass legislation applicable exclusively within their jurisdication. They were formally courts and not legislative bodies, and membership in the *Parlements* was restricted to the nobility – either inherited or purchased. Both the English and French governance systems, therefore, relied financially and administratively on offices and institutions extending from the throne through noble and enobled families. Those office-holders were, in principle at least, tied to the Crown by religious ties as well as those of patronage and politics.

Both the English and French monarchies claimed to be divine-right monarchies; that is, the ruler was understood to have been anointed by God, to be God's representative on earth. Government might was administered through the king's representatives, but the king himself was a father to his subjects, just as God was the father of all Christians (with this paternal metaphor becoming more complicated, of course, when there was a female monarch, or a regent). Subjects, from the wealthiest aristocrat to the humblest peasant, owed the king or queen their absolute obedience. This was to encourage loyalty in a world where the actual relations between kings or queens and their subjects were heavily mediated. The vast majority of the king's subjects would never have seen or heard him, and may never have seen a likeness of him. The monarch, in other words, was, for most of his subjects, effectively an absent parent.[12]

Given that parent–child metaphor of relations between ruler and ruled, it is not surprising that the overwhelming majority of the nation's population had no significant legitimate political role. The disenfranchised (as well as those whose enfranchisement in fact meant little) could and did voice their approval and their disapproval outside the legally constituted channels. The positive expressions took the form of celebrations at coronations, royal births and birthdays, and spontaneous toasts to the king.[13] The negative expressions sometimes took peaceable forms, such as writing petitions, pamphlets and songs, preaching, mockery during carnivals, or animated discussion in coffee-houses. Subjects would applaud the installation of royal statues, yet then also disfigure them or circulate caricatures mocking the king.[14] Disgruntlement could also be, and periodically was, expressed in other ways – poaching, stealing, smuggling, food riots, refusal to pay taxes or provide military service, and sometimes armed rebellion.

The Crown found it necessary, therefore, to reinforce *all* its subjects' loyalty by reminding them, as often and in as varied a manner as possible, of the King's sovereignty and power. Another strategy, as Roger D. Abrahams has argued for England, was pageantry and spectacle: "Public displays sponsored by the *prominenti* were produced constantly … Monarchs attempted to project an aura of personal power through encouraging pageantry … from this emerged the apparatus of the theater-state … James I and Charles I inherited this theatrical apparatus and used it in the dramatization of authority."[15] The early Stuarts also intensified the state's regulation of theater and other popular forms of entertainment, and elaborate royal funerals also provided an opportunity to reinforce, in the face of the individual monarch's mortality, the principle of the continuity of the institution.[16] Early modern French monarchs likewise sought to make their presence known throughout the nation. In addition to festivals and feast days, "[t]he royal name, inscribed on laws and invoked in public prayers, and the royal image, stamped on coins and sculpted in public squares, identified the largely invisible king as the embodiment of the kingdom and gave kingship real presence in the daily lives of his subjects, who celebrated the births of his children and the victories of his armies."[17]

Coinage provided a quotidian opportunity to bring those distant from the court into the royal ambit. In England, the issuance of money of any kind had long been the monarch's prerogative – a prerogative little challenged until shortly before Charles I's execution in 1649. (The first, anticipatory, non-royal coins, or "tokens" were struck in 1648 and, once introduced, were only successfully suppressed over a century later.)[18] While the primary reason for the royal monopoly on minting was no doubt fiscal, it also had important symbolic ramifications. The coin struck for Louis XVI in France shown in Figure 2.1 is exemplary of monarchs' usage of coinage to diffuse idealized, but nonetheless recognizable, renderings of their visages throughout the realm.

Monarchs could also use money as a means of political propaganda, or at least the dissemination of a political position. James I of England/James VI of Scotland, for example, issued a magnificent gold coin – appropriately dubbed "the King James Gold Unite" – conveying his hopes and ambitions that his reign would truly unite the two nations.[19] On the obverse, King James I was depicted in profile holding the orb and scepter. Not satisfied with this explicit representation of power, the royal visage and regalia were scarcely contained within the coin's circumference; the crown and scepter escaped the inner pictorial medallion, interrupting the legend running around the edge of the coin. A shield divided into four quadrants, each inscribed with the arms of England, Scotland, France, and Ireland dominated the reverse. That shield was surmounted by a crown and flanked – perhaps held together – by the letters I and R for Jacobus Rex. The message was further reinforced in words; around the edge of coin runs the legend, "I will make them one nation" (written in Latin). Both the political mission and the reinforcement of the king's power were thus reinforced in word and image, although this was a coin that, given its value, would have come into the hands of only a few.

Perhaps in part to facilitate the use of coinage to transmit political messages, James I also initiated the practice of silver and copper coinage. Earlier English monarchs had insisted on gold's exclusive usage, but base metal coinage had long

Figure 2.1 *Louis d'or* depicting Louis XVI, 1792 (gold), obverse. By French School (eighteenth century). ©Bibliothèque nationale. Paris, France. The Bridgeman Art Library.

existed in Scotland, and James I imported the practice, thereby vastly expanding the number of hands through which coins passed. Small-denomination coinage cast from less noble metals was also in circulation in France in this period, but Louis XIV appears to have had some reluctance to being pictured on the baser materials. While virtually all of the gold *écus* bear his profile, many of the florins and smaller coins do not.[20] Given that the English economy in the seventeenth century, and the French in the eighteenth, were highly monetarized – even as both also suffered regular shortages of specie – such pride might have been ill-advised. As the historian Gay Gullickson has pointed out, even rural dwellers in the Caux region in the mid-eighteenth century needed and used coins for their everyday purchases; perhaps regular sight of the king's profile on smaller coinage would have reinforced his authority among the poor.[21]

Coinage was far from the only double-purpose object mobilized by the monarchy for symbolic purposes. Proclamations had the dual virtues of both implementing desired policy and making the king's presence felt, both through the oral reading of the proclamation and through the printed texts. Virtually all such documents not only reproduced and disseminated the relevant *text* throughout the kingdom (or wherever it was applicable) but also, through the iconography that generally preceded that text, reinforced the power of the king. That visual reinforcement was achieved not only by means of the reproduction of the royal arms, but also through the elaborateness of the image itself. Such proclamations and declarations would have been circulated through the chain of authority, thereby also underscoring the local noble's role as a link between subjects and monarch.[22]

Both English and French sovereigns were very conscious of the power of the printing press on the one hand to increase their power and presence, but also on the other to provide opportunities for contestation. They therefore tried both to limit the number of publishers and to censor the material produced. The uses to which pamphlets, newspapers, and tracts were put in the years leading up to revolution and during the revolutions themselves would, of course, prove them right. Those works were often censored, and their authors brutally punished; but as the punishments generated outrage both licensing and censorship in Britain proved to be ineffective and even ultimately dangerous to the Crown.[23] Even printing itself escaped from royal control. There were, for example, in principle only twenty publishers in early seventeenth-century London – that is there were twenty *licensed* printers. The actual numbers were far greater, however, and by the 1620s, as a result of new technologies that reduced the cost of printing, pamphlets came to play a crucial role in mobilizing support both for the king and for the opposition. While far from everyone could read (estimates run at approximately 30 per cent of men in the countryside and 80 per cent in London, and the rates for women were much lower), there were enough so that most social worlds would contain a reader or two.[24] Once texts were read they were discussed and debated, potentially becoming the foundation of new visions of society and polity.[25] A parallel, and indeed an intensified, story, given the hundred and twenty years separating the English and French revolutions, may be told for Old Regime France. By the second half of the eighteenth century, those protesting against royal authority in France were using the print media far more effectively than the Crown. Even here, however, it is arguable that the revolutionaries took a leaf out of the Crown's book, turning its use of the print media to their own ends.[26]

Although the Crown's major preoccupation, as will be discussed below, was the loyalty of the small body of people who constituted the political nation, it would clearly be inaccurate to characterize the French and English monarchies in the early modern period as having made *no* effort to render the royal presence tangible among their ordinary subjects, even in rural areas far removed from the court. Coinage, tokens, medals, published laws and proclamations, prints of the king and of the royal dwellings all disseminated emblems of the Crown and of the king's authority throughout the realm. The Crown, furthermore, infiltrated popular festivals and attempted to assure that at those moments of festivity its own role was not forgotten.

These strategies were all efforts to reinforce the *king's presence* or vertical ties between subjects and the monarch. There was far less attention paid, on the part of the state, to creating a sense of *national identity* and its accompanying horizontal attachments among subjects in the population at large.[27] While an obvious explanation for this neglect on the part of the monarch would seem to be that inculcating a sense of national identity was simply not needed in a nearly homogeneous, indigenous population with few immigrants, that would be false. This period, and the century preceding it, saw some immigration into both England and France, and their native populations were quite heterogeneous, sharing few cultural forms. They spoke several languages and many dialects, had radically different food cultures, celebrated holidays differently (and did not share them all), and had different musical and different agricultural practices, different demographic and dwelling patterns, and different styles in architecture and the decorative arts. They were also often divided in their religious practices and beliefs. Furthermore, when the battle of Nottingham announced the beginning of the Civil War in England in August 1642, the archipelago over which Charles I ruled included the polities of England, Wales, Scotland, and Ireland. His power over each varied: within the British Isles, he was king of the two separate kingdoms of England and Scotland, Wales had been incorporated into England, and the relationship between England and Ireland may best be characterized as imperial. To these clustered nations of the archipelago for the British case, and the hexagon in the French, must, of course, be added the overseas colonies or trading settlements in America, Africa, the Caribbean, and the East Indies.[28]

Language policies provide a key illustration of both preoccupation with the maintenance of vertical ties between rulers and ruled, particularly among elites, and the neglect or even discouragement of such links among the ruled. While, for example, efforts were made to ensure that the English aristocracy residing in Ireland continued to speak English rather than shifting into Irish, most historians agree that efforts to anglicize the Irish were very limited. Likewise, the Welsh were allowed to continue speaking Welsh (after Wales had been annexed in 1284 and even after the link had been further strengthened by Henry VIII between 1536 and 1543), and the Crown, in fact, supported the translation of the Bible into Welsh, although it did impose English law and granted English rights. Some efforts were made to produce a unified, consistent "King's English," but the focus was on the governing elites.[29] English did, nonetheless, become more widespread: by 1700, the historian John Morrill estimates that 85 per cent of the population spoke it as a second, if not a first, language.[30] Similarly in France, as the classic work of Michel de Certeau, Jacques Julia and Jacques Revel has shown, no effort was made to create a unified French language among the populace in the Old Regime. There was, however, a concern with standardizing administrative and royal French – spoken and written only by the elites.[31]

The neglect of everyday practice as a strategy for nation-building may be seen in the utter absence of standardized weights and measures in both countries in this period. The same word could refer to units of very different size, varying from town to town, to say nothing of region to region or colony to colony. Travelers and migrants needed to learn and adapt to the "foreign" systems as they relocated, and peddlers and merchants had to have agile mathematical minds to convert prices and measures as they went from place to place.[32] Despite their numbers, therefore, it was not the mass of the population that most preoccupied early modern monarchs, it was the small group who constituted the political nation, along with the ambassadors and other influential foreigners.

Thus even the uniting of the crowns of England and Scotland in one person through the accession of James VI of Scotland to the throne of England in 1603 did not generate any systematic effort at the cultural unification of the two nations. This was in part because this was a multiple monarchy – the linkage of two separate kingdoms under one ruler – rather than a unification of the two polities. James I did have aspirations to produce a British, rather than an English, court (as well as ambitions for a more thorough union); but even the effort to create a united elite largely failed. Despite the presence of significant numbers of Irish and Scots aristocrats, the courts of James I and Charles I remained culturally English: the Scots had to conform to English norms, and the court had little impact on Scotland's political elites or its culture.[33]

In France, not only did the Bourbons try to create administrative centralization and a standard bureaucratic language, but they also attempted to create or defend distinctively French aesthetic forms in the domain of courtly culture. For example, the French Académie royale de musique resisted incorporating Italian music into its repertoire from the 1670s to the 1730s, when it gained popularity elsewhere in Europe. The music played in an institution sponsored by the French Crown was to be French, and even French technical terms had to be found to replace the Italian, e.g. *sonade*, *concert* and *rondeau*. This pattern only changed in the 1770s – just as the whole structure was falling apart.[34] An Italian aesthetic was also rejected in the domain of gardening, where a characteristically French style was created in the hopes of fostering a strong identification with the French Crown.[35] As the historian Chandra Mukerji has demonstrated, this elaboration of a French style was reinforced when forms used in the creation of gardens subsequently served as models for designs on manufactured goods. The French courts were systematically adamant in their promotion of national culture. This extended even to foreigners brought into the royal family through marriage: for example, when the Spanish princess, the Infanta Maria Teresa, became queen of France, her Spanishness was stripped from her, replaced by French clothing and hairstyles and a French name. It is noteworthy that this nationalism did not characterize seventeenth-century English courts. James I and Charles I had consciously and explicitly emulated Italian gardens, for example, just as they imported Italian architectural style, thereby creating a link between the Roman Empire and England.[36]

Within the world of the political elite *all* was political; it is a truism that early modern monarchs had no private life; their every gesture, their every act, their every possession had public meaning – the meaning of state. What is less often noted is that a corollary of the saturation of the monarch (and his or her court) by politics, was the near absence of politics (in this sense) from the everyday lives of the vast majority. Both because they had no formal political voice, and because they were understood to be tied to the nation by the links of paternalism and dependence, the gestures, habits, and dress of the populace were understood to lie outside politics. It did not matter, in the Old Regime, what language a peasant in Brittany spoke, nor that she had no sense of affinity with a shepherd from the Pyrenees. As long as she was loyal to her lord, who was the local embodiment of the king, then all was well. I would like to suggest, therefore, that it is inaccurate to say that there *was no division* between the public and the private in the early modern world; *rather, the division between those domains was differently conceived* than it would be later. Among other things this had radical implications for the gendered division of labor within both the state and the home. Women were not formally, categorically, excluded from political power under monarchical regimes.[37] In England, women could be heads of state; and although the Salic law made that an impossibility in France, they could wield tremendous formal power there as wives, regents, and noblewomen.[38] This would be challenged in fundamental ways during both revolutionary moments.

Given the ideology of divine right and of a society of orders, given the constraints placed on maintaining royal authority among the vast majority of the people imposed by the dispersal of the population in both England and France, and by the thinness of bureaucratic presence in the English, the task of maintaining the political order fell heavily to the intermediaries between the king and his people, and it was upon these intermediaries, and foreign governments, that the monarchs concentrated their attention.[39] There was considerable, although by no means complete, overlap of the political, economic and social elites in both realms, although, as has been discussed in the last chapter, not all who had wealth in seventeenth-century England or eighteenth-century France had political power or place, and not all of those with titles of nobility and the accompanying obligations had the means with which comfortably to fulfill them. Whether or not those with political position really could assure the loyalty of those lower down the political hierarchy, they were expected to do so through ties of patronage. And, within each household, the father was to assure the loyalty not only of his wife and children but also of the apprentices and laborers working there.

Both the English and the French Crowns not only used patronage to tie the elites to them and to their courts, but literally performed their power for them as a way of transmitting it to the lower orders.[40] As the historian R. Malcolm Smuts has written, "...costly objects ... were normally visible only to those with access to the king's palaces: courtiers, English peers and gentry, ambassadors and foreign visitors of rank. These were the people who mattered in seventeenth-century society and thus the ones the king had to impress."[41] A similar observation may be made concerning the place of music in French courtly life: "Musical experience ...

served an ideological function similar to that of the balls, banquets, coronations, and ceremonies of absolutism by representing the invisible power structures of the regime in visible displays."[42] Where one sat in the hall and by whom one was seen mattered more than what one could see and hear. Taste itself was determined by rank; one liked what it was appropriate that one should like. That understanding is seconded by the historian William Weber, who has argued that music in France was a vehicle of patronage (and therefore politics) from the sixteenth through most of the eighteenth century.[43]

That patronage thus included the granting or sale of offices, allocation of monopolies, and access to the king's person, but also invitations to banquets, spectacles, and concerts, which were simultaneously entertainments and political events. In England, Charles I commissioned, helped to stage – and appeared in as his own allegory – masques that combined theater, opera, ballet, music, *tableaux vivants*, very elaborate scenery and spectacular special effects, all mobilized around the celebration of the monarch's qualities.[44] Vaughan Hart has even made the intriguing argument that the very proportions used by Inigo Jones in his set designs for the masques were designed to "...reflect the absolute, divine right of Jones' royal patron to rule."[45] At the conclusion of the masque, the actors, in all their finery, would mingle with the crowd, thus blurring the boundary between the divine and the profane, the imaginary and the real. French royal performances, whether in the seventeenth or eighteenth centuries, while equally magnificent, did not blur those boundaries in the same way. The early Stuart kings were far more intimately involved in the creation of these masques than were their French counterparts, and saw this moving between roles as reinforcing rather than diminishing their power. Whether in England or France, these performances were staged in spectacular buildings, palaces equipped with luxurious furniture and tapestries, decorated with fine paintings and sculptures, and surrounded by fabulous gardens and well-stocked hunting grounds. James I in fact sponsored the creation of a new tapestry workshop at Mortlake, and allowed the immigration of fifty Flemish weavers and their families, in order to assure a stable source of high-quality tapestries to supply the court's needs.[46] Royal expenditures on the fine arts, music, dramaturgy, architecture, and furnishings, as well as clothing, jewelry, and food and drink, were predictably vast.[47] One of the strategies was the production and diffusion of objects embedded with symbols of royal power, the royal visage, or objects commemorating key historical events. Thus, the Lord Keeper of the Great Seal was allowed to keep a casting of the Great Seal and could have it transformed into an object of decoration or use. Sir Thomas Coventry (1578–1640), for example, had the Seal transformed into a cup, made out of silver gilt, featuring "the rose for England, the fleur-de-lis for France, the thistle for Scotland and the harp for Ireland, all crowned with the Stuart crown." Monarchs had portraits of all scales – from the monumental to the miniature – painted so that their likenesses could gaze down from the wall, but also be carried in a pocket or, in the case of engraved silver medallions, worn on a ribbon close to the heart. Drawing and painting were, in fact, among the talents of the courtier, and those skilled in these arts, like Sir Balthazar Gerbier, could use their skills to ingratiate themselves by painting miniatures of the royal family.[48] All of the Bourbons and Charles I also had a keen interest in sculpted portraits and commissioned a substantial number in a variety of sizes and materials – some in marble and some in bronze.[49]

What may appear simple extravagance or self-indulgence – James I's court was one of the most luxurious in Europe – was actually a rational investment in political power.[50] The same may be said of the very substantial expenditures on clothing and jewelry worn at court, by both the royal family and others. To borrow Smuts's formulation, "Feathers and livery coats were essential to the ceremonious majesty of kingship; when they failed to grace a major public event, royal prestige suffered." A simple black suit to wear at court cost £50; those same £50 would pay the annual rent on a town house in London. That sum was, nonetheless, modest compared to the £1,500 that Lady Arabella Stuart paid for her gown, or the few hundred pounds more that the princess Elizabeth spent just for the lace adorning a single robe.[51] Charles I's personal clothing expenditures for a year were about £5,000. Other expenses on luxurious display, however, were also very substantial; over a sixteen-year period during the reign of Charles I, purchases of gold plate came in at £74,000, each major public ritual would cost around £30,000, and his patronage of the fine arts cost £55,000. Both the Bourbons and the early Stuarts were important patrons and collectors, supporting a vast array of artists and artisans through their commissions and acquisitions.[52] To say that these expenditures had a logic, is not, however to say that they were affordable. Overall, in the 1640s, the cost of the English court's display – in all its manifestations – was enormous, with a household budget of about £400,000 annually; it was second only to the amount that was spent on war.[53] Such expenditures closely paralleled those in France. Marie Antoinette had an annual dress budget of 122,000 *livres*, and in 1786 she spent more than double that.[54] The significance of these figures may become clearer when one learns that only around 20 per cent of the population in the eighteenth century had accumulated wealth of more than 3,000 *livres* at the time of their death, although obviously the very few at the peak of the pyramid had much more. Her contemporary Arthur Young, for example, put "…the annual cost of living for a household with four servants, three horses and one carriage living in a country manor-house at 7,000 [*livres*]."[55]

An appropriate setting was needed for the display of such clothing at masques, balls, and concerts; both English and French monarchs spent vast sums on palaces both in or near the seats of government and elsewhere in the country. In France, new standards were set for courtly luxuriousness by Henry IV in the late sixteenth and early seventeenth centuries, when he had the Place Dauphine and the Place Royale (1605–1612) built and furnished, as well as renovations done to the Louvre and the Tuileries.[56] These French Renaissance courts were in turn rapidly emulated by the English monarchy in the sixteenth and seventeenth centuries, including Inigo Jones's reconstruction of Covent Garden in 1631 as a response to Henry IV's Place Royale. Charles I had greater ambitions, hoping to transform Whitehall, the main residence of the English monarchs since 1529, from a sprawling complex of buildings into a palace on the Continental model, although that never came to pass.[57] Whitehall, unlike European palaces, incorporated within its 1,500 rooms accommodations for the royal family, their entourage, high-ranking nobles and servants, but also many of the Kingdom's administrative offices and considerable other residential property. At Whitehall, as in Louis XIV's Versailles, courtiers vied for space close to their patrons. Royal palaces, theatrical performances, and dress were, therefore, quite literally instruments of diplomacy and domestic and international politics.

James I inherited from Elizabeth I a policy of tightly policing building in London, a policy intended to limit congestion and facilitate security but also to assure the aesthetic qualities of the royal seat, so that it would be an appropriate stage for the monarchy. He continued that strategy, but invested far more in building projects, improving already existing palaces, including spending £50,000 on Whitehall, before going on to commission the celebrated Banqueting House.[58] Not only did he make substantial expenditures on architecture, but he also took pride in supporting innovative design. Inigo Jones's Banqueting House, for example, is generally understood by architectural historians to have broken new aesthetic ground. Jones introduced Palladian proportions as well as window and roof treatments to England, thus departing from Elizabethan and Jacobean traditions. James I also intensified regulation, specifying building materials and forms, down to the size of the bricks used. A further element in this project of aestheticizing the capital was to attempt to render London's urban landscape more unified and harmonious. The architectural avant-garde was to be found, in other words, largely in the works commissioned by the Crown.[59]

This conviction that both royal palaces and an improved urban fabric were critical to the maintenance and expansion of royal power was shared by his son. Among other projects, Charles I had the Banqueting House, which had been damaged in a fire in 1619, rebuilt and ornamented with a ceiling by Peter Paul Rubens celebrating the achievements of his father. James is represented there as a Solomon-like figure, but a Solomon who brings two children together into one (Scotland and England into Great Britain) rather than resolving the dilemma of dividing one child into two. The room was used for masques and many state events (and would ultimately be the room from which Charles I went to his execution). By rebuilding the Banqueting House and devoting it to images of his father, Charles reinforced his power, in part by sheer expenditure, but also by reminding visitors of his lineage.

Louis XIV, consistent with his efforts to consolidate and centralize royal power, devoted most of his architectural energies to a single site – the Palace of Versailles, upon which work started in 1662. Louis XIV's Versailles was built around a not particularly impressive château, erected in the middle of swamplands by Louis XIII earlier in the century. Historians have argued that it is not an accident that

Louis XIV chose a singularly inhospitable location for his showpiece.[60] The lack of natural beauty only threw his accomplishment into greater relief; through the transformation of wasteland into beauty the king demonstrated his domination of nature itself. The forms of the gardens were, furthermore, in part derived from the designs of military fortresses, and they were built with the help of engineering skills developed to build fortifications – a fact that would be visible to any visitor with military training.[61] Military prowess and horticultural skill were thus melded to maximally emphasize the omnipotence of the Crown. The monarch himself devoted a great deal of time and attention to the buildings, their furnishings and decorations, and to the surrounding gardens.[62] According to the historian Anne-Marie Lecoq, he took the building and grounds as the "visible manifestation of the royal will, on a par with legislation, the navy, war, and diplomatic treaties."[63] In the eighteenth century, with the place of Versailles firmly established, and a growing, active and ambitious elite in Paris, the center of royal expenditure would shift to the capital, and to an increasing focus on creating a public, monumental, urban presence for the monarchy.[64] By the sixteenth century in England and the seventeenth century in France, those of old noble stock, those recently ennobled and also simply the rich sought to emulate these royal possessions and cultural productions.[65] Royal palaces also set the norms for the goods within the dwellings of the nobility and the aspiring gentry and bourgeoisie. In mid-eighteenth-century France, the nobility numbered approximately 400,000 (out of a total population of about 2 million, making two nobles for every 100 people). There was an elaborate hierarchy within the nobility determined by proximity to the king, starting with those who resided permanently in the royal household, and then those who had been presented at court, themselves divided into three categories – the highest were those admitted to the *cercles de la cour*; next came those who were allowed to ride in the king's carriages; and last those who had simply been presented. Those who had been presented at court totaled about 20,000 in the late eighteenth century. The remaining 380,000 or so nobility were also hierarchically ordered depending on their distance from the Crown, the office occupied, and other criteria. They ranged greatly in wealth, with the court nobles generally the wealthiest (having yearly incomes of between 100,000 and 150,000 *livres*).[66] They were, however, also the most indebted, given the costs of maintaining their position, with large expenditures on servants, carriages, and clothes. For example, an ordinary dress for one of Louis XVI's balls could easily cost 2,000 *livres* and the expense of emulating the interior decoration and gardens of the royal châteaux (learned about through engravings diffused throughout France and beyond) enormous.[67] There was also in this period, of course, both emulation and cultural innovation beyond those who were in direct contact with the court.

Here the stories of England and France at the eve of their revolutions, divided by over a century, diverge. As will be discussed at greater length in the next chapter, although the court and aristocracy were certainly not able to completely dominate the world of theater, music, dance, fashion, architecture and the visual arts under the Stuarts, an autonomous public sphere would only mature after the Restoration. The same could be said for France in the same time period under the reign of Louis XIV. The eighteenth century brought, however, in France as well as in England a vast expansion of the cultural, intellectual, and commercial world beyond the court. That world would be a site of lively intellectual discussion and cultural innovation, much of it articulated around a critique of luxury.[68]

This expansion in available goods should not be exaggerated, however. The studies of both rural and urban dwellers in seventeenth-century England and eighteenth-century France show that the vast majority of the inhabitants of both kingdoms were still living in minimal comfort. Margaret Spufford and others who have studied consumer patterns in this period in England describe the appearance of manufactured pins, pewter, fabric and a few other items.[69] Most dwellings were still small and minimalist in their decoration and most women still had at best two outfits for each season seconded by some changes of linen. This is obviously far distant from the world of starched ruffs and dresses of silk. While far more was available a century later in France, the gap between royal, aristocratic, and wealthy non-noble and the vast majority of the population was still very great. The following evocative description of rural life may be generalized beyond this local case: "Most families lived near the subsistence line, and their lives included few, if any, luxuries. Houses were small, damp, and dark. Heated by poorly ventilated fireplaces, the walls were blackened with smoke, and it was often impossible to see across even small rooms. Visitors frequently had to call out to see if anyone was home even if they had already come in the door. Pictures and curtains were unheard of luxuries, and furniture was sturdy but in short supply."[70] Even Parisians were not living in much greater luxury. The historian Daniel Roche, who has done the most detailed work on popular consumption in that city in the eighteenth century, after making a strong case for the increasing access to goods in this period, goes on to note that: "Of course, their décor had none of the Regency charm, Louis XV refinement or the theatricalism of the neo-classical age..." and there was a considerable time-lag, "Servant homes were nearly fifty years behind the aristocracy, and the affluent labouring class almost a century."[71] Even the historian Cissie Fairchilds, who argues for the diffusion of "populuxe" items into the lower middle class and lower class in the Paris of the second half of the eighteenth century, limits her discussion to a very narrow range of goods – particularly umbrellas and stockings.[72] It is, in sum, clear that the goods to which the poor and the middling most quickly had access were clothing and smaller home furnishings, and even then in limited quantities. Thus, although the many warnings of historians that one should not be "miserabilist" about the English seventeenth century or the French eighteenth are well taken, it would be anachronistic to interpret the incontrovertibly great increase of a certain range of goods, particularly among relatively well-off urban dwellers and servants, to mean that these were full-blown modern consumer societies.

Controlling Emulation

The conceptualization of the king as father to his people, and the theoretically absolute and omnipresent nature of the Crown's power involved the unity of two domains whose relation would be reconfigured in each nation's revolution – the public and the private. Monarchs had no private lives in the modern sense of the term. All moments of their existence, whether going to bed or getting up, or relieving themselves, were part of public life – an affair of state. The frequency of pornographic representations of monarchs and courtiers by the end of this period bears vivid testimony to the publicness of royal bodies.[73] In parallel to the minimal separation between spaces of dwelling and working in the lives and structures of most ordinary people, monarchs were always in public and all of their goods were public goods, designed to represent the splendor and power of the monarch, although only those part of the political nation had access to the vast majority of those representations.

The hierarchy among elites was reinforced by the monarch's efforts to regulate and control the right of emulation. Given the importance of goods to the maintenance of royal power and competition from the expanding commercial world, it is not surprising that all monarchs in the early modern period attempted to regulate access to the objects that were both becoming available on the market *and* understood to be of heavy symbolic weight. Sumptuary legislation was promulgated to assure that personal possessions, particularly clothing, were suited to individuals' political rank and social station. The logic of this legislation was very similar across Europe. Clothing was not worn simply to express individual taste or wealth. Indeed, most of the laws restricted access to certain fabrics – cloth of gold was for royalty, velvet for the aristocracy and silk for the gentry. Colors and variations on silk were also the subject of regulation. As one sixteenth-century French law put it, "…so that princes and princesses have – as is only reasonable – some difference in their appearance, we will permit them to wear clothes in cranberry red silk, which no other man or woman will be bold or arrogant enough to wear."[74] Royalty should dress differently from the nobility, who, in turn, should dress differently from the gentry. Even servants were fitted out in livery to represent the status and ambition of their masters, although that was not mandated by law.[75]

The reasons given for the necessity of legal regulation were equally explicit: "…And because a part of the excess usage of silk has been observed on the part of a large number of bourgeois women, who thereby transformed themselves into ladies from one day to the next, we have prohibited and again prohibit, these women to change estate, if their husbands are not gentlemen."[76] The existence of this legislation indicates that some had acquired the means and the desire to dress "above themselves." As one historian put it, these laws were passed in the period, "…before the industrial revolution built economic growth into people's expectations, but after that in which very limited economic horizons obtained, as they did up to the late

Middle Ages."[77] In an effort to circumvent such transgressions, Charles I used the law to add a further refinement to the display of noble rank when in 1627 he introduced new robes for the Order of the Garter with its embroidered star, constructed out of silver thread and silk appliqué. These stars were to be worn "…upon the left part of their cloaks, coats and riding cassocks, at all times when they shall not wear their robes, and in all places and assemblies … a testimony to the World, of the honour they hold…"[78]

Sumptuary law also bears witness to the fact that the courtly stylistic regime was in trouble. If there had been true consensus that goods should reflect rank, then no one would have attempted to "dress above themselves" and there would have been no need to pass laws prohibiting them from doing so. Likewise, had it not been socially or personally possible and useful to dress as someone else, then no one would have been inclined to do so. That so many laws of this nature were passed, with such frequency (and each containing complaints about the failure of previous efforts) is an indication that people were both able and determined to appear as they were not and thus flout the courtly system.

But sumptuary legislation is equally an indication that the courtly stylistic regime was – at least in part – alive and well. Even as late as the final years of the seventeenth century in England and the mid-eighteenth century in France, it was widely accepted that the Crown had the right and perhaps even the obligation to legislate on such intimate (and what would later be thought of as private) matters. The historian Steven Kaplan has made a related argument concerning the liberal laws of 1763–1764 in France: "Renouncing a stewardship it had exercised, so it seemed, from time immemorial, the royal government broke an unwritten covenant with consumers and proclaimed that subsistence was no longer its overriding responsibility… Subsistence became a matter for the individual to work out on his own."[79] Sumptuary laws were obviously concerned with the other extreme of consumer practice from subsistence; but the principle of the monarch intervening in the domain of domestic consumption to assure the moral and physical well-being of his people held until twenty-five years before the Revolution. Many popular insurrections in this period were, in fact, sparked by a sense that the monarch had failed in his royal/paternal obligation to provide food.[80]

Not only did contemporaries feel it was the monarch's right and obligation to regulate consumption, but he had that right because there was little distinction to be made between the interests of individual families and the interests of the state. The French law of 1649 put it as follows, "…there is no more certain cause of the ruin of a state than the excess of unregulated luxury, which by the subversion of individual families, necessarily brings about the ruin of the public…"[81] The English had said much the same a century earlier in a 1533 Act:

> the necessary repressing, avoiding and expelling of the inordinate excess daily more and
> more used in the sumptuous and costly array and apparel customarily worn in this realm,

whereof hath ensued and daily do chance such sundry high and notable inconveniences as be to the great, manifest and notorious detriment of the common weal, the subversion of good and politic order in knowledge and distinction of people according to their estates, pre-eminences, dignities and degrees, and to the utter impoverishment and undoing of many inexpert and light persons inclined to pride, mother of all vices...[82]

The nation was indeed, at this date, the family writ large. The monarch had the right and obligation to regulate family life so as both to ensure its health and that of the nation as a whole. But these laws were difficult to enforce, and there is little evidence that there was ever any serious attempt to do so. In fact, in both England and France, although in somewhat different ways, the state had created the conditions for the erosion of its own power.

The heyday for sumptuary legislation in England was the sixteenth century (although laws were passed there from the fourteenth century through the early seventeenth) and in France the late seventeenth, when twelve laws were promulgated in just over twenty years. Not coincidentally, those were also the years of a boom in courtesy book writing and translating in England.[83] While sumptuary law tried to prevent people from appearing to be other than they were, courtesy books of this period taught them how to do precisely that, but then to become as they seemed. Courtesy books provided detailed information – and how metaphorically or literally one should read that information is the subject of scholarly debate – on how to dress, how to eat, how to sit, or to stand according to the position one had or the position to which one aspired. While in fifteenth- and sixteenth-century Italy and France the *civilité* these books attempted to teach was associated with the expression of one's essence, that was already changing by the seventeenth century. In the earlier period, courtesy books had been, and had been read as, metaphorical maps for a just polity and a just society. And, most fundamentally, people were to be as they seemed and seem as they were. By the seventeenth century, *civilité* had radically changed. Roger Chartier has argued that it was "...poles apart from a conception that perceived outward behavior as an exact and necessary translation of the disposition of one's inner being, [rather it] is best understood as above all a social seeming."[84] This was not an encouragement of hypocrisy; people were to try to live up to their appearances. In a sense, one's own outward appearance and manners could serve as a model to one's inner being. By the eighteenth century in France, however, "[b]eing and seeming were ... totally separated, and when *civilité* was equated with an amiable courtesy that demanded no authenticity of feeling, the rupture was complete."[85] This transformation of manners into appearance would be sharply critiqued in each revolutionary moment, and in each, efforts would be made to reimagine the relation of inner essence and outer surface.

This ambivalent detachment of being and seeming is also apparent in transformations in the theater in this period. The historian Jean-Christophe Agnew has demonstrated that English theater in the sixteenth century showed a heightened awareness that what was happening on stage was *representation*. "For the first time, perhaps, theater made ... the 'idea of the play' its cardinal concern..."[86] Thus, beginning in the sixteenth century in England and the seventeenth in France saw a new awareness that people could somehow be different than they appeared to be. In the theater, characters on a stage would not only act a part, but one moment tell the audience that they knew that they are "only" acting that part and the next moment fully "be" the character. Similarly, in buying and wearing clothes, people would buy the clothing they knew to be the outward sign of a station other than their own, whether in the hopes of deception or simply for pleasure is hard to know. Finally, the aristocracy would learn from courtesy books how to appear better, more *civile,* than they were, in the hopes of actually becoming that which they appeared to be. This was certainly not yet a world where all could be purchased, where all was representation, and it was not yet one entirely given over to the pedagogic value of appearance – that appearing was a good way of becoming what one appeared to be; but, as we have seen above, commercialization was proceeding apace and having some surprising effects. These new meanings of representation and appearance would become crucial parts of the repertoire, along with the older meanings, during the revolutionary years in both countries – albeit to different ends.

The seventeenth and eighteenth centuries coincided with the extensive sale of noble office in France and the intensive development of overseas commerce in England. Putting previously hereditary offices up for sale, in order to raise money for the Crown, radically changed the definition of what money could buy. The source of nobility, of rank, was no longer in the blood, but rather in the purse. If money could be used to purchase an office, why could it not be used to buy the clothes appropriate to that office, even if the office itself had not, in fact, been acquired? Venality of office was obviously not viewed favorably by those who came from noble lineages; and those recently ennobled also quickly came to feel that nobility had been extended far enough. Raising money in this manner was, therefore, dangerous for the Crown. Selling offices raised revenues, but in so far as the value of offices depended on their scarcity, it also depleted their worth. Such sales also helped to create a fractious and competitive nobility. The sale of office was not much used in England to raise money for the Crown, but the allocation of monopoly rights was.[87] As trade to the Middle and Far East, South Asia, and the Americas expanded, English merchants became wealthier and wealthier and competed ever more intensely among themselves and with those of landed means. The Crown mediated among these interests, attempting to play them off each other to its best advantage, much as the French Crown did with the sale of offices.

Both English and French monarchs were, then, seriously constrained in their exercise of power. The inherent poverty of the Crown, its dependence on individuals and groups who were competing among themselves, and the trials of international diplomacy, meant that the Crown had to be careful – as it learned to its peril – not to overstep the boundaries. If Charles I gave certain monopoly privileges to one group of merchants, he had to balance that gift when dealing with rival merchants or find himself without their support. And one of the main favors the monarch could offer was tax-relief; but money lost in one domain had to be found in another. Intensive religious conflict further complicated the dynamics of rule. Thus, over the course of the early seventeenth century in England, and the late eighteenth century in France, the Crown progressively lost control of the courtly stylistic regime. This erosion of royal power was exacerbated by the elaboration of political theories opposed to divine right and absolute monarchy, and perhaps even more critically, by the development of commercial and colonial economies.

The American Colonies: English, Colonial, or Creole?

Moving across the ocean to the world of British North America considerably changes our angle of vision; we shift from metropolitan to overseas territory, and from metropolitan nations whose societies, for all their diversity, look quite homogeneous compared to the thirteen colonies. While the motivations of successive English governments for imperial expansion were quite consistent, those Europeans who actually undertook the Atlantic voyage in the seventeenth and eighteenth centuries were disparate, ranging from a quest for religious freedom or service as missionaries, to flight from poverty and lack of prospects at home, or a desire for adventure. Many came involuntarily either as indentured servants or convicts. Their religious affiliations included all the various forms of Protestantism and Catholicism, and they even included a few Jews. The English colonists, with their individual histories, found themselves, furthermore, inhabiting colonies of differing form – some proprietary, some royal, some chartered – each with its own mode of governance. The thirteen British colonies stretching down the Atlantic coast were furthermore both often very different in climate and landscape from England and internally greatly varied. By 1700, for example, while the Southern colonies were dominated by the cultivation of tobacco, rice, and indigo on plantations made possible by a warm climate and slave labor, New England had little by way of exportable agricultural products and functioned far more as a cultural broker and producer of manufactured goods. In their effort to adapt to local circumstances, even colonists who had started much alike rapidly became quite different, since these varied natural, economic, political and social structures brought with them specific habits of life, including residential patterns, work rhythms, architectural styles, and modes of entertainment.

The settlers were also, particularly after 1700, far from entirely English. Holland's loss of New Amsterdam in 1664 and the French cession of New France to the British in 1763, as well as that of Louisiana to Spain a year earlier, did not stop the flow of refugee Protestants (and some Jews) from those countries as well as elsewhere in Europe. In addition there were substantial German, Scots, Irish, and Scots-Irish populations across the colonies (although these were concentrated in certain regions). Each of these groups brought their own languages, religions, political traditions, and customs. The massive importation of African slaves in the eighteenth century was equally, if not more, crucial to the distinctiveness of North American society.

This combination of a population composed of groups with their own cultural, religious, social and political inheritances and a varied climate that shaped agricultural and settlement practices has produced a long and intense debate among historians concerning the nature of the American colonies. Some have argued that a distinctively "American" society and character developed early in the colonial period; others have claimed, rather, that the colonies are best understood as parts of provincial English society; and finally, some have found evidence for the significant influence of Native American, African, Dutch and German cultures within the dominant English matrix. Each of these understandings of the colonial period has important implications for interpretations of the American Revolution. Those who see a unified American society emerging organically in the eighteenth (or even seventeenth) centuries tend to understand the Revolution as a war of independence, a "people" seeking political autonomy appropriate to their unique identity.[88] There would, therefore, be no need for a "cultural" revolution to create a unified nation (although there would still be a need to transform monarchists into republicans). Historians who conceptualize colonial America as a variant on provincial English society tend to understand the Revolution as resulting from the British government's mismanagement of the colonists' demand for the "rights of Englishmen."[89] In this case, the Revolution would entail the forging of a cultural nation as well as a polity based on new principles. Finally, those who stress internal diversity within the colonies in combination with a distinctively colonial experience suggest that that diversity distanced colonial society from the metropole without going so far as to suggest that a unified "American" society or nation had emerged by the 1760s, when conflict with England intensified. This distance created the conditions of possibility for political mobilization in the face of English demands, but neither made the War of Independence inevitable nor determined the shape of the emerging nation.[90] In this case as well, a cultural revolution would be needed, but one based on heterogeneity and a shared colonial experience rather than a betrayed provincial heritage. It is the last that I find most persuasive, and it is to this, in some detail, that I will now turn.

The territory with which we are concerned here was, from the defeat of Dutch in 1664 until the Peace of Paris in 1783, juridically English. The earliest settlements had had the support of the Crown, and subsequent colonization was done in the interests of the metropole. Because of differences of climate, of landscape, of religion, of population, and of circumstances of founding, however, this Englishness did not produce cultural homogeneity across the thirteen colonies. Both the earliest English settlers and those who followed brought with them a wide range of experience and expectation. The location of the homes they had left behind in England shaped both;

Londoners were unique, and urban and rural dwellers in general had different skills and habits. Within England, the highlands and the lowlands had distinct cultures, as did the North and the South, and important differences existed within those regions.[91] Age, gender, class, occupation and religious affiliation were all further factors shaping the expectations and capacities of individual settlers. Adults brought with them trades, crafts, and abstract knowledge. They also brought different religious beliefs and practices and different political convictions. Some came as indentured servants, others as free men and women. And, although white migration to the English-owned colonies in the seventeenth century was overwhelmingly from England, the Dutch arrived in New Amsterdam in 1621, only fourteen years after the founding of Jamestown, and the French were trading in what would become Canada during that same period. By the eighteenth century, there was also very substantial non-English immigration, including Scots, Irish and Germans, and the accelerated importation of enslaved Africans. Each of these groups brought their own customs and practices, which the ruling English, despite the Navigation Acts, made virtually no effort to influence.

The Navigation Acts were a combination of prohibitions and tariffs regulating production and commerce within the North American colonies, between those colonies and other parts of the Empire as well as with Britain and Europe.[92] For example, in 1732 the exporting of hats to England as well as to foreign countries and from one colony to another was rendered illegal, and a limitation was put on the size of hatting shops and tight restrictions were placed on iron forges. The motivation for this legislation was economic rather than cultural; the hope was to maximize the export market for English manufactured goods and to minimize potential competition from the colonies. Unlike later colonial policy in India or Africa, the "civilizing" of (a small fraction) of the indigenous population was not at stake.[93] Colonial subjects were not punished for wearing the "wrong" clothing, nor was all colonial production eliminated, nor all smuggling stopped. Consumption of English goods and the practice of English customs thus varied greatly from colony to colony, and among individuals and groups within those colonies. Over the long term, the result was a series of complex hybridizations of a variety of English and other aesthetic, political and social forms.

The Dutch who settled in New York and New Jersey, for example, persisted in Dutch customs – including religious toleration, forms of Christmas celebration, and separation of Church and State, as well as styles of architecture and interior décor. This may be seen clearly in domestic architecture. The underlying logic of Dutch and English house-framing differed throughout the early modern period. While in the seventeenth century almost "pure" forms of both were built, by the mid-eighteenth century hybrid forms were to be found in New York, New Jersey and occasionally elsewhere, as those of Dutch descent adopted English and Huguenot forms and vice versa.[94] These Dutch families also brought with them and continued to make distinctively Dutch objects of interior décor, most familiarly the piece of cabinetry called the *kas*. Their dwellings were, furthermore, marked by the acquisition of goods from the entire Dutch Empire, including Indonesian tapestries and Sumatran serving dishes.[95] In parallel, French Huguenots maintained close contacts with Protestants in France and continued to make and purchase goods marked by a French Protestant aesthetic, while those who migrated from the German lands in the eighteenth century did the same.[96] In Pennsylvania, where they settled heavily, German immigrants and their descendants brought highly decorative patterns based on the natural world, particularly tulips, pomegranates, and fuchsias, which can be found on furniture, fabrics and pottery. Not only was the pottery far more colorful and decorative than that made in New England, but there were also distinctive forms, such as the fruit pie dish called a *poichissel* and apple butter pots called *epfel buther haffa*.[97] Similar examples could be provided from the intersections of Scots, Irish and Swedish cultures and others with whom they intermingled.

Not only did non-English immigrants bring different aesthetic forms and linguistic practices, but they often brought the Gregorian calendar, which was in use on most of the European continent by the seventeenth century. Thus by 1751, when the British calendar was changed by law from Julian to Gregorian, "... perhaps as many as one in five white colonial Americans [the proportion of colonists of continental European extraction] was already selectively using the Gregorian calendar."[98] The historian Mark Smith suggests that many colonists moved back and forth between the Julian and Gregorian calendars depending on the context of a given event. He also notes that some Native Americans and Africans apparently did the same. North American colonists in the eighteenth century would not, therefore, have been brought together across the thirteen colonies by shared religion, shared calendars, shared language, shared domestic interiors or conceptions of appropriate building or architectural practice. New hybrid – and thus perhaps "American" – cultural forms did emerge, but those were in this period regional, or even local.

The story is complicated further by the African and African-American presence and influence. While there had been Africans living in North America since almost the beginning of the Virginia colony, it was from the turn of the eighteenth century that white settlers, particularly although by no means exclusively in the South, started to import vast numbers of African slaves to do agricultural, domestic, and artisanal labor. They came from a wide range of African societies and cultures. Some had been captives long before their sale on Africa's west coast, while others had lived freely having experienced different forms of political and social organization. Their lives once they landed were equally varied. In some colonies, like South Carolina, there came to be ten blacks to every white and, at the other extreme, there were parts of New England where there were one hundred whites to every five blacks. The work slaves had been acquired to do also of course varied regionally, as did their degrees of autonomy, and the structure of slavery itself. Despite all those differences, however, life throughout the colonies in the eighteenth century was marked by the slaves' presence.[99]

Although African-Americans were very numerous in the thirteen colonies in the eighteenth century they were, until fifty years ago, most often understood to lie outside history. African-Americans were thought either to have been so traumatized by their capture, sale, and passage across the Atlantic that they had lost the culture they had possessed or, even if it was thought that their minds and psyches had survived the voyage, it was assumed that the dependence generated by their enslavement removed them from history.[100] More recent work has demonstrated that African-Americans did indeed bring cultural practices from Africa with them and that slavery did not, in fact, remove all initiative and drive. Slavery did not, furthermore, generally isolate blacks from white culture, but rather created the conditions for the making of a variety of creole cultures.

The possessions Africans brought with them across the Middle Passage were in their heads rather than their hands (although some were able to bring small musical instruments, amulets, items of clothing, or statuettes). They brought languages, naming practices, agricultural and architectural techniques, sometimes fishing and hunting strategies, recipes, hairstyling and dressing practices, religious beliefs and rituals, and knowledge of music and of how to make musical instruments. Narratives written by slaves provide first-hand testimony to the continuity of the self, and a multitude of examples definitively demonstrate the capacity of their cultures to survive the trauma of enslavement. Venture Smith, for example, arrived in Narragansett in 1737, and although he was very young at the time of his enslavement the narrative he wrote shortly before his death not atypically starts with his memories of his life in Africa.[101] Likewise, at the end of the eighteenth century, free blacks often chose African names, and in that same period "...a significant minority of New York blacks spoke a language that was nearer the African end of the linguistic spectrum."[102] Religious practices and beliefs, too, survived. The literary scholar Harryette Mullen vividly demonstrates the ways in which African conceptions of spirits and spirit possession encouraged irregularity and broken lines in the visual arts created by African-Americans, as well as fostering a milieu that "valued a script for its cryptographic incomprehensibility and uniqueness, rather than its legibility or reproducibility."[103] In parallel, archaeologists have demonstrated that African building, basket-making, and quilting techniques, as well as architectural forms, traversed the Atlantic.[104] None of this knowledge remained static, however, once its possessors reached American shores. "Interaction with slaves from other cultures, with Native Americans and with whites, as well as adaptation to a new environment, forced variation in the form and sometimes content of these cultural possessions."[105] Thus the West African *nkisi*, or "sacred object that embodies spiritual beings," found carefully placed between the inside and outside walls of slave quarters in North America was a bottle (rather than the traditional "gourd, pot, bag, or snail shell") and it was filled with "a button, several cloth sugar and tobacco bags holding plant material, and an iron knife" rather than the contents that would have been used by the Bakongo when they were still in Africa.[106] The historian Shane White has demonstrated – from evidence of a black creole in New York that mixed English, Dutch, and African languages, as well as specific clothing and hair styles – that even in the Middle Atlantic States, where they were far less numerous, African-Americans constructed their own style and their own sub-culture.[107] It should be noted that these differences were, to some extent, encouraged and enforced by slaveholders. In 1735, for example, "…South Carolina's 'Negro Act' attempted to legislate against African-Americans who wore clothing described as being 'above the condition of slaves.'"[108] Black Americans were, in other words, required to dress distinctively, receiving few cast-offs from their masters. The particular place of slaves was further inscribed sartorially by the fact that while white women would never have been seen in public without stays, that was the norm for slave women.[109] Africans continued, in sum, long after the Middle Passage, to make culture, albeit under terribly adverse circumstances.

Not only did African Americans come to meld African, European and Native American forms in their own cultural productions, but they also marked the evolving cultures of the colonies, with enduring effects in the post-revolutionary period. Music may provide an example. Evidence – both from surviving melodies and instruments – for African-American influence in music in North America is very strong. As Nicholas Cresswell put it in 1777: "A great number of young people met together with a Fiddle and Banjo played by two Negros…"[110] The banjo – in the form of a lute with a calabash body, fretless neck and gut strings – originated in West Africa and was brought by slaves to the American South in the eighteenth century. By the end of the century, it was used in concerts, along with the fiddle and sometimes drums, for white audiences.[111] African-American influence on colonial culture may also be seen in the built environment. African architectural influences first appear in the South and spread out later from there. The anthropologist Jay D. Edwards has persuasively demonstrated that the vernacular architecture of the colonial southeastern coast must be considered a creole architecture, with a strong African (by way of Caribbean) influence. These architectural forms then spread both inland and north.[112] The forms of the dwellings of most white and black Virginians became very similar, with African construction techniques strongly influencing both, most probably because it was the same slaves who built the dwellings of both whites and blacks.[113] Finally, in the early national period a form as seemingly "all-American" as the front porch, and a style as widespread as the "shotgun house" were almost certainly importations brought by blacks from Africa or the Caribbean (in the case of the front porch) and Yorubaland (in the case of the shotgun house).[114] It was not only the built environment that was bi-racial and therefore bi-cultural, however, but also the daily life that occurred there. African-Americans were present within the home, as midwives, wet nurses and nannies, as cooks and as seamstresses. A strong case can be made, then, for eighteenth-century Southern American culture as a creole of European, Native American, and African traditions. Finally, as will be seen in the case of the Native Americans, blacks were an "other" against whom whites imagined themselves.[115] Thus, as with the simultaneous preservation of some cultural idioms and the melding of others among white colonists of different origins, the co-existence of Europeans and Africans created a new array of distinctively "American" but plural cultural forms ranging from hybrids to distinctively white or black styles.

From the establishment of the first English settlement in Jamestown, Virginia in 1607, diversity of population was matched by diversity in the conditions and circumstances of founding of the thirteen colonies. Religious differences were critical. Some colonies were established as Anglican, some as Presbyterian, some as Congregational. Quakers constituted an important community in Pennsylvania; and in one, Maryland, Catholics were a significant presence. In yet others multiple religions were in competition. The fact that by 1700 there were over 400 colonial congregations, and that that number had risen to over 3,000 by the eve of Independence in 1775, is indicative of the extent of religious diversity. Not only were many denominations represented, but so too were divergent viewpoints on religious practice and the relation of Church and State. Questions concerning appropriate means of honoring the Sabbath, singing in church, or the location and form of churches created strife within communities and differences from one colony to the next. Even into the eighteenth century some northern colonies required presence at church, and forbade drinking and play on the Sabbath, even if these rules were not strictly enforced.[116] Throughout the colonial period, those with influence within the Church tended also to have political power, and each colony supported dominant religious practices. While religious affiliations and rituals could thus, in theory, have helped to forge ties across the colonies (or linkages back across the Atlantic), their role seems more powerfully to have been the consolidation of local and perhaps regional identifications. Given that Church and State were far from completely distinct in the colonial period, religious differences often mapped on to and consolidated differences in forms of governance.

Political status was equally fundamental; some colonies were founded as proprietary colonies, territories granted to an individual or a group of individuals for their profit and pleasure, and others were founded directly as royal colonies (under the closer control of the Crown), while yet others were charter colonies (under the control of a metropolitan-based corporation). These differences in origin were, in turn, matched by differences in systems of governance. By 1752, eight were royal colonies with Crown-appointed governors, two, Connecticut and Rhode Island, were charter colonies with locally appointed governors, and Pennsylvania, Delaware, and Maryland were colonies with governors appointed by the proprietor with the consent of the Crown. In addition, most had some form of locally elected assembly and royally appointed councils.[117] In the words of the historian Richard Beeman, "The colonies, on the eve of the Revolution, lacked a common political culture; the rules of politics – of electoral politics in particular – varied widely not only from one locality to another but also among groups within the same locality."[118]

Although, in all cases, formal political power – the right to sit in and vote for assemblies in the colonies in which they existed – was possessed only by white, propertied, adult men, the qualifications for the franchise were very varied. Some colonies, like Rhode Island, were quite open – about three-quarters of free adult men met the property qualifications for voting, and they elected many of their public officials – but most other colonies limited suffrage to an elite.[119] Each developed its own rituals and systems of governance, as well as local interpretations of the meaning and content of the English constitution.[120] Thus while Maryland and Virginia, once representative political bodies had been established, quickly ordered a mace, as well as robes for the speaker and the clerk, other colonies chose to do without these symbols of power. Even institutions shared across the colonies – militias, and their accompanying muster or training days, for example – took quite different forms in each region.[121] By the 1760s, therefore, as conflict with England intensified, colonists engaged it from quite divergent experiences of governance.

Divergence in forms of governance and religion was matched by diverse calendars, holidays, money, and weights and measures. Given that each colony was, by definition, autonomous from the others, the British government of course made no effort to encourage a sense of a shared "colonial American" identity. It also did not try to create or reinforce a sense of Englishness amongst the North American colonists. As noted above, before the reform that replaced the Julian with the Gregorian calendar throughout the British Empire, the imperial government tolerated the continued use of the Gregorian calendar by immigrants of Continental origin.[122] And, while most of the colonies celebrated Christmas, Coronation Day, and Election Day, the forms of those celebrations varied greatly. These shared holidays co-existed and competed with many local events. Some of these were imports and some newly invented. Finally, there was no common coinage across North America, and some colonies, starting with Massachusetts in the 1690s, took the radical step of issuing a wide variety of paper money.[123] Those differences were reinforced by the creation of highly local associations and institutions to provide health and educational services, to foster cultural development and knowledge, and to promote sociability. These included bar associations, hospitals, libraries, churches, fraternal organizations, learned societies and universities.[124] Far from producing an American culture or solidarity, these institutions were often engaged in intense rivalry.

There were, then, many forces and institutions dividing the thirteen colonies from England and from each other, but there were also some forces that unified them as well as some that reinforced their ties to the metropole. None of these can be described simply in terms of a shared British-ness nor a fully emergent American-ness. The pre-revolutionary developments that made an American identity a conceivable project were often indirect and always complex. The colonists' experience with the continent's original inhabitants is a case in point.

The invasion of North America by Europeans in the seventeenth century marked both the end of an epoch in Native American history and the beginning of a transformation in the European settlers' cultural repertoire. The most immediate and long-lasting of European imports to the continent were diseases to which the indigenous inhabitants had no resistance, and vast numbers of Native Americans succumbed to them. In the South, for example, the population of indigenous inhabitants declined by 75 per cent between 1685 and 1790. This is particularly striking in a period in which the white population multiplied by 28 and the black by almost seven.[125] Thousands more indigenous people died in wars against the settlers. These statistics vary from colony to colony, but the decimation of the native population and the radical transformation of pre-invasion modes of life were widespread in the thirteen colonies.

This demographic catastrophe has caused some historians to argue that the impact of Native Americans on colonial society was minimal.[126] This position has, however, been effectively countered by a very substantial literature demonstrating four critical sites of Indian influence: (1) borrowings of Indian material culture, language, and practices by the colonists, extending as far as what anthropologist Fernando Ortiz has called (in reference to Cuba) "transculturation";[127] (2) reactions (often contradictory, e.g. fear and admiration) to the Indian presence; (3) side-effects of both violence and often failed efforts at conversion and assimilation; (4) and, finally, functioning as an "other" against whom a white/European/settler/American identity was forged. While it is clear that the European (and European-enslaved African) settlement of North America utterly transformed indigenous societies, settler society was also shaped by the Native American presence. To some early settler eyes, in fact, the influence was largely one way. As Cotton Mather rather ruefully put it:

> Tho' they saw a People Arrive among them, who were Clothed in *Habits* of much more Comfort and Splendour, than what there was to be seen in the *Rough Skins* with which they hardly covered themselves; and had *Houses full of Good Things*, vastly out-shining their squalid and dark *Wigwams*; And they saw this People Replenishing their *Fields*, with *Trees* and with *Grains*, and useful *Animals*, which until now they had been wholly Strangers to; yet they did not seem touch'd in the least, with any *Ambition* to come at such Desireable Circumstances, or with any *Curiosity* to enquire after the *Religion* that was attended with them.[128]

During the seventeenth and eighteenth centuries, Native Americans provided needed goods, knowledge, and techniques, thereby profoundly marking colonial life. The first and most obvious Native American influences were in the domains of foodstuffs, agricultural, fishing and hunting techniques, medicinal plants, tobacco, and forms of transportation. Indians initiated the settlers into the uses of corn or maize, squash, maple syrup, tomatoes, cranberries, pine-tree candles, and Jerusalem artichokes. Indians taught the English to plant beans and squash along with the corn so as to fix nitrogen in the soil (as well as to use fish as fertilizer). They instructed them how not to scare the game they were trying to hunt, which berries, nuts and fruits were edible and which not, as well as what ailments could best be treated with what plant. Hemlock and alder bark, "soyles oyl," earth nuts, water-lilies, clowne's all-heal and garden patience were all found useful. Once their pupils had learned to grow their own corn and vegetables, to successfully fish, hunt and gather, their native instructors taught them how to process, preserve and cook the new ingredients. These became the foundation of the diet of both whites and blacks: "He [the slave] is called up in the morning at day break, and is seldom allowed time enough to swallow three mouthfuls of hominy, or hoe-cake, but is driven out immediately to the field to hard labor ... about noon he eats his dinner... His meal consists of hominy and salt, and if his master be a man of humanity, he has a little fat, skimmed milk, rusty bacon..."[129]

Settlers not only adapted their diet from that of the Indians, but also their clothing and modes of transport. Moccasins, furs, and leather clothing were all sometimes worn by immigrant rural dwellers, and without light-weight canoes crafted from birchbark, toboggans, and snowshoes made from bentwood and rawhide, settlers would have found their mobility in both warm and cold weather far more limited.[130] Some male colonists borrowed a hairstyle (called the macaroni – men wearing one lock of hair longer than the rest over the forehead) from Indian men.[131] They also found Indian pipes, baskets and bowls both practical and beautiful and incorporated them into their households. Finally, the cultural transfer did not occur only in the domains of material culture and husbandry: settlers also chose to adopt Indian names for places (e.g. Massachusetts, Connecticut, Shenandoah) and for the new animals and foodstuffs they encountered, such as moose, skunk and raccoon or hominy, and some even came to adopt Indian worldviews.[132] The historian Colin Galloway has in fact argued that cross-influences were such that archaeologists have difficulties distinguishing eighteenth-century Indian and colonial villages.[133]

The knowledge that these goods had been appropriated from Indians tainted them as far as many in the metropole were concerned. Thus, King James famously criticized tobacco in the following terms: "His Majesty wisely fore-seeing the evil consequences that would follow, by such immoderate sucking in the foul smoke of this *Indian* Weed, and He being the Physician of the Body Politick, doth by many strong and excellent Arguments, disswade his Subjects from imitating the practice of the Heathen *Indians*, in drinking in this noxious fume."[134] The notion that people would become what they ingested, sat on, or wore was commonplace; given that the Native Americans were generally perceived by the English as primitive and barbarous from the seventeenth century well into the eighteenth, it is not surprising that these borrowings provoked suspicion at best and outrage at worst. Even those colonists who lived in areas from which Native Americans and their culture had been eradicated, however, and whose everyday lives were virtually untouched by them, were shaped and influenced by their presence on the continent.

This foundational importance of the Native American presence in Colonial America may be best demonstrated by following historian James Axtell's counter-factual thought-experiment. He has proposed that we attempt to imagine how settlement would have been different had the continent been uninhabited.[135] He suggests that historians need to grasp "…the changes wrought in Anglo-American culture … by reacting negatively and perhaps unconsciously to the native presence, threat and challenge."[136] A key absence the lack of an Indian presence would have brought about is that of missionaries. Without the "heathen," they would have had no mission, and the strong evangelical current in American culture would have been lost.[137] Perhaps even more important would have been the absence of a certain kind of violence.[138] Early settlers lived in fear of Native Americans and of their alliances with the French; they also had to live with the violence they committed against the indigenous peoples. "Having the American natives as frequent and deadly adversaries – and even as allies – did more to 'Americanize' the English colonists than any other human factor…"[139] Most colonial men (white and black) served in the militia during the incessant conflicts that started with King Philip's War of 1675 and continued through the eighteenth century; most therefore had the experience of fighting both with and against Native Americans, in wars that melded the most violent of Native American, English and Continental battle techniques, reinforcing an "…image of the Indian as a dangerous and incorrigible warrior."[140] Scalping, for example, was invented by Native Americans but encouraged – through the offering of bounties – by the colonists.[141]

Finally, Native Americans modeled another relationship to nature, to property, to religion, to governance, and to society itself to which the settlers necessarily compared themselves. That alternative was sometimes vilified and sometimes sanctified, but it was always present and helped settlers to forge a sense of commonality among themselves that their diversity had otherwise made far from inevitable. In Britain during the first half of the eighteenth century Native Americans were generally characterized as naïve, innocent, vulnerable, childlike, and very distant from British culture. Correspondingly, the American continent was allegorized as a female Indian. The frequent choice to represent the colonies as a young Indian woman unified and homogenized the colonies but also cast them in an inferior position.[142] In the 1760s and 1770s, as rebellious settlers distanced themselves from Britain they appropriated a re-worked version of the Indian allegory; in the place of the modest maiden came to stand a masculine Indian hero.[143] Whether as innocent savage or terrifying warrior, however, the Indian was a crucial, unifying, symbolic presence in metropolitan, colonial, revolutionary and early national imaginaries.

The fact that the land the Europeans "settled" was already populated had, therefore, an enduring effect on the culture of the colonies. Even as their individual and regional experiences varied widely – by the mid-eighteenth century, some were in daily contact with those "others," while others knew them only as illustrations in books, as symbols, or as characters in stories – they did all share in the history of complex negotiation with the peoples who had been there first. They all inhabited a matrix of borrowing, distance, admiration, contempt, and guilt; a matrix that provided a common ground against which the juridical status of each colony, its religious affiliations, the origins of its inhabitants, and its climate all deeply influenced the cultural forms that evolved there.

Commonalities across the thirteen colonies created by this complex and paradoxical shared experience of violently settling a settled land were reinforced by more mundane means, including the print media and the postal system (created in 1710). The *Boston News-Letter* was founded in 1704 and became the first enduring newspaper in North America; it was followed shortly by others. These papers were all local in production but broader in distribution. Almanacs, most famously Benjamin Franklin's *Poor Richard's Almanac* published between 1732 and 1757, containing a wide range of useful information, also helped lay the groundwork for a national culture. In the domain of religion some historians argue that the religious movement known as the Great Awakening (1734–1744), disseminated through North America in part by itinerant preachers, provided a shared spiritual experience.[144] And, added to cultural institutions of local or regional reach were those, like the American Philosophical Society founded in 1743 in Philadelphia (also by Benjamin Franklin), that gave educated colonists a locus in America for collective intellectual engagement.

The specificity of this world as a settler colony created, in sum, common experiences across the seaboard. All had to negotiate their relation with the Crown and metropole, with the Native Americans, with white neighbors with very different origins from themselves, and with life in a society in which slavery and wage-labor co-existed. Nearly all had either themselves traversed the Atlantic or grown up with people who remembered and could recount another life. The fact that they or their parents or grandparents had chosen to take the huge risk of crossing the Atlantic (or had been forced to do so) makes it also likely that their first priority might not have been the emulation of the place they had left behind.[145] Thus, although the diversity was real, some historians would argue that the importance of the differences was diminished by the colonies' colonial status. The great range in the founding structures of the colonies, were countered by the considerable efforts made in the eighteenth century to smooth out these differences and to model colonial governance more systematically on the English paradigm, although significant variation remained.[146] Finally, strong ties to the English Crown were shared across the colonies. The elaborate celebrations held on the monarch's birthday and coronation day bear witness to those emotional attachments.[147]

Some scholars, most notably Richard Bushman and T. H. Breen, argue that the colonies, at least by the mid-eighteenth century, should, in fact, be conceptualized as an extension of Britain, analogous to the British provinces.[148] The colonists were, correspondingly, ultimately overwhelmingly English in attitude, orientation, and self-conception.[149] Or, in the words of the textile curator, Linda Baumgarten: "The same types and colors of heap Welsh woolens were used for slaves in Maryland, south to the Carolinas, and later in Mississippi and Georgia; British osnaburgs were available in stores through the colonies. Expensive items such as silks were sometimes duplicated as well."[150] These historians have persuasively shown that not only did the colonists avidly acquire English domestic objects such as china, small metal goods, mirrors, furniture, rugs, draperies and silverware, they also dressed themselves, their servants, and their slaves in English fashions, cooked from British cookbooks, learned how to behave from English etiquette books, and designed their homes according to British pattern books.[151] The evidence for these acquisitions is irrefutable; what is more debatable is their context and their meaning.

First of all, while it is clear that colonists bought substantial quantities of English goods they were far from the only things they chose to purchase.[152] It would appear, for example, that many of the Boston elite – as well as others up and down the Atlantic seaboard – acquired their furnishings from local artisans rather than having them brought from England.[153] These local cabinetmakers based their designs on English patterns, but altered them in some subtle and less subtle ways to create a distinctive local style (whether or not that style should be labeled *American*, as some historians do, is another problem).[154] Their local variations were significant enough that it is easy to "…differentiate Boston, Newport, Connecticut, New York, Hudson Valley, Philadelphia, and Baltimore 'schools' of cabinetmaking…"[155] Likewise, local productions of silver and pewter, of distinctive and characteristic design, were heavily patronized.

Crucially, the English goods most eagerly sought by the colonists were those that either English legislation or local lacks made either expensive or unavailable. Regulations limiting North American cloth production tremendously limited the development of the textile, clothing and upholstery industries.[156] The relatively late discovery of clay appropriate to fine china, combined with British taxation policies, fostered the dominance of British table services. Given, therefore, that the British had succeeded in creating a monopoly of certain goods, definitively determining the motivation for their purchase is difficult. How can one know if colonists turned to English goods because they identified themselves as English? One could argue just as plausibly that the colonists were, to some extent, "buying English" because, if they wanted certain manufactured goods, they had no choice.[157] Ultimately, the argument that the thirteen colonies should be conceptualized as a more distant English province is refuted on the one hand by the heterogeneity of the colonial population and of the colonies themselves, and on the other by the shared experience of cohabitation with Native Americans and enslaved Africans as well as the colonial experience itself (including the sense of being on a frontier).

When conflict with England broke out in the 1760s, the American colonies were different from the metropole in their social, economic, and cultural lives. Their diversity of origin, the consequent reciprocal shaping of culture, and the ways in which they adapted to the exigencies of life in North America ensured that they could no longer be "English." In fact, in the decades preceding the Revolution, visual images of the colonies circulating in England, America and France depicted the

American colonies as a "singular body politic" with its own identity and interests.[158] Those images were anticipatory rather than reflective, however. The colonists, being acutely aware of their subjection to the British Crown and Parliament, were however certain that that status assured them of certain rights. They were not, therefore, "Americans" just yet either, fighting for a state of their own as colonial subjects around the world a century and a half later would. As will be seen in Chapter 4, from the 1760s onward American colonists built on this complex repertoire of cultural forms, lived experience, and institutions to mobilize contestation and to begin to create a sense of what "America" and "Americans" could be. They were, however, also deeply influenced by the mother-country's own example a bit over a century earlier, when the Scots, English, and Irish decided to revolt against what they saw as an arbitrary exercise of power; and it is to that story that we now turn.

−3−

England's Unfinished Revolution
Challenges to Monarchical Culture

The inhabitants of the British Archipelago, from the outbreak of the Civil War in 1642 through to the restoration of the monarchy in 1660, experienced what may perhaps best be characterized as an unfinished cultural and political revolution. Very radical positions concerning political, social and economic organization were circulated, more representative forms of governance were attempted, and transformations in the relation of culture and politics essayed.[1] The most extreme positions were held only by a few, the Commonwealth was short-lived, and the revolutionaries were ultimately unable to agree on a non-monarchical form of governance or political culture. Unlike the almost equally short-lived French First Republic, the Commonwealth did not succeed in creating a symbolic repertoire, enduring new holidays or rituals, or a political culture recoverable by succeeding generations. Indeed, in the immediate aftermath of the coronation of Charles II, the old forms of governance and religion – hereditary monarchy, the peerage, state religion – were all reinstated, destined to remain in place to the present day. The monarch's profile would adorn the coinage of the realm, the scepter, crown, and orb would return as symbols of state, the royal palaces would be refurbished and a courtly culture would be recreated. That monarchy and courtly culture would not, however, in fact be the Old Regime restored.[2]

The rupture of the Civil War and regicide in tandem with the experiment with parliamentary rule and the expansion of cultures beyond the court at the end of the seventeenth century and into the eighteenth ensured that the old political culture could never be resurrected. One could argue, in fact, that the very resilience of the divine-right monarchy attests to the depth and significance of the experience of the Interregnum. It is as if, having attempted an experiment in republican governance before having the means to effect a cultural revolution and thereby create a republican polity and society, the country found that the trauma was too great ever to go down that road again. The limitations on the Crown's power effected in the Revolution of 1688 and later may also have made such a gamble seem unnecessary. This chapter will sketch both the cultural transformations and their limits in this first modern revolution; for despite those limits, this moment did bring significant innovations.

There was creativity and a long-lasting heritage of the mid-century upheaval in Britain but rather than finding expression in new *political or social rituals, iconography* or *material culture*, its greatest impact would be through *words*.[3] The visions for political, social, and economic transformations contained in the sermons, pamphlets, petitions, poems, and broadsheets would have enormous impact throughout the Atlantic world and beyond.[4] The radical Protestantism that would be a driving force behind political change emphasized the importance of the word because it was deeply suspicious of embodied practices and ritual. Thus, the central role played by religion in the tensions leading up to war, during the conflict, and throughout the Interregnum provides part of the explanation for the limited nature of that revolution in culture broadly defined.[5]

A second crucial element was the still limited nature of commercial society in the first half of the seventeenth century. Cultural production (in the conventional aesthetic sense) was still dominated by the court. Although, as was discussed in the preceding chapter, there was very substantial economic development in the late sixteenth and early seventeenth centuries, it did not yet translate into the availability of a wide variety of goods to the non-elite population, nor did it generate the advertising and marketing strategies that would lead people to reconceptualize the place of goods in their lives. Thus, the two domains of material culture to deviate substantially from the style established by the early Stuarts – clothing and architecture – were marked by a religious (Puritan) rather than a political aesthetic.[6]

That religion should have been so important and so generative of divisiveness in seventeenth-century England is hardly surprising. Henry VIII's schism with the Catholic Church had taken place a century earlier, leaving behind unresolved conflicts concerning the relation between Church and State, church governance, religious practice, and toleration. These played out, with theme and variation, and with differing degrees of destructiveness, in each successive reign. England continued, furthermore, to be home to a sizeable Catholic population and Protestants divided among many sects and tendencies. After James VI of Scotland became James I of England in 1604, the situation was further complicated owing to the significant divergences between Scots and English religious practice and in the relations between Church and State in the two polities. The continued commitment to a religion of state coupled with profound differences in belief divided the monarch's subjects and created a highly volatile situation. Contrary to what one might have expected, however, given the attempt to assassinate James I in an effort to safeguard Catholic interests, the most disruptive conflicts in seventeenth-century Britain were not between Catholics and Protestants, but among Protestants.

Just as it is impossible, in this period, to separate religion from politics, or, as we saw in the last chapter, culture from politics, it is impossible to separate religion from culture, in both the aesthetic and the anthropological senses in which I use the concept in this book. Religion is itself part of people's "culture," and in certain historical circumstances, of which the seventeenth century was certainly one, it can profoundly shape other domains of culture. Religious beliefs concerning idolatry, modesty and humility influenced the stances taken toward the arts and clothing, music, alcohol, the naming of children, the meaning of sex, and attitudes toward the poor. Religious beliefs concerning charity framed conceptions of luxury. The calendar of religious holidays shaped people's daily lives, including cycles of labor and rest, of sociability, and of food consumption. That most people knew great portions of the Bible by heart shaped their use of language and the metaphors at their disposal. Key to the seventeenth-century conflict was the fact that two Protestant tendencies, the Puritans and the Arminians, were deeply divided in their vision of Godly culture.[7] The Puritans held that swearing, drinking, smoking, "immodest" dress, holiday-making, gambling, the theater, music and art in Church, and secular entertainments on the Sabbath – all everyday cultural practices – were anathema, a sign of imminent damnation. The Arminians, by contrast, believed that beauty in music, art, and clothing celebrated God, as did joyous pleasure in holidays. Protestants also did not share a vision of the appropriate roles for men and women in the home, in the church, or in politics. Disagreement among the Arminians, and Presbyterian, Congregational, and Radical Puritans, as well, in some cases, within each of these groups fundamentally shaped the revolutionary process. Conflicts over religious practice then, were also and inevitably, conflicts over cultural practice.

This, the first modern revolution, was defined by the central place of religion, by the violence of the war itself, and by its very precocity. War is by definition destructive of life and property. The English Civil War, however, was, when compared with the American and French revolutions (although not with contemporary Continental wars), especially violent. Equally crucial was the fact that this was the first of the revolutions. While neither those who joined the Boston Tea Party nor those who participated in the storming of the Bastille had any idea either that their rebellion would end in revolution, the English, Scots, and Irish could have even less sense of an alternative to monarchical rule and culture. The early date of this conflict also meant that the commercialization of society was less developed and there was less of an imaginary of an elite culture beyond the court than would be the case for the later revolutions. Thus while contingency, accident, and improvisation played key roles in all three revolutions, and while all three relied heavily on past models as they tried to imagine their future, that was particularly true in this case.

The Religious Revolution

The imbrication of politics and religion was pervasive from the beginning of this conflict; all the participants were fighting for their vision of a Godly, God-fearing polity. Since religion permeated virtually all aspects of everyday life, that meant they were also fighting for their vision of a pious society. While tolerance of difference varied from one group to the next, and freedom of conscience was a topic of hot debate, religious pluralism was far from a widespread commitment. All, by contrast, were deeply concerned with Church–State relations, church governance, and religious practice both within the church walls and in everyday life. This is not to say that efforts to enforce religious precepts always took precedence over other interests. As in the case of James I, a convinced Calvinist, but also a political pragmatist, political exigencies sometimes trumped religious conviction. He was firmly convinced that an episcopacy – not part of Calvinist doctrine – was necessary for effective Church–State relations, and therefore endorsed that institution. But even James I's pragmatism had its limits: his vision of the powers God had granted him as a monarch by divine right caused continuous and serious clashes with Parliament, laying a foundation of mistrust between Parliament and Crown for his son to inherit. Charles I proved even less able to sense which of his religious beliefs could be imposed upon his realm. He attempted to remold both the English and Scots Churches according to the precepts of Arminianism, thereby exacerbating an already-fraught religious, economic, and political situation. Parliament, and the opposition more broadly, found the relation between religion and politics equally treacherous: sometimes religious differences fractured what might have otherwise been solid coalitions; sometimes such differences were overcome.

Arminianism was an early seventeenth-century reaction to the Calvinist doctrine of predestination. Followers of the movement held that people could have some influence in their own salvation – that free will and God's sovereignty were compatible. Arminianism also put greater emphasis on faith and the place of prayer and ritual in the maintenance of that faith, and on the sacraments, as well as on the role of the clergy and the Church hierarchy, than did mainstream Calvinists. The differences proved too great to be tolerated and the Calvinist leadership explicitly rejected the Arminian position in 1618. In England Arminianism was starkly set against the most visible form of Calvinism there: the radical Protestantism pejoratively labeled "Puritan" by its opponents. These radical Protestants were unhappy with the *via media* between Catholicism and Continental Protestantism worked out during the reigns of Elizabeth I and James I, and they sought to "purify" the established, or Anglican, church. They were opposed to efforts to centralize religious practice through the *Book of Common Prayer* and wanted to rid churches of ornamentation, ritual, and instrumental music, in order to focus attention on the word. They believed in the importance both of individual reading of Scripture and of sermonizing, in which the word of God was brought orally to the congregation. Radical Protestants also advocated more rigorous pursuit of the teachings of the Bible in everyday life. Finally, some radical Protestants sought a congregational and others a presbyterian model of Church governance, but all advocated an elected rather than an appointed leadership, as well as a central role for the laity. Given that Charles I's Arminianism would incline him to reinforce the Church of England's already hierarchical and ritualized nature – going in precisely the opposite direction to that desired by the Puritans – the stage was set for conflict.

King Charles I had different religious convictions from his father, but was also less tolerant, and sought to impose his vision upon the nation. He enacted reforms intended to remove power from the laity, centralize church authority and create tighter links between the Crown and the Church. It was, in part, that impulse that led him to elevate the widely hated high-church Archbishop Laud, who would come to serve as a lightning-rod for those opposed to these moves away from what they saw as the true Church. Under the leadership of Archbishop Laud, the Church made a number of highly controversial changes in the organization of religious life. One such innovation was the displacement of the wooden communion tables present in most churches from the center of the nave to the eastern end. Not only were the tables displaced, but wooden altar rails, dividing the communion table from the congregation, were often erected. Non-Arminian parishioners were hostile to this because they understood it to have theological implications; that the placement of tables and their separation from the congregants indicated that the Laudians believed that the actual body and blood of Christ was present at communion (rather than communion being a commemorative event).[8] This provoked a powerful reaction; in 1641 Puritans, like William Dowsing, the Commissioner for East Anglia, set about ripping out the altar rails that Laud had had installed in churches. These efforts at purging English churches of what was viewed as the stigmata of papacy foreshadowed further iconoclasm during the Civil War.[9] As seriously, Charles I did not confine his efforts at religious change to England, but in 1637 tried to impose a new set of ecclesiastical canons and the English prayer book on the Scottish church, a move that was met with enormous hostility that quickly turned into war. Thus it was Charles I's interventions into religious life, as much as his military defeats, mishandling of Parliament, and arbitrary use of power, that ultimately created the conditions of possibility for regicide. As will be seen in greater detail below, however, religious differences among Charles's opponents, in combination with difficulty in agreeing on a non-monarchical form of rule, also limited the constructive possibilities of this revolution.

The nine years (1642–1651) during which the three civil wars were intermittently fought saw numerous efforts by the parliamentary and army forces, as well as pamphleteers and petitioners, to restructure and re-imagine England's religious life. One of the most immediate and direct strategies was to continue to attempt to rid the landscape of what were thought to be signs of idolatry; but reforms in church practice were also implemented, as well as efforts to renew, transform and purify the practices of the inhabitants of the British Isles in accordance with Puritan principles.[10] The years 1643–1646 thus saw repeated instances of iconoclasm, including the destruction of religious statues, woodwork, and stained glass. More dramatically and definitively, some churches were burned to the ground, while in other locations monumental public crucifixes were removed. Celebrated cases of the latter include the removal of Cheapside Cross in London in 1643 as well as the demolition of the cross in Abingdon's marketplace in 1644.[11] While some of this destruction was no doubt a result of the hazards of war, some was clearly intentional, designed to remove objects and buildings deemed offensive to God and to produce religious sites appropriate for radical Protestant worship.

The more peaceful interventions built on earlier strategies and practices: moral suasion through preaching and pamphlet publication; reformed everyday practice, such as in dress; and, legislation. Many of these efforts appear, at least at first glance, to have been concerned only with religious matters, and reactive rather than creative in approach, refusing of change rather than advocating it. And, indeed, the rhetoric was often religious and one of return, return to the true Church and the true commonwealth. Closer examination nonetheless reveals both an agenda much broader than religion and much innovation only partially masked by the language of a call for a return to an earlier, authentic practice. Arguments, for example, often started with morality and concluded with either mercantilism or concerns with economic efficiency. A pamphlet defending the role of the theater as a force for religious pedagogy thus also claimed that closing the theaters put many out of work and was therefore opposed to the national interest.[12] Many of the diatribes against the evils of alcohol emphasized that not only did drink offend God, it also rendered workers much less competent. In parallel, a pamphlet endorsing the use of coffee cited its benefits as a replacement for beer; it kept artisans lively and alert. God and profit sat side by side in these texts, attesting to their place in a world more and more preoccupied with economic expansion and the rationalization of production, but still justifying their interventions in the name of God.

Scripture was mobilized to argue for social, as well as economic change, notably in the domain of gender relations as may be seen in John Milton's *The Doctrine and Discipline of Divorce*, published in 1643. *The Doctrine and Discipline of Divorce* is a forty-page argument for the legalization of divorce on the grounds that there was nothing to be gained by incompatible people being forced to remain together.[13] In brief, God created woman to be company for man; if she was not company then it was not God's will that the couple remain united. The argument was very radical in content; not only was hostility to the dissolubility of marriage in this period great, but the strength of the endorsement of companionate marriage was highly controversial. The form of the argument was, by contrast, conservative, the justification and demonstration based almost entirely on biblical authority. Milton's text is but one example. The period saw a profusion of pamphlets and petitions by and about women in which claims were made not only for changes in marriage, but also for women's right to participate in politics, all with a thorough grounding in Scripture.

Substantial numbers of women took advantage of radical Protestantism's emphasis on the individual reading of Scripture to seek in it justifications for a transformation in their role.[14] Some historians have argued that the Reformation, in its de-centering of Mary, and refusal of the intercession of saints (thereby removing female interlocutors between women and a God always imagined in paternal form), and the dissolution of convents, disempowered women, or at least distanced them from religion.[15] Although the patriarchalism of most varieties of seventeenth-century English Protestant radicalism cannot be denied, the evidence (and, as we will see, that from colonial America) belies that claim. It supports, rather, those who have made the opposite argument, seeing in the elimination of the celibacy of the priesthood an elevation of women's status, and in the emphasis on the individualized relation with God an opportunity for women's independent thought and action.[16] While asserting only their desire to return to a prelapsarian moment, women in the radical Protestant sects used both their moral obligation to read Scripture and the important place that everyday, including domestic, morality played in Puritanism to carve out space for novel kinds of speech, writing and action. In addition to submitting petitions, they turned their traditional needlecrafts to religious ends (although not, as far as I have been able to determine, explicitly political ends). Domestically produced embroideries from this time, virtually always done by women, most often depicted a scene from Scripture, sometimes accompanied by the text.[17] A piece of lace, for example, created in the first half of the seventeenth century by a woman who signed her work B.E.B, depicts the temptation of Adam and Eve in the Garden of Eden.[18] The maker of the pillow cover in Figure 3.1 was even more ambitious; her work brought four scenes from the Old Testament into the household's daily tactile life. The scenes were all from the book of Genesis and included: God creating Adam, God creating Eve from Adam's rib, the temptation of Eve, and the expulsion from the Garden of Eden. These scenes were both particularly well adapted to embroidery and conveyed an appropriate moral message.

It took months, if not years, of patient stitching to produce these embroideries, lace panels, crewel-work pieces or tapestries. Although needlewomen often used

Figure 3.1 *Pillow cover*, England, early seventeenth century. Linen, embroidered with metal thread and silks (Victoria and Albert Museum, London). Museum number: T.115-1928.

canvases or fabrics upon which an outline had been traced, or looked to patternbooks for ideas, the colors, stitches and details were always the product of their imaginations. The work itself was very slow and repetitive, requiring great bodily discipline. When done alone, by someone of religious conviction, it could no doubt have been labor conducive to a meditative state. Imagining this as a spiritual exercise is not, therefore, difficult.

After completion these needleworked pieces were often tacked on a wall, or they served as a table-covering, or were used as a cushion, thus providing a daily reminder of their content and the work, and perhaps prayer, behind them. These handicrafts, therefore, had two lives, one while they were labored over and a second when looked at, used, and admired. These women may not only have engaged in a form of religious meditation, therefore, but asserted the importance of women's domestic labor to the family's righteous life.

Sometimes, however, Puritan hostility to a given cultural form did limit the reformers' imaginative capacities, and they became purely repressive and reactive. The parliamentary ordinance suppressing the theater in 1642 is a case in point: "Whereas the ... distracted Estate of England, threatened with a Cloud of Blood, by a Civill Warre, calls for all possible meanes to appease and avert the Wrath of God ... and whereas publike Sports doe not well agree with publike Calamites, nor publike Stage-playes with the Seasons of Humiliation, this being Exercise of sad and pious Solmnity, and the other being Spectacles of pleasure, too commonly expressing lacivious Mirth and Levitie: It is therefore thought fit, and Ordeined by the Lords and Commons in this Parliament Assembled ... that Stage-playes shall cease."[19] In this case, sports and the theater were associated and both deemed inappropriate distractions when the nation was traversing a fraught and dangerous period. It is, at first glance, a surprising association, for one could have imagined a move to eradicate spectator sports, which presumably had no moral pedagogic power, while allowing the theater to continue, but mandating the performance of uplifting rather than lascivious or frivolous plays.

This absence is particularly striking, since theater's capacity to persuade was enough part of common sense for those protesting the prohibition to use precisely that argument. Thus the author of the 1643 *Actors Remonstrance* wrote that: "wee have purged our Stages from all obscene and scurrilous jests..." and that plays are now performed "...in which, vice is alwayes sharply glanced at, and punished, and vertue rewarded and encouraged..." The text promises furthermore that if the theaters were reopened they would ban women unless accompanied by their husbands and forbid the use of tobacco.[20] The author then implicitly acknowledged the association of the theater with what was considered gender disorder and other "vices," but claimed that it could have a new life. The defense of theater was taken further in a 1661 (post-Restoration) text with the argument that while there had been, without question, excesses in the theater, there was no intrinsic evil in it any more than there was in clothing, food, drink or even sleep, all of which could be abused.[21] Neither were persuasive; the ban on the theater remained in place until the Restoration, although performances did, in fact, continue to occur. It would appear, then, that there was such a distaste, mistrust, and fear of some cultural forms, particularly the theater, that its obvious capacities for moral pedagogy were ignored. This position had changed by the last third of the eighteenth century, at least among American and French revolutionaries, who also felt that theater in its current manifestation was highly dangerous, but that precisely in that danger lay its power.

If theater were deemed hopelessly corrupt, the spoken word in church and beyond was considered a powerful persuasive tool. Sermons, broadsheets, and pamphlets abounded with exhortations to moral renewal in an astonishing range of domains. Among the milder and the more predictable were arguments that people should, for the sake of God and the well-being of the English nation, be honest and honorable in their business dealings, taking no more than a just profit, and be generous to the poor. George Fox, for example, extended morality into the world of business when he harangued the merchants of London to be just in their business dealings, to "...ask no more for the thing than you would have..."[22] He was, further, appalled by their extravagance in the face of poverty: "...you going in your gold and silver, yea in your very shooes laced, and the poor want bread, want stocking and shooes; and you your many dishes, change of dishes, and that you call novelties, and the poor cannot get bread; spare one of your dishes, and let it be carried to the place for the poor, and do not let them come begging for it neither..."[23] Writers and preachers felt entitled not merely to urge correct business dealings and a charitable disposition toward the poor, but also to intervene in the domain of dress, food, pets, entertainment, and sexual habits.

Moral suasion was deemed an appropriate strategy, but so, too, was legal coercion. Laws were passed concerning an equally vast range of everyday activities, including swearing, cock-matches, horse-races, dueling, drinking, consumption of tobacco, dancing, the theater, holiday celebrations, marriage, birth, and burial. These interventions, in some cases concerning life far outside the walls of the church, were, depending on their nature, sometimes phrased in purely religious terms, and sometimes melded a concern with Godliness with the need to protect or to generate a sound political order. The reappearance of efforts to transform (or ban) many of these same everyday cultural practices in both the American and French revolutions attests both to the influence of the English Revolution and to the potential these seemingly apolitical practices bore for political transformation.

The series of statutes passed in Parliament over the course of 1644, for example, restricting behavior on Sunday and prohibiting cursing and gambling, were framed as necessary only because such behavior was offensive to God. Thus: "...as all prophane Swearing and Cursing is forbidden by the Word of God, Be it therefore enacted... That no person or persons shall from henceforth prophanely Swear or Curse..."[24] Very similar language was used to justify regulating behavior on the Sabbath: "Forasmuch as there is nothing more acceptable to God then the true and sincere service and worship of him according to his holy will, and that the keeping of the Lords Day is a principall part of the true Service of God... Be it enacted that ... there shall be no meetings, assemblies or concourse of people..."[25] The list of prohibited activities included those generally thought of as secular entertainments: bear- and bull-baiting, games, sports, interludes, wrestling, shooting, dancing, bowling, bell-ringing for pleasure or pastime, and common plays. Also to be eradicated were wakes (otherwise known as feasts) and church-ales. Sometimes the religiously-based criticism of these activities was that they were held on Sundays and distracted people from their proper activities of church attendance and prayer. Some of the cultural practices were viewed, like the theater, as hopelessly corrupt and corrupting whatever day of the week they were indulged in (this was true of dancing for many). Finally wakes were condemned, because although occasioned by funerals they were thought to be moments for excess of all kinds (particularly in food and drink). The vision of religion in these texts is one characterized by a radically austere everyday and by the saturation of both private and public life by the codes of piety.

Some of the texts in this same collection of statutes made the connection between morality and politics explicit. For example, several of the laws punishing drunkenness moved from religion to the domain of politics more narrowly defined: "Whereas the loathsome and odious sinne of Drunkennesse is of late growne into common use within this Realme, being the Root and Foundation of many other enormous sinnes, as Bloodshed, Stabbing, Murder, Swearing, Fornication, Adultery and such like; to the great dishonour of God and of our Nation; the overthrow of many good Arts and Manuall Trades; the disabling of divers Work-men; and the generall Impoverishing of many good Subjects, abusively wasting the good Creatures of God..."[26] Alcohol was thus displeasing not only in the sight of God; not only did it, as alleged above, discourage efficient labor, but it led to the dishonor of the nation itself.

These years of war also saw substantial revisions of Church practice. Parliament mandated the close monitoring of the content of sermons and a new emphasis on the importance of individual reading of the Bible, on the participation of lay elders in Church governance, and on the centrality of preaching. In 1645, for example, the Episcopacy was abolished and the Prayer Book banned, followed by the 1650 repeal of the Act of Uniformity. The Act had required the use of the *Common Prayer Book* as well as weekly attendance (upon penalty of a fine) in the parishioner's Established Church. Once it was repealed, people could worship where they so pleased, founding the principle of religious freedom, although it was not, as the restrictions on participation in Holy Communion indicates, a freedom without judgment.

Access to Holy Communion was now to be limited to those whose outward lives were judged to be consistent with an inner faith. It was, furthermore the parishioners, not the clergy, who were to determine who was sufficiently pious; all were thereby subjected to the surveillance and judgment of their neighbors. Outward behavior was understood to reflect an inner state; any misstep would be understood to be a sign of impiety. This was a different conception of bodily practices than that of some of the courtesy books discussed in the previous chapter, but also than the conception that would appear in both the American and French revolutions. Here bodily practices were reflective, not pedagogic; one *was* what one seemed, one could not *come to be* what one appeared. Acting pious would not make one pious.

These changes would have had a mixed effect on people's everyday life. They found themselves freer in some respects – free to read the Bible, free to attend the church of their choosing. Some, as they policed their neighbors, would have had more power. They also obviously found themselves restricted in many ways, called upon to use their bodies and voices differently, to pray differently, to drink less, to work more. The body of a radical Protestant was not, in other words, the same as an Arminian or even pre-Arminian Established Church body, nor were their relations to either God or their fellow humans unchanged. This was a far less hierarchical organization, one less mediated by ritual, one that placed much responsibility on the individual, whether male or female.

While the repeal of the Act of Uniformity was presumably very popular among many, other regulations were not. The list of activities to be repressed on Sundays, the varieties of forms of the theater to be banned, the enormous detail in which ale-houses were regulated, all are testimony to the place of these leisure activities in people's lives. The repetitive nature of these statutes, passed year after year, with more severe punishment mandated in each, is indicative as well of the continued attraction of popular entertainments throughout the period.[27] Even more serious in its impact, perhaps, was the elimination of certain holidays and wakes, as well as the removal of much ceremony from the rituals marking the major life-transitions of birth, adulthood, marriage, and death. People were left to face these moments starkly, without the softening of embodied collective practice.[28]

Given the willingness to attempt to mandate many aspects of life, it is intriguing that Parliament balked at the legal restriction of everyday clothing. Existing legal limitations on clothing use – sumptuary laws – were allowed to stand, and laws regulating who could wear what at political events, as will be seen below, would be renewed under the Protectorate; but no new constraints on styles, fashions, or fabrics were passed. Such regulation was deemed too great an infringement on individual liberty. This debate, too, concerning the power of clothing to represent, and even create, political and other identities (and therefore its status as a matter of state) and its being a matter of private concern (and therefore beyond the state's interest) is one that would recur in the American and French revolutions. Despite this reticence, it is striking that there appears to have been widespread *voluntary* participation in a Puritan clothing code, which could, but did not necessarily, coincide with one's parliamentary allegiance.[29] Beyond the domain of law and discourse, there was, by the 1640s, a long tradition of the practice of distinctively Puritan dress. Rather than cover their bodies with the bright colors, reflective materials, embroideries, and revealing (whether of breast or of calf, depending on gender) clothing that characterized the court and fashionable society, they favored somber colors, ample forms that tended to mask the body, and an absence of figuring either in the weave or through embroidery. The contrast may be seen by comparing the images in Figures 3.2 and 3.3.

In Figure 3.2, Hester Tradescant is depicted in a gray dress, most probably of a high-quality wool, and, in any case, of a non-reflective, rather stiff fabric, unadorned by any patterning or embroidery. Following the condemnation of "gaudy and vain clothing … wantonness and lightness in them, which is especially in nakedness, as to such and such parts of the body, which modesty are hid," the cut of her dress flattened her chest and thickened her waist, while the ample and layered skirts would

Figure 3.2 Thomas de Critz, *Hester Tradescant and her stepson, John*, 1645 (Ashmolean Museum, Oxford).

obscure the movement of her hips as she walked.[30] She was very thoroughly covered, with only her face, wrists and hands visible. Leaving her hands free of gloves, since gloves were often among the most luxurious and highly decorated of clothing items, increased rather than decreased the modesty and austerity of the image.[31] Her face, by contrast, was left only minimally visible, her neck was hidden by her collar, and almost all of her hair by the cap worn beneath her hat. Her face was clearly devoid of any makeup and she appears to have been wearing no jewelry. This austerity was reinforced by the painter's decision to make the background almost the same shade of gray as the dress, a technique that while not uncommon in the period, underscored the drabness of the cloth.

Figure 3.3 William Faithorne, *Print of Margaret Hewitt, Lady Paston*, 1659 (Victoria and Albert Museum, London). Museum number E.914-1960. Given by Edgar Seligman.

It would, however, be a mistake to read this or much other Puritan dress as either inexpensive to produce or intended to convey an impression of economy. Even the treatises, like James Durham's *The Law Unsealed,* advocating the elimination of "costliness and excessive bravery of apparel," quickly qualified their positions so as to allow for variations by rank and class. Thus immediately following his condemnation of extravagance, Durham went on to write "Which saith not that we are to foster sordidness or baseness, or that men in all places or stations and of all ranks, should, as to their apparel, be equal, but that none should exceed."[32] In this case, as in other clothes of radical Protestants of high rank, the quality of the fabric was most probably excellent, her collar and cuffs made of quality linen and edged with lace while her classical conical high-crowned "Puritan" hat in this period may easily have cost as much as the plumed, flat-crowned broad brimmed hat commonly worn by courtiers. Not only could the cost be comparable to those worn at court, but the complexities of the political location of these clothing forms should not be understated. Hester Tradescant was the second wife of John Tradescant, gardener first to Charles I and later to Charles II. Her attire, as in many other cases, would appear, therefore, to reflect a religious rather than a political allegiance.

Cavalier clothing, by contrast, was characterized by fabrics that draped beautifully, reflected light well, were often brocaded or embroidered, and rendered the body's movements visible and graceful. Men wore knee-length breeches and covered their calves only with stockings, revealing their shape. Their jackets were also form-fitting, displaying fine waistlines and broad chests and shoulders. The feathers adorning their hats moved as they traversed a room or engaged in animated conversation, thus underscoring again the body in all its movements. As may be seen in the engraved portrait of Margaret Hewitt, in Figure 3.3, women's garb was also designed to display their bodies. Characterized by dresses with low-cut bodices, narrow waists, and full skirts, they too were made of silk, velvet, and brocade. Women's hair was often uncovered and elaborately dressed; they wore pearls or precious stones to show off the luminosity of their skin, and the clasps on their sleeves and bodices were often crafted from gold or silver. The division between the Puritans and the Cavaliers was not one of means – while not all Puritans came from the elite, those whose painted portraits have come down to us certainly did – or expenditure or luxury, but of the nature of the expenditure and the relation of the body to the clothing. Those who dressed like Hester Tradescant were not seeking to look poor or to emulate popular dress, but rather to embody their beliefs.

This may be further illustrated by Ann Jones's and Peter Stallybrass's brilliant discussion of the radical Protestant criticism of the fashions of the period of James I. That critique was composed of several parts. First of all, the fashion for ruffed collars – which required starch for their shape – transformed a foodstuff into an adornment. To this terrible waste of a commodity that could nourish the body by using it to indulge in vanity were added the iniquities of the color yellow. The yellow in starch was produced from saffron, which arrived in England from Spain or the Middle

East via Ireland. "As a culturally freighted color, saffron yellow linked luxury and contaminating waste; at the same time, it was seen as originating with England's traditional enemies, Spain, Ireland, and France..."[33] Yellow starch, associated with waste, with women, with foreignness and with Catholicism, was contrasted by the anti-court faction with good English wool, like that worn in the portrait of Hester Tradescant.

As much at stake as avoiding lust and encouraging women's modesty was responding to an anxiety about masculinity. Again, John Durham: "There is in clothes a base effeminateness amongst men (which some way emasculateth or unmanneth them) who delight in those things which women dote upon, as dressing of hair, powderings, washings..." Long hair, cross-dressing, and too much finery among men would create a confusion between the sexes understood to be prohibited by the Bible.[34] This was far from the only critique of court fashion, and courtly consumption in general, as effeminate. As the historian David Kuchta has argued, this rhetoric was as much intended to undermine the court as to effect sartorial change; but it may have accomplished both at once.[35] The use of the epithets "effeminate" or "unmanly" as a strategy for the delegitimation of political enemies proved to be a common one. By the late eighteenth century, political pornography would be widely diffused by those opposed to the Crown in France, and in America of the early national period, patriots would condemn European fashion as effeminate.

In the last decades of the seventeenth century the portraits, literary descriptions, and engravings of men and women dressed in sumptuous fashion and the innumerable pamphlets railing against the evils of lascivious extravagant dress indicate that radical Protestants did not succeed in creating long-term changes in English sartorial habits. I would like to suggest, however, that by building on their juridical, political and cultural inheritances of sumptuary laws regulating who could wear what where, and the careful calculations necessary within court society to ensure that one's attire represented an appropriate expenditure in relation to one's patrons and one's clients, the radical Protestants and the parliamentarians created a code of luxurious austerity compatible with the complexities of their religious, economic, and social identities. In so doing they expanded the political semiotics of clothing. By using clothing practices to represent themselves and their politico-religious position outside the courtly context they created a precedent upon which many others contesting the established order would continue to rely thereafter.[36]

Clothing and the fabric arts appear to have been the dominant domain of everyday *material* culture that was constructively – as opposed to destructively, as in the case of iconoclasm – influenced by radical Protestantism, but some impact may be seen in architecture as well. The historians Timothy Mowl and Brian Earnshaw have argued for a style they at times call "Puritan classicism" and at others "Puritan minimalism," which they note appeared under the early Stuarts and continued after the Restoration.[37] It was a style characterized, like the radical Protestant clothing, by austere lines and a renunciation of ostentatious decoration, but not necessarily by modest materials. There was no official call for Puritan or Commonwealth architecture, no contests held, and no official buildings built, again unlike the subsequent American and French revolutions. The impact of this style appears, furthermore, to have been relatively slight, and it does not seem to have been accompanied by innovative designs or techniques in the arts of the home. Even the new iconography of the Commonwealth and Protectorate would be more republican and nationalist than Puritan.

This general lack of domestic Commonwealth or republican style speaks to the greater importance attributed to material culture that had a public, as opposed to an exclusively domestic, presence, as well as to the particular properties of clothing and needlework. While household furnishings remained very expensive in the first half of the seventeenth century, there was far greater availability of more affordable fabric, ribbons, lace, and other notions. That increased availability, in combination with the long and particularly intense politicization of clothing, gave it a special status. While the idea that there was a radical Protestant form of dress and of many everyday life practices seems to have met with considerable agreement among the leadership, once one left the world of Puritan morality and entered the Church itself, there was far more disagreement among the anti-Laudians.

Particularly fraught were the questions of the organization of the Church, and social, and for some gender, equality. The central issue concerning the organization of the Church was that of the autonomy of congregations. Could each church self-govern, deciding on admission to the sacraments and membership itself, or was the model to be a Presbyterian one, with much power given to a council of elders providing regional and national oversight? These differences were profound and would, as early as 1644, spark serious divisions within the Puritan-parliamentary forces between the Independents and the Presbyterians. This emphasis on religious and moral reform and conflict should not be read to imply that nothing was at stake in terms of governance formally speaking. This story unfolded within the context of a war when the conflict between the Crown and Parliament, as well as within the Opposition itself, intensified concerning the form polity and society in Britain would take.

As would be the case in the French Revolution later, Charles I was forced by financial exigencies to summon Parliament in 1640, and after a final brief meeting and a brief dissolution (the Short Parliament) it was to remain seated until dissolved by Oliver Cromwell in 1653. Attempts were initially made, including the Grand Remonstrance of 1641, to negotiate *a modus vivendi* between the Long Parliament and the Crown. The contents of these efforts reveal the complex melding of religion and politics in this conflict. The Grand Remonstrance strongly echoed the Petition of Rights of 1628, but with far more impact on the Church; it would have deprived bishops of their vote in Parliament, eliminated the influence of the Catholics, purged some of the king's advisers understood to be corrupt, repealed forms of taxation perceived to be unfair and restored Parliament's control over taxation, reformed the judicial system, stopped the billeting of soldiers as well as arbitrary and cruel imprisonment, and ended royal monopolies on necessities. Charles I's response was to silence the demands by accusing the five leaders of Parliament of treason and attempting to arrest them. Undaunted, Parliament went back to work on June 1, 1642 and passed the 19 Propositions, which, while far from imagining the end of the monarchy, did seek to limit its power radically. Charles I once again simply responded negatively, lifting on August 22, 1642 his standard against the forces representing the Parliament.

War: Radicalization of Religion and Politics

In the war that raged intermittently from 1642 to the regicide in 1649, both sides saw themselves as fighting on God's side and their cause as righteous and pious. It is perhaps this quality of a holy war that made this Civil War so extraordinarily destructive of both life and property. This belief may have both encouraged some to fight – most of the soldiers were conscripted but some volunteered – and may have made them take greater risks and be more violent once at war. Almost a quarter of all adult men served as soldiers at some point in the conflict, and as many as 200,000 men died in combat or from war-related illnesses. The religious groundings of the conflict would be especially important by the time the New Model Army was formed in 1645. Four of five generals in the Army were devout Puritans, and high standards of moral conduct were enforced. The New Model Army also proved to be a locus of political and religious radicalism, as well as military innovation.[38]

The Army was organized nationally (rather than locally or regionally), thus combining men from all parts of the country into the same units and promoting allegiance to the cause, rather than to one's neighbor.[39] It also, crucially, practiced promotion on the basis of talent rather than birth. This was particularly important since the Army had a strong representation of men of modest means, and significant numbers came from areas that had seen an increase in rioting against enclosure in the early 1640s. Enclosure – that is the removal of land from agricultural production and its devotion to sheep grazing to feed the wool export economy – had displaced many, some of whom became susceptible to political argument. The historian John Walter suggests that: "Enclosure riots were not an indiscriminate attack on the landed classes. The overwhelming bulk of the riots were directed against those who were directly associated with the discredited *ancien régime* of Charles I."[40] And, radical pockets were to be found elsewhere, in "...areas of forest and pasture with the absence of a resident gentry, the presence of the cloth industry and an earlier tradition of radicalism and, above all London..."[41] Thus many soldiers, including some who rose to leadership positions, had a prehistory of political radicalism that was nurtured in the New Model Army.

By 1646, in fact, the Levellers had become more numerous in that army. The Levellers were both politically and religiously radical; they sought the abolition of the monarchy, the House of Lords, and the State Church, election of the sheriffs and justices of the peace, opening the enclosures, and the elimination of conscription, excise taxes and privileges associated with the aristocracy and corporations. Furthermore, like even more radical groups, they argued for the spiritual equality of women and men.[42] Meanwhile, those other groups, the Diggers and the Ranters, pushed political, economic, and religious reform even further than the Levellers. The radicalism of the Army troubled many, and in the long term these internal differences, in combination in some cases with different economic and social interests, would prove very damaging to the opposition's capacities to act in unison to create a new form of governance.

By 1647, a struggle for control between Parliament and the New Model Army had commenced. The Independents (Congregationalists and dominant in the New Model Army) were more radical politically and more tolerant religiously than the parliamentarians. Parliament, by contrast, was dominated by the rural gentry and the London elite, who favored a compromise with the monarchy, the control of the army by the gentry, a presbyterian model of Church governance, and little tolerance of religious variation. Initiated by the Army, what historians have called a "second" Civil War broke out in 1648, culminating in the execution first of Archbishop Laud, and then of the king himself, and the creation of the Commonwealth in 1649. It would also ultimately lead to the suppression of the Levellers and the other radical sects; but that is a story to which we will return.

The tactics used in the Civil Wars were not only bloody, but particularly destructive of the built environment. The historian Stephen Porter recounts that "at least one in ten of those living in provincial cities and towns saw their houses destroyed in the Civil War."[43] In other words around 11,000 homes were destroyed, leaving 55,000 homeless people scattered across some 150 towns and fifty villages. The wars were so destructive because this was a conflict in which siege warfare played a crucial part (about 30 per cent of the military actions over the course of the war).[44] Both the preparation for sieges and their enactment destroyed the urban fabric. Elaborate fortifications were built around cities; structures that interfered were removed, and the surrounding countryside rendered barren so as to deprive besiegers of nourishment. To these destructive protective measures must be added punitive destruction. Fires were set, and buildings were pillaged and plundered. Townships across England attempted to cope with not only the inevitable strain of the increased numbers of homeless, but also the destruction of churches, schools, libraries, and almshouses.[45] Following these ravages, the parliamentary government was so inundated with requests for assistance from dispossessed citizens that they were forced to create a "Committee for Burning" charged with processing these petitions. The Civil War not only effectively destroyed a large segment of the population's homes but also instituted the purification of the Church through the removal of relics, and left towns without the physical presence of civic institutions.

The void left by this massive destruction would seem to have created an almost unique opportunity to develop a new built environment, including styles for civic, religious and domestic structures, based on new principles. The shock of that destruction, however, the brevity of the regimes, and financial straits limited what could actually be accomplished. Following such wholesale destruction, the process of rebuilding was slow and the costs very great. Parliament authorized "briefs" to raise money for rebuilding as early as 1645, but little funding was made available – perhaps because it was assumed that the destruction was largely of the property of royalist sympathizers.[46] Efforts at rebuilding were limited, moreover, by conflicts among the victorious parliamentary forces, and also perhaps because the need for a political iconography (for both pedagogic and representational purposes) preoccupied them. The newly declared Commonwealth thus inherited a country battered by six years of brutal warfare during which little had been rebuilt. It also faced the very profound challenge of self-legitimation after the regicide. Charles I went to his death from the Banqueting House he had had refurbished to celebrate the life of his father King James I. The regicide not only ended a reign but marked the first moment of the new regime's quest for legitimation and its continued reliance on the symbols and forms of the Old Regime.

The Republican Experiment: Legitimizing the State, Making the Nation, 1649–1653

Not only was the monarchy abolished, but so too were the House of Lords and the Bishoprics, and England was declared a Commonwealth. Church lands were seized and sold; cathedrals commandeered and put to other purposes; and ministers, if deemed insufficiently rigorous, were removed from their livings. Efforts were made to undo the patronage system and replace it with careers open to talent. The Parliament achieved supreme power: "In Constitutional terms, the Commonwealth established parliamentary supremacy based on popular sovereignty, but reduced popular sovereignty to little more than parliamentary supremacy itself."[47] It should be noted, however, that in 1650, *all* adult males were abruptly brought into the political body of the nation. They were required to endorse the changes by "taking the Engagement," that is, swearing an oath of allegiance to the Republic that included public acknowledgement of the legality of the abolition of monarchy and the House of Lords. Although more moderate economic policies prevailed – there was no effort or intent to undermine private property under either the Commonwealth or the Protectorate – there was a very substantial enlargement of the political nation. Both regicide and the founding of a Commonwealth were, indeed, politically very radical, and the Rump Parliament was intensely aware of the need for a whole new "representational language of political signs and symbols."[48]

The first task to which the Rump Parliament and its Councils of State immediately gave their attention was the *eradication* of the symbols of royal power. Thus the Crown Jewels and images of the monarchy were destroyed, and the king's statue at the Old Exchange was first beheaded and then removed; but that still left the urgent charge of legitimizing the new Commonwealth. Such an undertaking was complicated by the regime's fundamental suspicion of material culture, images and ritual. Some of the objects and institutions inherited from the monarchy were simply dispersed or abandoned. Thus, as was noted by the historian John Brewer, while there had been a plan to create a public library from Charles I's collection of books there was no analogous project, as there would be in the French Revolution, to use the very impressive royal painting collection to found a public museum.[49] Since the paintings were understood to be decadent, much of the collection was simply sold to raise funds, while the rest remained in government hands. The triad of the Great Seal of the English Commonwealth, the Mace of Parliament, and the Arms of the English Commonwealth fulfilled the essential symbolic task previously served by the crown, scepter and orb. Just as the latter had established the monarch's political presence, the new seal, mace, and arms established the Commonwealth's political capacity: "[On]17 March 1649, the day the Rump issued its justification of the regicide and subsequent constitutional revolution, a parliamentary committee was ordered to look into redesigning the mace used in the House," a timing indicative of the importance that this symbolic work was understood to bear.[50] The new maces no longer carried the coronet, orb and cross, which had been the Stuart emblems, laden with now thoroughly inappropriate political and religious valences. In their stead were the "arms and insignia of the free state. Branches of oak supporting escutcheons with more arms, with an acorn replacing the traditional orb and cross."[51]

Even more dramatic, in some sense, was the new seal. Parliamentary forces had, much earlier, attempted to create unity out of division, and legitimacy in what was fundamentally an insurgent moment by the appropriation and reproduction of the culture and symbols of political power. Thus, after the flight in 1642 of the Lord Keeper Littleton, who held the Great Seal that was required for the exercise of government, a vote was called in Parliament, in January 1643, to invalidate that seal. By May a decision was reached to create a parliamentary seal and new keepers were appointed. On August 11, 1646 that seal, too, was destroyed and its "fragments were divided between the Speakers of both houses."[52] The destruction was purely symbolic – although importantly so – because the new seal that was put into use looked just like the old, complete with portrait of the king and the Stuart Arms. This seal remained in use until the supremacy of the Commons was declared, followed by the issuance of a seal of novel design commissioned in January 1649.[53] That new Commonwealth Seal bore on one face – which before had carried the portrait of the king – an image of the assembled House of Commons engaged in active debate (see Figure 3.4).

Not only is the replacement of the king by the Commons significant, but so too is their exact representation. In earlier images, the "Commons had been depicted as an anonymous lumpen mass huddled at the bar of the upper House, spectators of the important and dazzling ritual bonding between monarch and peers."[54] On the new

Figure 3.4 Thomas Simon, *Struck silver military award for the Battle of Dunbar* (Trustees of the British Museum).

Great Seal, the members were individualized and shown as an active, engaged group. The reverse side now bore a map of the Commonwealth, including (optimistically or arrogantly) areas that had not yet been won to the parliamentary side. The new seal was commissioned and ready one week after the king's execution, and the 1646 seal was ceremoniously destroyed. Figure 3.4 shows the Commonwealth Seal rendered as a medallion that was offered to soldiers who fought for Parliament at the Battle of Dunbar. The new government thus appropriated the royalist tradition of carrying precious images close to the heart, as seen in Chapter 2. Not only was the seal to serve more distanced state tasks; it could also be used as a talisman.

Finally, the arms of the Commonwealth incorporated the cross of St. George and the Irish harp of Erin in escutcheons. In part, no doubt, to repudiate Charles I's reinvention of the Order of the Garter (borrowed from the French), the imagery mobilized on this new iconography was thoroughly nationalist: the cross of St. George, oaks, use of English rather than Latin, and maps of the Commonwealth.

This new symbolism of state was not only present at sittings of Parliament but was diffused across the Commonwealth: "…urban, educational and charitable corporations all across England had new maces made, and erected the arms of the state in town halls, on city gates, in school rooms and hospitals."[55] The reinforcement of the legitimacy of the Commonwealth through iconography was to be seconded by a new currency upon which "One face of the coins would depict the cross of St. George on a shield, with the motto 'The Commonwealth of England,' whilst the other would bear the arms of the Commonwealth and the words 'God with Us'."[56] Ships were retrofitted with the Commonwealth symbol, and there was even republican silver plate made in the period.[57] It is, furthermore, significant that, like the adoption of Puritan dress, the deployment of the Commonwealth arms was generally voluntary rather than imposed by the government.[58] The desire to see the new government properly symbolized appears to have been strong, even, perhaps, among those who would have preferred a continued monarchy. The habit of seeing coins, seals, maces and statues that embodied the form of rule was very powerful. This period also saw experiments in republican dating, although they were never widely implemented. Furthermore, despite Puritan understandings of the evils of theater, elegant food, and luxury, Commonwealth politicians were realistic enough about the nature of politics and power in the seventeenth century that they also strove to produce a form of spectacle appropriate to a republic.[59] Banquets, state funerals, successful diplomatic negotiations, and military victories were all lavishly celebrated.[60] Another continuity lay in the very locus of Parliament; it continued to sit in St. Stephen's Chapel, Westminster, where the Stuart Parliaments had sat. Plans were made for more extensive visual representations of the Commonwealth, including redecorating the Banqueting House with images of military victories, on the one hand, and portraits of Cromwell on the other.

The process of eradicating the monarchical presence and replacing it with a new, republican one, was long, difficult, and of necessity always partial. As was discussed in the last chapter, not only the early Stuarts but centuries of English kings and queens had marked the landscape and the built environment. Removing a coat of arms or taking down a statue left an absence rather than creating a presence. Further complicating the task, and illustrative of the power of the old semiotic system, was the profusion of commemorative royalist objects produced after the regicide. These objects included heart-shaped silver lockets bearing Charles I's profile, sealing-wax cases ornamented with royalist symbols, and firebacks (used to protect the brickwork in chimneys) memorializing the dead king, as well as the more predictable watercolor or embroidered miniatures to be carried intimately in a pocket or worn around the neck.[61] Less discreet was royalist pottery like the plate shown in Figure 3.5.

Although the charger was obviously intended for display within the home and not in public, it was a much bolder statement of defiance than a miniature portrait or a sealing-wax case both of which were easily and quickly hidden in a pocket. The very subject matter – Charles I in full battle armor flanked by his male heirs – was provocative. It also exemplifies the circulation of images across genres in this period; the portrait providing inspiration to the pottery-painter was first produced

Figure 3.5 Pickleherring Pottery (probably), *Tin-glazed earthenware charger* bearing a portrait of Charles I and his three male heirs. Southwark, England (probably) 1653 (Victoria and Albert Museum, London). Museum number C.71-1998. Purchased with the assistance of The Art Fund, Sir Harry Djanogly CBE, and an anonymous donor.

on an engraving in Holland in 1639 and later circulated as a print. A particularly ostentatious defiance of the current regime, it was far from unique.[62] It is noteworthy that the vast majority of extant commemorative and representational objects of this period are *royalist*. Although historians have found some documentation of republican dinnerware and state iconography, including a wide variety of portraits of Oliver Cromwell himself, these are few compared with memorializing the early Stuarts. The fans, sealing-wax cases, lockets, pen knives, embroideries and other objects seem to have largely been produced for those who had been in the habit of carrying this kind of memento in honor of their king before the Civil War. And even those forms created to fill the gap on the Parliament side were as much reminiscent of that gap as productive of imaginaries of the new political regime.

Once the Commonwealth was declared in 1649, the institutional transformations and not fully successful efforts to create a new iconography were quickly followed by a close regulation of everyday life. It was almost as if the difficulty in finding an effective form of governance, political culture, or symbolism for the Commonwealth was channeled into a radicalization of the state's efforts to control everyday life, ritual practice, and lifecycle events. The year 1650 alone saw the passage of acts mandating the punishment of: adultery, fornication, swearing, blasphemy and neglect of Sunday observance. That year also marked the making of female adultery a capital crime. This legislation, as would that that followed Cromwell's dissolution of Parliament in 1653 and his taking on of the title of Lord Protector, underscored a pattern of a more stringent enforcement of the Puritan moral code at the same time as lifecycle events were further stripped of their ritual and ceremonial content. Thus, for example, the 1653 *Act Touching Marriages and Registering thereof; and also touching Births and Burials* mandated that marriages would henceforth be carried out with the minimum of ceremony by the Justice of the Peace.[63] People were asked to accept a more and more austere life in which they had little recourse to traditional forms of comfort or pleasure in difficult moments of life transitions. This regime was not long-lived, but the Protectorate that followed largely built on its tendencies.

Consolidation and Ambivalence: The Protectorate, 1653–1659

With the dissolution of the Parliament in 1653 and the establishment of the Protectorate, governance took a paradoxical turn, becoming simultaneously more radical and more conservative. The Protectorate marked a return to a leader-dominated, mixed regime in which power was in theory to be shared among the Lord Protector, the Parliament and the Council of State. The Lord Protector, however, was appointed for life and had, in fact, great power. The new Instrument of Government, or Constitution, limited, for example, the vote to non-Catholic men over the age of twenty-one who possessed at least two hundred pounds in property and had not been opposed to Parliament or participated in the Irish Rebellion. Shortly after dissolving the Rump Parliament, Cromwell reconvened it, in considerably reduced form, as the Barebones Parliament. There was much continuity with the previous Parliament: this one, too, continued to meet in St. Stephen's Chapel in Westminster, and its speaker was also Francis Rous. It was, however, despite its limited suffrage and greater domination by the Lord Protector, much more active, passing in five months thirty statutes concerning law and tax reform and attempting to bring Scotland under tighter English control. It was also, as a body, intolerant of dissenting Protestant religious beliefs and practices.

Although in formal terms, the Protectorate seemed to resemble the preceding Stuart monarchies, its accomplishments and forms of production and reproduction of power reveal some notable differences. Very significantly, the period saw the unification of the three kingdoms. In the words of the historian David Armitage:

> The Cromwellian union achieved what the Stuart kings had failed to provide: the consolidation of England, Ireland, Scotland, and all the territories belonging thereto, into a political unit under a single head. Within the history of the British Isles, such an agglomeration of dominions had been unparalleled since the days of King Arthur, and would not be seen again until parliamentary union joined Ireland to the United Kingdom after 1801.[64]

Communication and infrastructure were much improved, including a reform of the post office. The fiscal system was modernized and efforts to eliminate corruption and the extension of the "reformation of manners" continued. Cromwell, furthermore, remained committed to liberty of religious conscience. It is, however, crucial to note that the regime was most marked by religious or moral radicalism, not economic or political transformation. Cromwell was not engaged in a struggle for the reform of either property or hierarchy.[65]

These changes were accompanied by the partial monarchization of the Lord Protector, despite the fact that Cromwell always refused the royal title itself.[66] This monarchization was particularly marked after Cromwell's re-investment as Lord Protector in 1657, which was much more elaborate than the first; he wore an ermine-lined robe, and received the sword of state and a golden scepter. At first glance it appears that this was more than a partial monarchization; and in fact the dominant historiographic position is that this was simply the re-establishment of a mixed monarchy under a different name.[67] Even Cromwell's first term had been marked by extensive borrowing from the royal repertoire, as had the Commonwealth itself. In 1653 Cromwell was granted all the former royal palaces; and he chose Whitehall – the principal royal residence under the Stuarts – as his court, with Hampton Court as his personal retreat. Not only did Cromwell give these buildings back their former usage, but they were largely refurnished and redecorated with Charles I's possessions (the total value exceeding £35,497).[68] Some of the furniture, tapestries and works of art that had been sold off were repurchased, and those that had been in use by the Commonwealth were also given to the Lord Protector. Even the royal tapestry workshop that had been established in 1619 at Mortlake continued production throughout the Interregnum. Support for music resumed. Although organs had been removed from churches and music in cathedrals had been prohibited, the Cromwellian court was an important locus of musical composition and performance, and it was in these years that the first full-length English opera was written and performed.[69] The Lord Protector also renewed the tradition of patronage of the arts by providing a living at court for three major poets (John Milton, John

Figure 3.6 Silver pattern crown (5*s.*) of Oliver Cromwell, London, England, 1658 (Trustees of the British Museum).

Dryden, and Andrew Marvell). Cromwell furthermore followed royal practice in the staging of his visits to the City of London and in diplomatic negotiations.[70] Finally, the Commonwealth Seal was replaced with one that linked the three nations with Cromwell's arms, and the Parliament disappeared from political symbolism.

Despite these similarities in the use of culture and iconography under the Stuarts and the Protectorate, the differences, as the historian Roy Sherwood has argued, are at least as significant.[71] For example, the coinage issued under the Protectorate followed a classical republican rather than the royal British model, with Cromwell pictured in profile, wearing a toga and crowned with a laurel wreath (Figure 3.6).

There was, then, a creative and selective appropriation of monarchical and courtly forms. This may also be seen in the continuity or revival of traditional sumptuary systems, including the use of rare and expensive fabrics for those in high office, all continued or revived under the Protectorate, but with twists and changes. The smaller court, new patronage networks, and religious reforms all required modifications in the traditional system. The new criteria for the right to clothing connoting high position, for example, may be seen in the following 1656 protocol elaborating the dress code for the election of the Master Chamberlain and Bridge Masters:

> The Lord Maior and those Knights that have bourne the office of Maioralty ought to have their cloaks furred with gray Amis, and thos Alderman that have not been Maiors, are to have their cloaks furred with Calabie. And the wife of such as have been Maiors are to have their cloaks lined with changeable Taffata and the rest are to have them lined with green Taffata...[72]

Unlike earlier sumptuary laws in which clothing was to be determined by both office and *birth*; here it was office and *service* that determined the grade of luxury.

Those who held high office during the Protectorate generally did so not because they were aristocrats but because of their performance during the Civil War period. The new religious calendar also imposed changes as may be seen by juxtaposing the 1656 edition of these protocols and that for 1692 (after the Restoration). The two editions are identical, except that All Saints' Day, Christmas Day, Twelfth Day, Candlemas Day, Innocents' Day, Good Friday, Low Sunday, and Monday and Tuesday of Whitsun Week have reappeared in the 1692 text (indicating that the wearing of velvet tippet was required on those holidays).[73] Thus the Protectorate retained the forms of sumptuary and courtly life, but selectively excised offensive holidays from the calendar.

The 1654 renewal of the prohibition on dueling is another indication of distance from the Old Regime: "Where the fighting of Duels upon private Quarrels is a thing in itself displeasing to God, unbecoming Christians, and contrary to all good order and government..."[74] Dueling was to be prohibited *both* because it was displeasing to God *and* because it was "contrary to all good order and government." Given that dueling had been central to the courtly code of honor, and a ritual from which commoners were explicitly excluded, the continued prohibition on dueling is also indicative that this regime was not simply imprinted on the old monarchical forms.[75] Furthermore, despite the Lord Protector's religious rigorousness, he – unlike the Stuarts, who understood themselves to have been anointed by God – conceptualized a distance between the Godly and the political order. This did not stop Cromwell, however, from justifying juridical interventions and other gestures by reference to both the secular and sacred good. A further important difference between the Protectorate and the monarchy came in the separation between the State and the Lord Protector. Under the Protectorate, unlike under the Stuarts, there was a separate account for the household, rather than the royal household simply being a state function. Finally, to quote Sherwood:

> One of the more fundamental differences between a royal and the protectoral court is that whereas a royal court of the seventeenth century was very much a social and cultural institution that of the Protectorate was not. The protectoral court tended to reflect current society rather than set patterns for attitudes, manners and customs for society, or at least sections of it, to imitate as royal courts did.[76]

I argue further, following Laura Lunger Knoppers's persuasive analysis, that even in the realm of portraiture and representation something more complicated than mere imitation was going on.[77] Portraiture is often used as the ultimate demonstration of the derivative quality of the Protectorate. Protectorate-era portraits of Cromwell exist in virtually all genres and at all scales. There were miniatures painted on ivory, prints to be reproduced on broadsheets, and full-sized oil paintings. These portraits of Cromwell during the Protectorate look, at first glance, as if they are simple reproductions of earlier royal and aristocratic portraits, but with a different face.

Figure 3.7 *Thomas Wentworth, 1st Earl of Strafford*, studio of Sir Anthony Van Dyck. Oil on canvas, *c*.1636. 54⅛ in. × 43 in. (1,374 mm × 1,091 mm). Given by Sir Gyles Isham., Bt, 1967. © National Portrait Gallery, London.

Knopper, in her elegant close analysis of Robert Walker's 1649 portrait of Cromwell (the most widely circulated likeness of Cromwell, juxtaposed it to Van Dyck's 1636 portrait of Thomas Wentworth, the first Earl of Strafford (see Figures 3.7 and 3.8).

The men are given virtually identical poses in the two paintings. Both stand against a dramatic sky, and are wearing armor, with face framed and the neck protected with a linen collar. Knoppers points out that the similarity ends at the neck.

Figure 3.8 *Oliver Cromwell*, by Robert Walker. Oil on canvas, *c*.1649. 49½ in. × 40 in. (1,257 mm × 1,016 mm). Transferred from British Museum, 1879. © National Portrait Gallery, London.

Strafford is given an elegant, idealized visage. His skin is smooth and flushed with health, his hair evenly trimmed, his features regular. Cromwell, by contrast, is pale, his hair somewhat disheveled, his beard tufty, and his nose rather closely resembles a potato. I would add to Knoppers's discussion that there is, furthermore, a noticeable difference in the hands in the two portraits. Strafford's hands are strongly drawn, their sinews, joints, and muscles clearly visible. One is strongly outstretched while the other firmly grasps a baton. Cromwell's hands are flaccid, his right hand, in the foreground, is limply holding a stick pointing downwards and off the canvas, while his left is drooping. The viewer's attention is further distracted from the central figure by the servant engaged in tying what looks to be a satin sash around his waist.

This portrait seems to embody Cromwell's ambivalence about claiming monarchical power. On the one hand he ruled in an authoritarian manner; on the other he refused to be crowned. Here he is represented in a classic pose, but that pose is undermined by the only visible parts of his body. That body is represented not only as weak and flawed, but also as definitively mortal, perhaps also signifying Cromwell's reluctance to found a ruling dynasty. While it cannot be said that such ambivalences and ambiguities are present in *all* the representations of Cromwell in circulation under the Protectorate, given that this was the most often reproduced image it is particularly significant.

Thus, the picture that emerges is one of partialness, of almostness. The Commonwealth and Protectorate succeeded in destabilizing but not displacing the older system of political power and symbolic representation. Cromwell's religious and political commitments and historical circumstances caused him to refuse coronation and to emulate, but only incompletely to copy, the royal courts he had fought to destroy.[78] He did not want to re-start a royal lineage, and yet his son inherited his position. This almost but not quite accomplishment is captured well by the historian Kevin Sharpe:

> ...if the royal regalia, melted in the civil war, had to be remade, that was true, to a degree, of the monarchy itself... A republican cause and a Commonwealth party were born from 1649 and, though they failed to establish a dominant culture and government, they remained to destabilize the English royal regimes of 1660 to 1688 and, both chronologically and geographically, some beyond.[79]

Including the Civil Wars, the Interregnum lasted a mere two decades. Oliver Cromwell could never fully distance himself from the symbols and signs of royal power. The parliamentarians could never fully establish themselves in a democratic government. They did, however, accomplish a great deal.

I would like to suggest that the English Revolution broke the ground and modeled some ways of connecting everyday and material culture with political transformation. While from the hindsight yielded by the American and French revolutions, the changes wrought in the British case may seem slight, that vision would be anachronistic. The parliamentarians did not at the outset, of course, intend to execute the king or to create a republic. The force of religion and religious conflict, and the violence of the war itself played a significant role in pushing the conflict so far and not only prompting reflection on the relation of religious and political culture, but enabling experimentation with new forms of governance. Yet, the fact that this was the first such revolution was crucial in limiting how far it could go. Oliver Cromwell's ambivalent position, in all senses of the word – like a king, but not quite like a king; creating a court, yet not quite creating a court – is a good illustration of the dual, radical-conservative nature of this revolution.

1660. The Restoration: What Was Restored?

The Restoration of 1660 – while a counter-revolution that restored certain institutions associated with monarchy along with the monarchy itself (the House of Lords, censorship, and bishops) and certain cultural and religious forms (theaters were officially reopened in 1660 and the *Book of Common Prayer* reintroduced in 1662) – could not restore the society, polity or culture to pre-1642 days.[80] There was a very strong sense among those supporting Charles II that popular enthusiasm for the Crown needed to be mobilized and sustained.[81] A first step in that process was the eradication of all traces of republicanism (echoing the period following the regicide), the prosecution of the opposition, and, most dramatically, the exhuming, hanging and dismembering of celebrated regicides. More positively, the coronation itself provided an ideal opportunity to establish continuity and legitimacy of the Restoration through the symbolic association of Charles II with Roman conquerors and gods as well as Old Testament figures.[82] Public pageants and the theater were two critical means by which this was done; but in fact both king and aristocracy had lost much of their control over both polity and society. Innovations in style, technical breakthroughs, and political initiatives in the eighteenth century would require the cooperation of the gentry, the new middle classes, the nobility and the Crown. The tradition of political critique in the press and in pamphlets that had started in the 1640s only continued and grew in importance. As the historian Gerald Maclean puts it: "The Restoration might have put an end to the English republican experiment, but it could not put an end to those competing traditions of radical and republican thought that English men and women had become accustomed to seeing debated in print since the 1640s."[83] The enormous expansion of the economy and commercial culture would enable a much wider diffusion of consumer goods and an ongoing debate about fashion and luxury.[84] The late seventeenth century also saw the considerable expansion of coffeehouses and other sites of public debate and discussion, as well as the increasing importance of cultural production and consumption beyond the court.[85] Their role in the Revolution of 1688 that brought the Restoration to a close is a topic for another book, but it is clear that as the eighteenth century yielded to the nineteenth, governance would also require the, at least tacit, acceptance not only of non-courtly elites but of the popular classes.

The Crown did, however, retain an important symbolic power into the nineteenth century and beyond. Its particular form of parliamentary monarchy may, in fact, have helped England escape revolution in the nineteenth century, in striking contrast to continental Europe. The monarch played a largely symbolic yet active role throughout the modern period. The English state continued into the twentieth century to devote considerable resources to the maintenance and reproduction of the monarchy as an embodiment of England and things English. The monarchy came to represent the nation, unified, pure and *above* politics, while Parliament became the locus of division and strife. Britain itself in the eighteenth century came to represent a potential alternative model to those across the Channel critical of French forms of monarchism.

Britain did then, in fact, forge a new nation out of revolution, but it was one that kept monarchy and Church, albeit a transformed monarchy and Church, at its core. It was monarchy consistent with a revitalized notion of citizenship ("freeborn Englishmen") that English colonists in America would draw on initially to formulate their own sense of grievance a century later. Given its limits, however, it was not a national form that required so radical a refiguring of the sense of self and of everyday life as would develop in America and France.

−4−

The Politics of Silk and Homespun
Contesting National Identity in Revolutionary America

News of Parliament's passage of the 1763 Stamp Act provoked great indignation among the North American colonists. The Stamp Act was the first of the Revenue Acts intended to help defray Britain's fiscal crisis by dramatically increasing the rate of taxation on English imports to North America. Colonists were outraged that neither American contributions to the well-being of England, especially the market the colony provided for English manufactures, nor the limitations the colonial system imposed on Americans were recognized by Parliament. Their reactions were all the stronger because the British government's involvement in colonial life had been relatively limited until the financial burden of war caused Parliament to turn a greedy eye across the Atlantic. When the colonists' demands for repeal of the taxes and above all for recognition – including political representation on a par with metropolitan subjects – fell on deaf ears they reacted strongly, starting down a road that would culminate in both national independence and a democratic form of governance. As was noted in Chapter 2, however, the colonies were indeed colonies in the plural, characterized by diversity, autonomy, fierce independence, and sometimes rivalries. Not only did the colonies differ one from the other, but their inhabitants were also very diverse socially, economically, religiously, and culturally. Some were free and some enslaved; some of the free owned slaves, while some fought for slavery's abolition. Some were Calvinists, some Lutherans, some Quakers, some Catholics, and some Jews. Some owned vast estates and some nothing at all. At the same time, however, all were united by their relationship to the British Crown and their uneasy cohabitation with the ever dwindling Native American population. In short, the politically articulate colonists, at the moment of crisis in the 1760s, identified themselves for political and economic purposes as English people who happened to live in North America. But they also had distinct cultures, rooted in the routines, aesthetics and practices of everyday social and political life, that gave them the resources and the repertoire to unify and to fight back.

Much more emphatically than the revolutionary regimes in seventeenth-century England, then, the Americans were participating in the dual task of nation-making *and* devising a new form of governance. The period of upheaval that may be taken to open with Parliament's passage of the Stamp Act in 1763 and close when John Adams became the first president to reside in the White House in 1800 was marked by simultaneous efforts to separate from Britain, to create a new national identity, and to reach consensus on the form of the new state. Of the three revolutions discussed here, then, the American had, in some sense, the largest and most complex task. Although the constructive project would prove immense, it started with a seemingly simple act of refusal.

When the American colonists learned that they were not, in the eyes of Parliament, entitled to the same rights as those who lived in England, they countered forcefully. To the more traditional reactions to perceived injustices (looting, theft, attacking government representatives) and formal political organization (congresses in which protests were written and petitions to Parliament crafted), American creoles quickly added a novel form of protest – organized refusal to consume the taxed goods. If the English were going to tax imports, they would simply not buy them. Thus, the boycott was key to the American Revolution.[1] From the mid-1760s through to the end of the century, patriots and republicans struggled to convince their fellow Americans that they could live better without English things. This was not a simple task. One domain in which the British government had always restricted colonial liberties was in the production and processing of industrial and commercial goods, so as to assure a market for commodities and raw material produced in Britain. With strategies ranging from the banning of the export of English sheep to the American colonies in 1660, through the creation of a permanent Board of Trade to supervise economic activities in 1688 and the prohibition of trade in colonial woolens a bit more than a decade later, Parliament had done its best to ensure American dependence on English goods. That effort had been only partially successful; both indigenous production and imports from other countries were available (as shown in Chapter 2). Nonetheless, North American lifestyles, particularly those of the elite, in the mid-eighteenth century were heavily dependent on British goods and on the events in which finery of fashion, furniture, and food could be displayed and consumed. Those seeking to persuade their fellow creoles and colonists to abstain from these goods crafted arguments from both classical republican tradition (via the French) and from religious tradition (via the English). Melding the two, political thinkers fashioned a uniquely American discourse on taste, luxury, and national identity. Austerity associated with Puritanism joined that associated with the Roman republics in their heyday: luxury was bad because it corroded the morals, effeminized, and caused national debt. A properly American taste and style would be classical in inspiration, but indigenous in its particular form. Americans, above all, should learn to admire and desire those goods and forms that could be produced on the continent.

But this was not just a discursive protest, nor was it just a negative one. In the words of the historian Michael Zakim:

Thus when in 1774 the first Continental Congress declared a general policy of 'non-importation, non-consumption, and non-exportation,' it was far less concerned with ascetic self-denial than with encouraging American arts and manufactures, 'especially that of wool.' Non-consumption, in other words, was not synonymous with anti-consumption, and political independence rested not on the sacrifice of property but on its industrious, that is, its virtuous use. Indeed the homespun protest was an implicit acknowledgment that the world of goods had become integral to any discussion of public happiness.[2]

Revolutionary and post-Independence Americans devoted a great deal of time and attention, therefore, to devising new American forms of everyday culture and practice, and new national holidays and symbols, many of which commemorated key revolutionary events and figures. Some of those attempts were official, government efforts, or less official discourses by political figures, but many, in part because of the nature of the boycott tradition, were popular in origin.

Boycotts are, by definition, voluntary gestures of protest dependent for their success on both an internalized set of beliefs and the fear of public opprobrium.[3] Political movements in which boycotts play a central role have, therefore, certain characteristics. First of all, anyone who consumes can participate. The boycott movement provided the framework for the creation of a political public, a public that was relatively open; and, unlike a political public shaped by a conception of the independent property-owner, one created by the mobilization for boycott and subscription lists included women and the poor (although not slaves nor the indentured). Boycotts also require the imaginative leap that an act of individual choice and in some cases personal deprivation can lead to the public good.[4] As the historian T. H. Breen has powerfully argued, the American Revolution turned, then, far more centrally than any other modern political conflict, around goods and the social practices with which those goods were associated.[5] The seventeenth-century English revolutionaries discussed in the last chapter were already enacting a politics of the everyday, arguing that abstaining from alcohol, gambling, theater attendance and other pleasurable pastimes could help bring about the good health not only of the individual but of the entire nation. These themes reappeared in the context of the American Revolution. The boycott of goods, however, as Breen has underscored, was new.

In late-eighteenth-century North America the politicized refusal of some goods seconded the active endorsement of others by and the production of new forms to create a new polity and a new culture. This chapter traces how taste, style, and everyday life were envisaged and reconfigured from the moment of crisis in the American colonies in the 1760s through the establishment of the United States in the last two decades of the eighteenth century.

Making Revolution: Boycott and the Invention of American Style, 1763–1776

The inflammatory Stamp Act of 1763 required colonists to print newspapers, diplomas, legal documents and pamphlets on specially stamped paper that was taxed. The inclusion of newspapers within the taxable goods was particularly offensive to the colonists, since it was perceived, if not as a form of censorship, at least as a constraint on the diffusion of knowledge. American colonists responded to the Act in 1765–1766 by boycotting the sale of these stamps. This initial consumer protest was followed by others responding to subsequent revenue acts in 1768–1770 and 1774–1776.[6] Through these boycotts colonists were mobilized and convinced of the injustice of English behavior and of the legitimacy of their protest.

Mobilization against the Stamp Act started in Boston, where the Sons of Liberty hung the local tax collector in effigy from a tree that later became known as the "Liberty Tree." Andrew Oliver suffered further indignities when his home was looted and the stamps destroyed. Protest against the Act quickly became more organized and more juridical, culminating in the "Stamp Act Congress" held in New York in the summer of 1765, at which delegates from nine colonies both confirmed their allegiance to the Crown and demanded the repeal of the Stamp Act.[7] Even as contestation moved from the street to the hall and from action to writing, protestors continued to elaborate new symbols and rituals to fortify and consolidate their actions. Delegates to the Stamp Act Congress, for example, not only drafted a document, but also designed a flag later known as the "Rebellious Stripes." This flag, composed of alternating red and white horizontal stripes representing the nine participating colonies, became one of the first representations of the colonies as a collective unit.[8] Tellingly, however, the flag borrows its colors and its stripes from both the British flag of the period and that of the British East India Company; those two elements would become constituent parts of virtually all subsequent American flags. Visible traces of both Britain and the major colonial trading company thus remain forever present in the key symbol of the United States. This practice of borrowing from an existing repertoire of forms, while turning those forms to new meanings, would characterize future revolutionary and post-revolutionary cultural practice.

Although the Stamp Act was rescinded a year later, it was followed in 1767 by the Townsend Revenue Act, which imposed duties on a number of commodities and raw materials, including glass, paint, oil, lead, paper, and tea. This news hit especially hard because the American colonies counted on these English imports. This dependence was, in part, a reflection of the colonists' increased prosperity, but was also a direct result of the English policies of limiting American manufacturing and trade with other Continental powers. That policy made it impossible for the American colonists to spend their new-found wealth on exclusively American-made goods. Those restrictions on manufacturing and on access to markets other than the

English had been acceptable so long as the American colonies were not made to bear what the colonists understood to be extra burdens, particularly taxation without representation. Some historians have argued, in fact, that Americans had never felt so British as in the 1750s and 1760s, when the tensions with Britain reached their peak.[9] Even if the degree of creole identification with England may be questioned, as I have shown in Chapter 2, there is no doubt but that the Revenue Acts were perceived as a betrayal. As the "Declaration of Rights" written by the Draft Act Congress in 1765 put it:

> 1st. That his majesty's subjects in these colonies owe the same allegiance to the crown of Great Britain that is owing from his subjects born within the realm, and all due subordination to that august body, the Parliament of Great Britain. 2d. That his majesty's liege subjects in these colonies are entitled to all the inherent rights and privileges of his natural born subjects within the kingdom of Great Britain. 3d. That it is inseparably essential to the freedom of a people, and the undoubted rights of Englishmen, that no taxes should be imposed on them, but with their own consent, given personally, or by their representatives. 4th. That the people of these colonies are not, and from their local circumstances, cannot be represented in the House of Commons in Great Britain.[10]

A similar sentiment was echoed in strong language by the Continental Congress nearly a decade later, in October, 1774 (shortly before the outbreak of war): "...the present unhappy situation of our affairs is occasioned by a ruinous system of colony administration, adopted by the British ministry about the year 1763, evidently calculated for enslaving these colonies, and with them, the British Empire."[11] The Continental Congress conceived the Revenue Acts as enslavement because they increased the colonies' dependence on England without granting colonists the same rights as inhabitants of the metropole.

Throughout the 1760s, the boycott movement combined pamphlets, newspaper articles, and public demonstrations to persuade people to abandon their use of English products. Trade associations created earlier in the century – like the Society for encouraging Trade and Commerce in the Province of Massachusetts – also provided important institutional contexts for these discussions.[12] Arguments in this period turned on the unfairness of English practices and on how resisting English goods would produce freedom and independence. In a 1765 pamphlet, John Dickinson first argued that the Stamp Act was unfair because the colonies imported far more from England than they exported and that therefore the Americans needed other outlets for their goods were they to be able to continue to pay for English goods. He then urged his fellow Americans to follow the example of the Swiss, and resist English and French taste: "[T]heir coarse clothes and simple furniture enable them to live in plenty, and to defend their liberty." And to make it seem more feasible he argued that it was, in fact "...already ... practiced by us. It is surprising to see the linen and cloth that have been lately made among us."[13] George Washington thought that "...it would be possible to check purchases 'if the Gentlemen in their several

Counties wo'd be at some pains to explain matters to the people, and stimulate them to cordial agreement.'"[14]

The American critique of luxury had elements, as the historian John Crowley and others have noted, of romantic pastoralism or primitivism: "Let us Eat Potatoes and drink Water. Let us Wear Canvass, and undressed Sheepskins, rather than submit to the unrighteous, and ignominious Domination that is prepared for Us."[15] Abigail Adams also sought to encourage the family to "return a little more to the primitive Simplicity of Manners ['of our Fathers'], and not sink into inglorious ease."[16] I argue, however, following Michael Zakim, that although there certainly are traces of nostalgia in this discourse, the American revolutionary and early national periods were characterized by the forming of an evolving American aesthetic that was not simply renunciation or a return to a fantasized simpler life, but rather an effort to shape a particular republican and a particular national self. The fractured, diverse, and conflictual nature of life in the thirteen colonies made this an especially difficult task, but it is crucial not to underestimate the forward-looking, constructive nature of the project. This was, moreover, not only a discourse, but also a practice; changes in dress and cultural forms were not simply advocated but also made. For example, the *Virginia Gazette* reported that at a holiday ball in December 1769: "the same patriotic spirit which gave rise to the association of the Gentlemen on a late event, was most agreeably manifested in the dress of the Ladies on this occasion, who, in the number of near one hundred, appeared in homespun gowns."[17] The cloak in Figure 4.1 shows homespun at its most elegant. This hooded cloak crafted from scarlet wool, partially silk-lined and ornamented with wool shag around the front edge belonged to Deborah Champion (1753–1845), daughter of the Colonel Henry Champion, of New London, Connecticut. According to tradition, as recorded by the Connecticut Historical Society, she wore this cloak during the American Revolution when she rode across British lines from her home to Boston to deliver the payroll to the American army. The cloak's amplitude allowed her to disguise the bulky package. The jacket in Figure 4.2 has suffered from the years it spent hidden under the floorboards of a house in Guilford, Connecticut, but one can imagine its simple elegance when new. It had been made for a young man from brown woven linen, and featured pewter buttons for its closure, a high turn-over collar, narrow sleeves, and deep cuffs. The front sweeps towards the back in a fashionable curve below the waist. Both these homespun garments are characterized by simple elegance. They were made of a single color, have limited ornamentation, and a lusterless finish. Like the radical Protestant clothing discussed in the previous chapter, however, their production involved substantial labor and expense.[18] These were not the clothes of those who could not import fine fabrics; they had been chosen to convey a political meaning.

The contrast with the dress shown in Figure 4.3, typical of those worn for evening social occasions by colonial elites, could not be starker. It is made of silk fabric, enhanced with elaborate embroidered bead-work, and the sleeves and bodice are

Figure 4.1 Woman's Cloak, *c.*1770–1800. Red wool broadcloth, with silk lining and wool "shag" trimming. Connecticut Historical Society. Gift of Elizabeth Alden Steele and Deborah Champion Steele Geier.

edged with very fine lace. The dress was also very closely fitted, requiring great skill on the part of the seamstress and many sittings.

The crucial shift to be observed here is not that homespun was being produced – historians have demonstrated that from mid-century many households spun and wove the rough cloth for sale on the market – but that it was being worn by elites.[19] Thus, many members of the graduating class at Harvard in the 1760s attended

Figure 4.2 Homespun Boy's Jacket, 1775–1786, brown linen with pewter buttons. Connecticut Historical Society. Museum purchase.

commencement exercises wearing homespun made, if not by their mothers or sisters, by servants within their households, whereas an earlier generation would have bought elegant English fabric with the money earned by the sale of the home-produced cloth.[20] Wearing homespun was the appropriation of an area of economic life from which the British had attempted to exclude them. By that act American

Figure 4.3 Sack-back Gown, *c*.1760. Silk, trimmed with silk fringe, lined with linen, hand-sewn (Victoria and Albert Museum, London), museum number, T.77 to B-1959. Given by John Sterling Williams.

colonists made the costume part of their collective identity, an act comparable to the appropriation of the rattlesnake or the Indian as an emblem of America, or to designing a national flag. It was a gesture that revealed a desire for distance from Britain, rather than an effort to return to an imaginary bucolic past. The political purposes of these sartorial practices are underscored by the fact that, in this same period, those elites dressing in homespun were clothing their slaves in imported

English fabrics.[21] The wearing of homespun by those who could easily afford satin and velvet was a claim to autonomy and self-possession. It was, therefore, appropriate festive garb for the ladies and gentlemen of Virginia or ceremonial dress for the solemn graduation of the next generation of colonial leadership from Harvard. The wearing of English cotton was appropriate for dependants, for those doomed to perpetual childhood, that is, slaves, literally or metaphorically.

This use of homespun obviously harks back, in some ways, to the Puritan dress discussed in the last chapter. There are, however, a number of important differences. While it was the case that Puritan clothes were tailored from wool rather than silk, they were not home-woven, nor was their national origin key to their meaning. As the historian Laurel Ulrich so eloquently depicts, the crucial quality of "Homespun" was that it was, indeed, spun *at home*. And, of course, home had the doubled meaning of being a literal home and a political home – in the American colonies rather than in England. Although it would appear that the boycott strategy was most often articulated by men, therefore, it was clear to contemporaries that it could not be implemented without women's participation.[22] Women were key consumers *and* (at least in some areas) domestic producers in late eighteenth-century America. With the call to boycott English fabric, creole women were asked to abstain from purchasing imported fabrics. While poorer women gave up their calicoes and other industrially produced imports, wealthier women were to forgo their silks, damasks, velvets, and taffetas, they had purchased with the sale of the much rougher fabrics made on their property and wear clothes crafted of that fabric instead. During the war years, women were also called upon to intensify greatly their production of cloth, not only for their own use, but to provide military uniforms. Thus, although American women's historians have tended to look at the French Revolution with a kind of envy, seeing a political initiative and independence they find to be lacking in the American context, for example, in texts like Olympe de Gouges' *Declaration of the Rights of Woman,* in actions like the Women's March on Versailles, or in French women's active participation, for a moment, in the clubs; such envy may be misplaced.[23] As will be seen in the next chapter, women do seem to have played a more active role in certain facets of the revolutionary process in France, but not in the production of the radical cultural change key to political transformation. In America, the particular melding of the public and the private, the importance of home in both the literal and political senses, the centrality of the boycott movement (and its corollary – an emphasis on domestic production), and women's importance in textile production and consumption seem to have given women a definable political place, and one that would long have resonance. Thus historians Linda Kerber and Mary Beth Norton underscore the importance of the "spinning bees," all day events at which women would spin, demonstrating their patriotism and discussing politics with participants and spectators.[24] Such politicization was not always well received. As some women made claims to extending their domestic politics into other arenas, they more and more often came under attack. This is a theme to which we will return. At this early stage in the revolutionary dynamic, however, there was still more openness about the formation of the political public.[25]

It was not only in the discourse about dress and clothing practice that political consciousness was formed in this period, but also in "public, symbolic demonstrations by crowds," in which the English king was often killed in effigy.[26] As had been the case in the English Civil War and would again be seen across the Atlantic a decade later during the French Revolution, these demonstrations and public rituals were critical in inspiring people to communal feeling and revolutionary action.[27] The historian Rhys Isaac has argued that in a period of limited literacy "...*tableaux vivants*, communicating more than words could do, worked to create a collective consciousness of belonging to a virtuous community unanimously roused in support of its dearest rights."[28] In the aftermath of the original revenue acts of the 1760s, English colonists started developing through debate, everyday practice, and collective action, a *political* sense of themselves as Americans distinct from both metropolitan English and inhabitants of other English colonies. But this sentiment was only nascent; the vast majority still hoped that the combination of political pressure from lobbying Parliament and economic pressure from the boycott would bring about a change in revenue policies. This was not to happen.

Relations between metropole and colony deteriorated further in the early 1770s. The statute of May 1773, permitting the East India Company to export tea directly to the American colonies free of all duties (except the three penny tax payable in America) thus giving it a practical monopoly, was the last straw. The New York Sons of Liberty passed a resolution on November 29, 1773: "To prevent a calamity which, of all others, is the most to be dreaded – slavery, and its terrible concomitants – we, subscribers being influenced from a regard to liberty, and disposed to use all lawful endeavors in our power, to defeat the pernicious project, and to transmit to our posterity, those blessings of freedom which our ancestors have handed down to us..."[29] This endorsement and further mobilization of legal boycotting was closely followed by an illegal act – the Boston Tea Party of December 16, 1773 – during which tons of tea were dumped into the Boston Harbor.

The fact that the rebels chose to act disguised as Indians is significant because it indicated that they had, in their minds, broken with Britain and were envisaging themselves as "American." In pre-conflict eighteenth-century British illustrations, America was often depicted in political prints and texts as a childlike, innocent Indian in need of protection. In this case, the personification was almost always as a young girl.[30] Though young and innocent, this girl was also defined as essentially foreign and essentially inferior to the British – the ultimate "other" of civilization. In the period before 1763, that image of the Indian was accepted by many creoles, who still identified strongly with Britain, although they found the representation of their home, America, as foreign, disturbing. As tensions heightened, but before it became clear that a break was inevitable, the young, naive, female Indian came to be depicted in British illustrations as an innocent victim of seduction; this conceptualization took away her childlike qualities, but left the possibility of her return to the British fold. Once hope of that return was abandoned, British allegories of America as Indian were transformed into, on the one hand, a bellicose, mature, savage, male Indian or, on the other, a no-longer innocent, but licentious "…female Indian who engaged in promiscuous courtship of France and Spain who sought to fulfill her desires for material well-being through her sexual favors to the enemies of Britain…"[31] To the rebellious colonists, however, the Indian – as the original inhabitant of the land – came to represent both authenticity and legitimacy. As people who lived lightly on that land, and had few luxurious habits, Indians came also to incarnate the refusal of a decadent and corrupt civilization.

Thus, as the historian Philip Deloria has argued, the colonists were to identify more and more with those who had been the alien other – the Indian. "As England became a them for colonists, Indians became an us."[32] Ann Little has furthermore demonstrated that at the time of the Boston Tea Party the colonists both shared the general understanding of the period that clothes did, quite literally, make the person, and had a long practice of clothing exchange with Native Americans.[33] In dressing as Indians, therefore, the colonists were becoming "natives" of a land they were differently asserting to be their own. This culminated in the moment of claiming Indianness at the Boston Tea Party. In that gesture, the colonists symbolically joined forces with the first Americans to fight against a newly alien other – the British.[34] Deloria argues further that colonists had recourse to Indian dress because there was not yet a clearly marked "American" dress – homespun not being thoroughly established in that role – through which to claim a national identity.[35] This very complicated, ambivalent, and ambiguous changing of sides would have echoes through the rest of American history. In the immediate present, Indians would be recruited to fight against the British and representations of Indianness (either figural or iconic) would be mobilized as part of the new American iconography.

The Indian, because of all the ambiguities of the image, could only be a component element of the symbolic repertoire for the new nation. The other heritage from British imagery – the child – was obviously completely impossible; a people seeking independence could not allegorize itself as a child in need of tutoring. The French and Indian War in the mid-eighteenth century had been an earlier moment when finding a new symbol around which the colonists could unite became urgent, and Benjamin Franklin had turned his not inconsiderable talents to this problem, coming up with the at first improbable idea of the rattlesnake.

Franklin justified his choice by characterizing the snake as unique to North America, particularly vigilant (not having any eyelids), magnanimous, in that it warns by rattling before it attacks, and, as he rather charmingly confessed:

> I was wholly at a loss what to make of the rattles, 'till I went back and counted them and found them just thirteen, exactly the number of the Colonies united in America; and I recollected too that this was the only part of the Snake which increased in numbers

– Perhaps it might be only fancy, but, I conceited the painter had shewn a half formed additional rattle, which, I suppose, may have been intended to represent the province of Canada. – 'Tis curious and amazing to observe how distinct and independant of each other the rattles of this animal are, and yet how firmly they are united together, so as never to be separated but by breaking them to pieces. – One of those rattles singly, is incapable of producing sound, but the ringing of thirteen together, is sufficient to alarm the boldest man living.[36]

Some historians have suggested that he also discovered, while looking in European emblem books, that in Italian iconography the snake represented democracy, and that a French book may provided the image of the cut snake accompanied by the motto: "Join, or Die." The snake was thus doubly legitimated; it combined a European genealogy and North American authenticity. It also incarnated Franklin's vision of the American character and his hopes for the future of the colonies. The image clearly resonated with his fellow colonists, for the rattlesnake, with each segment of the serpent labeled with the initials of a colony, became a much-reproduced call to arms, or at least to solidarity.[37]

The snake enjoyed a period of popularity as an emblem of colonial union, reused by Paul Revere two decades later on the masthead of the celebrated Boston newspaper, *The Massachusetts Spy*, and again on the Gadsden flag in 1775. The masthead, reminiscent of the royal edicts and proclamations discussed in Chapter 2, was substantial, very decorative, and bursting with allegorical references. The title of the newspaper had pride of place at the top of the page, printed in type old fashioned for the time, reminiscent of the lettering often used in printings of the Bible. The title was given further weight by the elaborate curlicues emanating from each letter, providing the words "Massachusetts" and "Spy" a framing like that that often used in the first letter of illuminated manuscripts. Under the slogan "JOIN OR DIE" in bold block letters, ran from left to right, a beautifully drawn rattlesnake, facing off against a winged creature plausibly interpretable as standing in for England. The masthead also featured a seated figure holding aloft a liberty cap on a staff. The masthead, like the snake itself and much other republican iconography, sought to re-use a familiar repertoire of symbols to legitimate creole claims. The snake was ultimately abandoned, but the theme of a national unity that respected the autonomy and independence of each of the colonies/states was maintained, with the rattles on the snake replaced by the white and red stripes and the stars of the "Betsy Ross" and later flags. The homespun movement, the spinning bees, the Boston Tea Party, and the elaboration of an iconography of Americanness all helped consolidate a sense of distance from Britain that was only reinforced by British actions.

Parliament's retaliatory legislation, known as "The Intolerable Acts" (1774), mandating among other things that the port of Boston be closed until the losses to the East India Company had been repaid, served to increase the rate of avoidance of tea as well as the other boycotts.[38] The culmination of the boycott movement was reached on October 20, 1774, when the Continental Congress voted the Non-intercourse with Great Britain Act. They resolved to refuse to import or consume goods from, or export goods to, Great Britain. The void in English goods was to be compensated for by a combination of abstention and encouragement of local production:

> We will, in our several stations, encourage frugality, oeconomy, and industry, and promote agriculture, arts and the manufactures of this country, especially that of wool; and will discountenance and discourage every species of extravagance and dissipation, especially all horse-racing, and all kinds of gaming, cock fighting, exhibitions of shews, plays and other expensive diversions and entertainments; and on the death of any relation or friend, none of us, or any of our families will go into any further mourning-dress, than a black crape or ribbon on the arm or hat, for gentlemen, and a black ribbon and necklace for ladies, and we will discontinue the giving of gloves and scarves at funerals.[39]

At first glance, the author's inclusion of a ban on entertainments – horse-racing, gambling, cockfighting, and theatrical performance – is startling on two counts. First, it reproduces, virtually verbatim, any number of documents from the English Revolution. Second, the activities it listed did not require English goods. In fact, one could easily imagine a contemporary making the opposite suggestion, that is, that his fellow Americans distract themselves from things English by greater indulgence in entertainments not requiring imports. But patriots quickly assimilated English products to decadent lifestyles in general and argued – as had English Puritan revolutionaries in the seventeenth century and as would the French revolutionaries in the 1790s – that political change required a transformation of social life. National unity was to be constructed both through an everyday life in concordance with Puritanism and in a political practice based in republicanism.[40] The radicalism of the position is further underscored by the one specific brake on consumption proposed – the drastic curtailing of mourning dress. It is true that funerals had been the site of great ostentation in colonial America, including as noted in the text above the distribution of tokens to those attending.[41] But the restriction did not simply concern the gifting at funerals, but the immediate families' dress. Asking people to abandon tea, to renounce velvet, to not go to the theater could all be made to seem trivial, but asking them to restrain their customs of expressing respect for their dead greatly raised the stakes.

A new value, which had arisen in the English Revolution and would be echoed in the French, was put on transparency and authenticity: "the non-Importers had long been endeavouring to discover who were true, and who Traitors to the Cause of American liberty, which nothing could so effectually discover as the present Measure: But since the Sons of Liberty have got all their Names, and *every Man who before wore a Mask, now appears with an uncovered Face*..." The new American public was, therefore, "...an imagined body of people who demonstrated virtue by renouncing British goods and thus earned the right to judge the behavior of the less virtuous."[42] There are signs here, as there would be later in the French context, of a tension between the revelatory qualities and the pedagogical capacities of cultural processes. On the one hand it was thought that people could be transformed by the food they ate, the clothes they wore, the songs they sang; on the other hand, the practice revealed an inner being, one already transformed. In the latter interpretation, only those who were already American and/or republican had a right to engage in American practices; others would be commiting fraud. This was an eighteenth-century innovation. While it is true that some medieval and early modern sumptuary laws regulating dress were justified by saying that people were appearing to be other than they really were, such anxiety did not appear in the Puritan/revolutionary texts. Radical Protestants, in their belief in predestination, were sure that one looked as one, profoundly, was.

Whether it was a question of being or becoming American, however, it required a remaking of one's entire way of life. How one enjoyed the living and how one mourned the dead were to be changed. Marking respect – of either the living or the dead – through dress or other goods was no longer legitimate. Rituals that marked time, like having tea, were to be abandoned. The recently discovered concept of leisure to be enjoyed at the theater or the races was to be left aside. And, all were to work. Even those who did not need to work should be industrious, because from honest labor came independence. The theme of independence, and independence through labor, was especially fraught because of the issue of slavery. Some even argued that the virtues of labor were such that those who owned slaves should free them, since slavery enslaved the master as much as the slaves by encouraging them in their luxurious habits.[43] The whole structure of polite society and gentility, including the increasing separation between public and private lives, was suddenly subject to radical questioning. This political and religious, republican and puritan tradition gave force to and sustained the boycott movement; the boycott movement made those traditions palpable in everyday lives.

Waging War, Making the Nation: Confederation, 1776–1787

The boycotts came to an end with the Declaration of Independence in 1776, and with the Peace of Paris in 1783 the new nation was definitively established. From the late 1770s until the ratification of the Constitution and the first elections in 1788, Americans faced the successive challenges of war, of fully elaborating what "America" was, who "Americans" were, and how America was to be governed. The end of the boycotts in 1776 did not bring an end to the mistrust of European luxuries or to discussions of how to develop a particular "American" taste for productivity and austerity.[44] If anything the debate intensified during the war and especially in the early national period, when the political model of confederacy was clearly failing, when "American" identity seemed particularly unstable and indeterminate, and demand for European products revived with a vengeance.

The decade following the Declaration of Independence in 1776 was dominated by the creation of interim structures of government and war. But in order for the war to be effectively waged, in order for the newly independent Americans to consolidate their sense of a shared identity, there was a widely perceived need for shared symbols, for a common aesthetic vocabulary, and for a unified set of values and everyday habits. That need was all the more extreme because not only did the new polity consist, in fact, first of thirteen separate republics tied togther into a confederation (only becoming a federal republic in 1787, but regional identifications and differences continued to be strong. Vermont, for example, was an independent country in this period, and Massachusetts created an uproar by abolishing slavery. There was truly little to bind the nascent polity. The new nation could clearly not rely solely on Britain's negative example to establish and sustain itself. After approving the Declaration of Independence and the Articles of Confederation, therefore, the Second Continental Congress (1775–1781) set about commissioning designs for the flag and the Great Seal, issuing paper money, as well as selecting the eagle as the national emblem.[45]

Determining the appropriate symbolic repertoire for the new nation proved a complicated task; in part influenced by the French example, designers put an increasing emphasis on European neoclassical forms, albeit accented with what was understood to be indigenous American detail. This may clearly be seen in the design of the Great Seal. Thomas Jefferson's first design (in 1776) balanced the "frontiersman" dressed in buckskins against a liberty figure holding a Phrygian cap atop a pike, and had the specificity of each colony identified by its initials surrounding emblems of American uniqueness topped by the all-seeing eye of the Enlightenment (Figure 4.4). By the time the official Great Seal was adopted a decade later, however, it had become considerably more abstract (Figure 4.5). The states had now become stars and stripes, with all mention of their specific and differentiated identities eradicated; both the figure of liberty and that of the frontiersman had disappeared, as if absorbed by an American eagle in whose claws were clutched the classical emblems of the olive branch of peace and the arrows of war. The image is visually much more arresting and, indeed, the emphasis *is* on its visuality. The motto "E pluribus unum" – which provided the grounding for the earlier sketch – has been reduced to a small ribbon in the eagle's mouth. The bald-headed eagle is, of course, a specifically American bird, but the Roman Empire had used a European eagle as its emblem, as had other more recent Continental regimes. By making a distinctively American variant of a species with a long tradition in European heraldry the national symbol, the early government thus underscored both its connection to the old world and its independence from it.

The Great Seal was an important emblem, but a more immediate representation of the nation was needed. As we have seen in earlier chapters, money – both

Figure 4.4 First design for the Great Seal, after Eugène du Simitière. Design for the Great Seal of the United States, 1776. Pencil on paper. Thomas Jefferson Papers, Manuscript Division, Library of Congress.

paper and coins – had long played that role for European monarchies, and for the Commonwealth and the Protectorate during the English Civil War; it was thus an obvious element in the symbolic repertoire on which to draw. There was also a strong American tradition upon which to rely, however. The American colonies had, in fact, been in the vanguard of the production of paper money – the earliest was produced in the Massachusetts Bay Colony in 1690 – and the individual colonies had also struck coins for local usage. The outcome had, inevitably, been an inconsistent multiplicity of competing specie, with the late colonial and early national periods being marked by monetary chaos. English, Spanish and French money coexisted with the money issued by each of the colonies. The banknotes authorized by the Second Continental Congress, known as Continentals, although still local and volatile, were both the first step towards a national currency and consciously used as a very immediate and direct way to spread political ideas. For example, an early Maryland note, designed by a silversmith from Annapolis, Thomas Sparrow, in the summer of 1775, depicted a figure representing Great Britain being handed a petition from the Continental Congress by an allegorized America. America, meanwhile, was busy stomping out slavery and holding liberty aloft, lighting the way for American soldiers. The perceived importance of these notes in symbolizing, even incarnating, the newly unified nation may be seen in the considerable efforts people made to maintain an intrinsically very fragile (because printed on soft paper) currency. The Maryland bill was, for example, carefully sewn together, while others were preserved by being glued on to newspaper. It would take independence and a constitution for a unified system of coinage and paper money to be created; but these early gestures indicate the importance granted to this means of everyday politics.

Figure 4.5 First publication of the Great Seal. James Trenchard, "Arms of the United States," engraving in book *The Colombian Magazine* (Philadelphia, September 1786), p. 33. Rare Book and Special Collections Division, Library of Congress.

   Even this multiplicity of currencies left a penury of specie and disorder. To answer both problems, the Continental Congress chartered the Bank of North America in Philadelphia in 1781 as the nation's first bank, which helped increase the money supply. Given its coexistence with the individual states' monetary production, however, it did nothing to produce more coherence. The problems this chaotic system posed for national development were noted by Robert Morris from the Office of Finance in a letter to the President of Congress, in 1782. After a long discussion outlining how fortunate it was that units of measurement were common across the thirteen colonies, he went on to decry the multiplicity of monies: "The ideas annexed to a pound, a shilling, and a penny, are almost as various as the states themselves. Calculations are therefore as necessary for our inland commerce, as upon foreign exchanges... Difficulties of this sort ... are perplexing to most men, and troublesome to all. It is however, a fortunate circumstance, that money is so much in the power of the sovereign, as that he can easily lead the people into new ideas of it."[46] Despite his optimism and the declaration in 1785 that the basic unit of American currency would be the dollar, it would be more than a decade before unified coinage entered circulation. Given the challenges facing the country in this period, it is not surprising that there was a gap between the call for the creation of this crucial element of the national symbolic system and its actual production and circulation.

Contemporaries were also acutely aware, however, that the official iconographies of state would never suffice alone to create a national spirit and weave the horizontal ties needed for solidarity. Thus, even in the middle of wartime, questions of austerity, luxury, and manly republicanism continued to preoccupy central political actors. For example, John Adams, writing home to his wife from France in the spring of 1778, described the attractions of life in France under Louis XVI, and both his admiration for and immense distrust of it: "The Delights of France are innumerable. The Politeness, the Elegance, and Softness, the Delicacy is extreme... But what is all this to me? I receive but little Pleasure in beholding all these Things, because I cannot but consider them as Bagatelles, introduced, by Time and Luxury in Exchange for the great Qualities and hardy manly Virtues of the human Heart."[47] Adams thereby associated the positive attributes of France (if such they really were) to two qualities America could not have – age and wealth (time and luxury), which he opposed to what America did have – character (great Qualities) and wholesome masculinity. He tried to make the difference between France and America intrinsic, but was clearly nonetheless deeply worried about contagion.

Adams's association of elegant manners, fine objects, skilled entertainment and effeminacy with royalist politics was common at the time, as was his fear of their eventually overrunning America. In 1779 Samuel Adams warned James Warren of an "...Inundation of Levity Vanity Luxury Dissipation and indeed Vice of every kind..." This moral decay was worrying less on a personal, than on a political, level: "This Torrent must be stemmed... A general Dissolution of Principles and Manners will more surely overthrow the Liberties of America than the whole Force of the Common Enemy." The solution as far as Adams was concerned was the creation of associations to enforce austere living and education: "If Virtue and Knowledge are diffused among the People, they will never be enslaved. This will be their great Security. Virtue and Knowledge will forever be an even Balance for Powers & Riches."[48] John Adams argued further that national solidarity itself depended upon "...the Education of the rising Generation, the Formation of a national System of Oeconomy, Policy, and Manners..." and feared "...the Contagion of European Manners, and that excessive Influx of Commerce Luxury and Inhabitants from abroad, which will soon embarrass Us."[49] In these texts the seductive quality of European vices was rendered explicit and the need for a moral pedagogy – as in the English Civil War – was explicitly stated.

John Adams envisioned a step even beyond what the Puritans had been able to accomplish when he wrote to his wife Abigail expressing his longing to have the power to "forever banish and exclude from America, all Gold, silver, precious stones, Alabaster, Marble, Silk, Velvet and Lace."[50] He added, however, that he feared that were one to reinstate sumptuary laws, the women would rebel! Thus, in their claims to move from the politics of the needle to politics *tout court*, women had apparently moved from the space of virtue to that of vice.

By the next decade, much of the argument against luxury specifically addressed the irony of the United States' having recently won their independence from England, only to once again become dependent on it for matters of taste and style, as well as once again paying England taxes on imported goods. James Warren wrote despairingly to John Adams, early in 1785, of a return to materialism and its accompaniment, European taste:

> Money is the only object attended to, and the only Acquisition that commands respect. Patriotism is ridiculed; Integrity and Ability are of little Consequence. Foreign Commerce has extended itself beyond its natural supports and, by its Extravagant Imports greatly Exceeding the Exports, drained off all the Money, embarrassed itself, and every other resource of the Country, while Luxury keeps pace with the manners of older and more affluent countries.[51]

A magazine article of 1787 predicted dire consequences from this dependence:

> What can we promise ourselves if we still pursue this same extensive trade? What, but the total destruction of our manners, and the loss of our virtue? Every man, in proportion as he falls into luxury, becomes more and more inclined to bribery and corruption. He finds wants and desires before unknown, and these wants and desires being merely artificial, become not easily restrained without proper bounds and limits.[52]

Even if goods could be imported more cheaply than domestically produced, in that direction lay perdition. The appropriate solution was a greater investment in the honest, manly, and independent activities of husbandry, agriculture and especially manufacture.

Not only did dependence on English goods spark concern, but the old anxiety about public entertainments, the theater, gambling and card-playing reappeared as well. An author who signed him/herself only, rather ironically as will be seen, as "A confident Republican," wrote in defending the prohibition on theatrical performances in Massachusetts in 1785:

> ... it would be highly imprudent to think of a theater, at least till we have broken an intimate connection, which too many, it is to be feared, are still fond of, with a nation which has exerted its utmost to ruin us, and therefore, a nation whom we have reason, more than any other, to abominate – a nation abandoned to every species of wickedness and folly ... let us all endeavour to unlearn and forget the destructive customs which we have learned of that mother of harlots, and secure to ourselves and posterity, that independence which, by the smiles of heaven we have purchased with our treasure and best blood.[53]

Echoing seventeenth-century worries about the power of the theater, the "confident" republican seems very much to lack confidence in his or her fellow republicans. The bad influence of the English was underscored in the *American Herald* the same year, "The manners of certain British residents are too prevalent: – We should cautiously guard ourselves against them..."[54]

These texts contain a fascinating amalgam of worries and anxieties. The authors were fearful that, finding a void where American culture should be, both women and men would be attracted to Europe and things European. They oscillated between arguments about the intrinsic qualities of the Old World and the New, but were clearly deeply worried that the New World would be made over in the image of the Old. This would be, above all, bad for the national character and perhaps the nation's very existence, because frugality, labor and a certain definition of masculinity and femininity were understood to lie at the heart of the Republic.

These fearful responses may be seen again in the polemics around the Sans Souci Club in Boston in 1785. Sans Souci was a nightclub, held up by Samuel Adams as emblematic of all that was wrong with post-Independence America. A play – *Sans Souci, Alias Free and Easy: or an Evening's Peep into a Polite Circle* – deeply critical of the club (along the lines argued by Adams) was printed and circulated. Partially, perhaps, because of much protest in the newspapers, it was never performed. The character given the name of "the republican heroine" railed especially against hypocrisy: "I did expect to find a cultivation of manners somewhat similar to their publick resolves; but ... I am greatly disappointed."[55] Blame is placed especially on the women of Boston for not having eradicated "british gewgaws – etiquette and parade". The valuing of freedom more than equality, or certainly republicanism, may be seen in the character Little Pert, who declaims:

Damn the old musty rules of decency and decorum – national characters – Spartan virtues – republican principles – they are all calculated for rigid manners, and Cromwelian days; – they are as disgusting as old orthodoxy: – Fashion and etiquette are more agreeable to my ideas of life – this is the independence I aim at – the free and easy air which so distinguishes the man of fashion, from the self-formal republican – the court stile – the *je ne scai quoi* – give me but this and away with all your buckram of Presbeterianism.[56]

Little Pert was, of course, right. These were remnants of "Cromwelian days" carried across the ocean and across more than a hundred years. The Little Pert character, however much disliked by the author, no doubt did represent a frustration and perhaps impatience at the perceived absence of a new, modern, adequate and positive American vision. The new United States, while heirs to England's Civil War, were in a new age, as the revolutionary strategies, particularly the boycott and the homespun movement, had demonstrated; but they were struggling mightily to invent a culture adequate to their reality.

A variation on this complaint may be found two years later in the first comedy to be written by an American and professionally performed by American actors in American theaters – Royall Tyler's 1787 play, *The Contrast*. The play's theme was succinctly summarized in its last lines, pronounced by the hero, Colonel Manly: "And I have learned that probity, virtue, and honour, though they should not have received the polish of Europe, will secure to an honest American the good graces of his fair countrywomen, and I hope, the applause of THE PUBLIC."[57] Throughout the four acts of the play, New York society – in the character of Mr. Dimple – is represented, in its effort to emulate the elegance of Europe, as effeminate, silly, debt-ridden, and duplicitous, while American (Yankee) society – in the personage of Col. Manly – is represented, as masculine, honest, sincere, frugal, and direct. In a dialogue between Letitia and Charlotte, it is revealed that men and women are indistinguishable from each other in this "Europeanized" society:

> *Laetitia*: Our ladies are so delicate and dressy.
> *Charlotte*: And our beaux are so dressy and delicate.
> *Laetitia*: Our ladies chat and flirt so agreeably.
> *Charlotte*: And our beaux simper and bow so gracefully...[58]

The virtuous heroine, Maria, closes the first act regretting that she has committed to marry Mr. Dimple: "...a depraved wretch, whose only virtue is a polished exterior; who is actuated by the unmanly ambition of conquering the defenceless; whose heart, insensible to the emotions of patriotism, dilates at the plaudits of every unthinking girl."[59] By contrast, Col. Manly would "ride, or rather fly, an hundred miles to relieve a distressed object, or to do a gallant act in the service of his country."[60] Col. Manly put nation and patriotism above gallantry and even above his desire to please his sister. European manners are not condemned outright; it is American efforts to imitate Europe that are seen as foolish: "In Paris, the fashions have their dawnings, their routine, and declensions, and depend as much upon the caprice of the day as in other countries; but there every lady assumes a right to deviate from the general *ton* as far as will be of advantage to her own appearance. In America, the cry is, what is the fashion? And we follow it indiscriminately, because it is so."[61] Finally, Col. Manly is made to condemn luxury as "the bane of the nation." Col. Manly in fact wears buckskins, retreating even further back into the American iconography of austerity and masculinity than homespun. As was discussed in Chapter 2, buckskins were borrowed from Native American sartorial systems, and were a synecdoche for authentic life on the frontier. Luxury, Col. Manly went on to say, "renders a people weak at home, and accessible to bribery, corruption, and force from abroad."[62] Luxury creates internal divisions, as can be learned from the lesson of ancient Greece: "They exhibited to the world a noble spectacle, – a number of independent states united by a similarity of language, sentiment, manners, common interest, and common consent in one grand mutual league of protection... But when foreign gold, and still more pernicious foreign luxury, had crept among them … The various states engendered jealousies of each other … The common good was lost in the pursuit of private interest."[63] The play was immensely popular, and subscribers to its printing included no less a personage than George Washington.

Unlike *Sans Souci*, *The Contrast* was not critical of women, but rather of effeminacy, luxury, and desires to emulate Europeans rather than to live like Americans. Effeminacy, once again, stood in for what was not indigenous, not natural, not appropriate, at the same time as traditional gender roles were, indeed, reinforced. In a good republic, men were men and women women; but as essential was Americans being Americans, even though figuring out what that was seemed to be very difficult. Critique of luxury and of European manners encouraged the quest to find an "art" that bore "…a physical relationship to the national character" and led to both a new interest in art and a quest for an American style.[64] The new nation-state would, of course, work to create its own iconography, but the citizens of the new country, both women and men, also took this task into their own hands.

Domestic, Popular, and Commercial Constructions of the Nation

In the years following independence, Americans both produced and consumed an astonishing array of everyday goods commemorating the Revolution and its heroes. The Revolution had "made private events public events, and private figures public men…"[65] Its heroes – starting with George Washington – were celebrated in portraiture. There are obviously echoes of royal and courtly portraiture in this practice; but the modesty with which American leaders, particularly America's first president, arrayed themselves pose a stark contrast to European courtly fashions. Washington was most often depicted wearing either his general's uniform or a plain homespun suit.[66] Some of the portraits were official and for government buildings; but national leaders were also present in people's homes, depicted in paintings or on buttons on clothing, or painted on pottery. Likewise, major events of the Revolution were represented on a wide variety of household items. Most of these objects were commercially produced, but some were homemade.

I would like to suggest that there is an important differentiation to be made between producing items for sale on the market and those that were labored upon in the home for one's own, or one's family's use, or to be given as a gift. And even the "commercial" is too broad a category: an object produced by one's neighbor to one's own design would have different meanings than one clearly produced in the new nation, but bought in a shop; the latter would be different again from a tea-set embossed with eagles imported from England or China. People thus paid to look at waxwork statues of George Washington in museums, or bought portraits of him; but women also commemorated his death in 1799, for example, by spending days, months and years rendering his image, or his dwelling, in needlepoint and

0embroidery.[67] Like the embroidery of Adam and Eve discussed in the preceding chapter, this embroidery would have represented many hours of labor. This kind of image – unlike some samplers, which were set work at girls' schools – would have been chosen and perhaps drawn, or at least transferred, by the embroiderer: Caroline Stebbins Sheldon, for example, embroidered a picture of Mount Vernon, either because it was moving or pleasing to her or because she thought it would be for its intended recipient.[68] It would then, of course, hang on a wall from one generation to the next, reminding those who saw it not only of George Washington's home but also of the devoted labor involved in the work itself. The name of the needlewoman who produced the early nineteenth-century embroidery in Figure 4.6 has been lost, but

Figure 4.6 American School, Memorial Embroidered Picture, *c*.1805–1815. Silk, linen and water color. ©Museum of Fine Arts, Houston, TX, USA. Bayou Bend Collection, Gift of William J. Hill. The Bridgeman Art Library.

her elaborate memorial portrait of George Washington bears witness to her desire to use her domestic skills to honor a public figure, while at the same time keeping a female figure (perhaps either herself or an allegory of the Republic) in center stage. The woman sitting at the base of the funerary monument in form of a pyramid upon which a classic medaillion portrait hangs, has tamed an American eagle bearing a shield with the emblem of the United States on its breast. The nation's primary symbol is linked to its first president by the staff held in the female figure's hand. The scene is pastoral, seemingly emphasizing the rural nature of the young country. This embroidery is somewhat unusual in its quality, scale and vividness, but not in its content. Women regularly turned their skills both to recording and commemorating significant people and events.

Quilting was another, distinctively American, mode of commemorating the Revolution at home. Some quilters chose to reproduce patriotic images on their covers, so that they, or their children, would quite literally sleep in contact with the nation's symbols. Quilt-making and embroidery were very slow work: these politically-charged symbols, visages and places first took form in women's minds and were then produced by their hands over months or even years. The quilt shown in Figure 4.7, for example, gives the Great Seal of the United States pride of place, but domesticates it by framing the eagle with bouquets and encasing it in a traditional quilt pattern. Others commemorated key revolutionary events in their domestic productions. The battle of Saratoga on October 17, 1777 in which almost 6,000 British soldiers led by General John Burgoyne were encircled and defeated by the American Army, was honored in a quilt pattern appropriately called "The Burgoyne Surrounded," an example of which may be seen in Figure 4.8.

Since a non-quilting viewer would be unlikely to make a connection between the abstract geometric forms of this pattern and a battle, this style of political quilting provided repeated occasions for recounting key events in the Revolution among the patriotic. Thus while patterns like the Great Seal conveyed their message wordlessly, others involved a melding of narration and visual form. Women's domestic production of patriotic and historical needlework, most probably building on the politicization of clothing during the boycott period, was prolific, apparently far greater than comparable work in revolutionary or post-revolutionary England or France. Women in America, at least women with the leisure to do so, took up their needles in the post-revolutionary moment; but they also rapidly built upon the politicization of domestic life. Once again they took to producing – not homespun this time – but a wide array of politicized textiles. Some of these, particularly the quilts, were collectively made, providing women a time and space to come together. Perhaps building on the experience of boycotts, of the homespun movement, and of the revolutionary spinning bee, women would work together to produce objects simultaneously private and public, political and domestic. Out of that domestic coming together would come other kinds of mobilization. Thirty years ago feminist historians argued about the relative importance of the abolitionist and the women's

Figure 4.7 Great Seal of the United States in appliqué, early nineteenth century. Brown-Francis family, Canterbury, CT, USA. National Museum of American History, Smithsonian Institution.

club movements in providing the grounding for the US women's suffrage movement. I would like to suggest that all three may well have been enabled by the particular melding of public and private during the revolutionary years.

A few women also politicized another traditionally female domain – the kitchen. At the interstices of the popular and the commercial lay the world of cooking and cookbooks. Amelia Simmons included in her *American Cookery* – the first printed cookbook adapted for use in North America (published in Hartford in 1796) – a substantial number of recipes using ingredients of indigenous origin.[69] The three variations on Indian pudding – based on cornmeal and molasses – are the most familiar; but *American Cookery* also included dishes based on pumpkins, cranberries, and notably the leavening agent pearl ash (produced by forest fires set to clear land).

Figure 4.8 Indigo and white latticework variation of "Burgoyne Surrounded" *c.*1835, 84 × 87 cm. Maryland Betsey Telford's Rocky Mountain Quilts, 130 York Street, York Village, ME 03909, USA, www.rockymountainquilts.com.

Scholars have persuasively argued that the book's author included those recipes as part of her project of establishing a specifically American diet and cuisine. In writing down recipes in which indigenous goods played a key role, she was both recording a distinctively American practice and encouraging its transmission. Amelia Simmons was most probably more self-conscious than many early American cooks and writers of recipes; but she was far from alone in this practice.[70]

In addition to women's commemorative labor within the home and to their cooking, and transcribing recipes for distintinctively American food, a wide variety of commercial products were made in the new nation, or abroad for consumption there, designed to remind Americans of the Revolution. The sign made for Stratton's Inn in Connecticut, was most probably locally made for the owner who chose the design. It is conceivable that it was made by the inn's owner himself; but the turning, the reference to Chippendale style, and the form – it could easily have been modeled on a chair-back – suggest that it was made by a professional furniture-maker. Its rusticness and its purpose make it unlikely that it was produced far away in a shop specializing in signage. Such labor, while presumably done in exchange for payment, would have been of a different nature than that of those producing non-commissioned everyday objects commemorating George Washington.

Representations of George Washington's face were, no doubt, the most ubiquitous revolutionary, national symbol in everyday life. In addition to the embroideries discussed above, his portrait was produced commercially in America and abroad (for the American market) and in virtually any medium imaginable. Thus a button was crafted in 1789 bearing his head – perhaps so that he could be worn close to the heart; the French produced a profile embedded in Baccarat crystal; and a New Jersey porcelain company decorated a plate (made in Silesia) with his visage.[71]

The degree to which the project of constituting the nation through commemoration of its founding event and the project of making a profit through the sale of commemorative items coincided is exemplified in the Chinese, and especially English, production of revolutionary souvenirs. While the Chinese created tea-sets decorated with patriotic scenes, English potters went so far as to produce goods with "American eagles tearing apart British lions."[72] Although it is important to differentiate among these objects according to the locus of production and the relation of their makers to the political cause, the motives of the consumers is somewhat, although not entirely, more straightforward. Although those who received these objects as gifts from someone they liked, admired or to whom they felt endebted may have kept them despite having no desire to participate in the making of an American nation, it is legitimate to assume that the majority who purchased them had.

The new nation – and the definitions of equality, freedom, and democracy – that emerged from the American Revolution were inextricably bound into a developing commercial, capitalist economy and culture. The United States, given its weak centralization and its lack of national infrastructure was particularly dependent on commercial and private culture for its national cultural consolidation. This investment in commodities and goods, even those emblazoned with revolutionary heroes or patriotic symbols, did not sit well with many politically active Americans, who had, after all, been through the quest for a particular American aesthetic based on austerity, simplicity, and frugality during the boycotts of the 1760s and 1770s. Since some of these were also firm adherents of federalism and states' rights, they may or may not have felt more positively about the national state's efforts to create solidarity through symbolic objects.

Making the Nation-state, 1788–1800

In the period from the 1780s through the early years of the nineteenth century, the government of the United States struggled with Americans' heritage of mistrust of government, very limited centralization, and the burden of a colonial past as it attempted to construct a repertoire of shared symbols, signs and rituals so that the inhabitants of the far-flung country would have a sense of shared mission and a shared past. There was no shortage of aesthetic genres or important events upon which to draw: the Revolution itself provided one rich repertoire of form, the classical world of Rome and Greece provided another, and the creolized forms that evolved over two centuries of colonial settlement provided the third. The style ultimately chosen was inspired by the classicism of the democratic city-states of ancient Greece and of republican Rome. As the historian Neil Harris has argued, neoclassicism, both because of its formal qualities and because of its historical associations with democracy and French republicanism, could come to stand for the antithesis of English luxury and decadence and as the embodiment of American simplicity and elegance. As during the French Revolution, neoclassicism was the style chosen to represent a break with the immediate past and the embrace of a republican present and future. As in the French case, there were ironies in the choice. The French revolutionaries praised a style that had, in fact, been endorsed by the last French monarchy. American visionaries, in their effort to endorse austerity, to choose a style appropriate to the new republican nation and to move away from European style, selected one that had in fact been brought to England from Italy by Inigo Jones under the patronage of James I.

Although contemporaries appear not to have been aware of the ironies, some considered the Greek and Roman republics to offer both a model and a warning. On the one hand, the ancient world was portrayed as offering all that was good and noble; on the other, Timothy Dwight was not alone when, in his well-known nationalist poem *Greenfield Hills* (1794), he claimed that Greece and Rome had been "spoiled by pageants, luxury, and gold."[73] Citizens of those republics had yielded to their desires for luxury and entertainment; those of the newly founded United States should take warning, and limit their emulation of these earlier political forms. No alternative model presented itself, however, so despite this anxiety, nearly all governmental building came rapidly to be in neoclassical style, and private individuals emulated the styles of their official edifices. The elaboration of a division between public and private, the relegation of the culture of the everyday to the private, and the exclusion of the state from that domain made full exploitation of that repertoire difficult, however. From the Peace of Paris until late in the nineteenth century, the most consistent aesthetic representation of America was found in coinage and the buildings of municipal, county, state, and federal buildings.

Very shortly after ratification, Congress chartered the First Bank of the United States with the authorization to issue paper money. This was followed by the creation of the first US Mint in Philadelphia in 1792 and the issuance of national American coinage the following year. At the time of the creation of the Mint, not only did Congress unify and centralize coinage, but it also decided on the most effective and desirable symbolic representation of the nation in the citizens' everyday lives. It mandated that US coins have on one side: "an impression emblematic of Liberty, with an inscription of the word Liberty, and the year of coinage; and upon the reverse of each of the gold and silver coins shall be the representation of an eagle, with this inscription, 'UNITED STATES OF AMERICA.'" While it would take many years for common bills to enter circulation, Americans had, passing through their hands on a daily basis, an allegory of the value considered most dear in the new nation – liberty (not fraternity, equality, or the republic). It was, like most of the national iconography, as abstract as possible while retaining its distinctively American features.

Another immediate consequence of the ratification of the Constitution, since it determined the basic structure of governance, was the construction of a national capital, along with the necessary administrative buildings. Given that the Capitol was to represent the people, Thomas Jefferson determined that its design should be chosen through an open competition (to which he himself secretly submitted a design!). The call for submissions in 1782 brought a substantial response, but all (including Jefferson's) were deemed inadequate, and ultimately a project in the neoclassical style merging the ideas of a number of different architects was built.[74] Washington, Jefferson and others involved in the process envisaged a seat of government in which European and American symbols and styles were joined, creating a new whole.

The new United States also encouraged the celebrating of holidays to commemorate major revolutionary events, most notably the signing of the Declaration of Independence on July 4, 1776. It was hoped that celebrating the same holiday at the same time across the nation would both counter class, regional, racial, and religious differences and make or strengthen horizontal ties of solidarity.[75] The federal state had only finite power, however; it declared the dates, but left local groups to actually organize the celebrations, which they did in varying forms and with differing levels of enthusiasm. Given the diversity of the population and the long-lasting commitment to older cultural practices, there were often very local and very particular forms of celebration to which people were more committed than the national holidays they were asked to honor.

The 1780s and especially the 1790s saw the names of public places and streets changed, with the corresponding redrawing of maps, and the development of a national post office. As was noted above, however, there was a limit to what the central government could do. Even under the federal system established in 1787, the national government was very weak; there was no federal income tax and no federal paper money, and the Congress had little power. Each state continued to print its own bills, and by 1836 there were over 30,000 different styles in circulation. The government did not have the means to create an American museum equivalent to the French Louvre; there was no possibility of creating a national school system; and there could be no national Church, as in England. The limits of the federal government were, however, compensated by popular commitment to both commemoration and the shaping of a new national culture. The post office, and the low postal rates, proved to be crucial in that process. The postal system provided the infrastructure for a national print and commodity culture. Thus the work, already started in the colonial period, of establishing links among people through the circulation of goods, and even more centrally, the circulation of print media carrying advertisements and information about those goods, continued apace in the early national period.[76] It would, however, take until the 1880s before public institutions attempted to create a national aesthetic; and even then, these were more often municipal than federal.

While the particular heritage that the independent and rivalrous colonies left to the new nation made national consolidation difficult, other dynamics of the American Revolution enabled women to make a unique contribution to that project. Consequently, I would like to suggest that, although historians have effectively demonstrated that women were excluded from most public political life in the early republic, women continued to build on the tradition of politicized domesticity and republican motherhood that they inherited from the revolutionary period.[77] The particular configuration of republican motherhood and the key place of domestic production and consumption in the American Revolution shaped the gendering of the American polity in a way different than that of either the British or the French.[78] Throughout the nineteenth and arguably into the twentieth centuries, women built successive generations of institutions situated at the border of the private and public, the domestic and the political in order to participate in the shaping of their nation.[79] The intersections of the Abolitionist and of women's suffrage movements would also give a distinctive cast to the forms taken by American feminism.[80] Although women in the French Revolution also mobilized strong arguments for political participation, the ways the boundaries were drawn in that revolutionary dynamic between the public and the private and the universal and the particular configured their possibilities differently.

–5–

Making French Republicans
Revolutionary Transformation of the Everyday

...names do many things, depending on their nature. They rally people to patriotism, to virtue, to error, or to fiction... When one reconstructs a government from nothing ... one should republicanize everything.[1]

Frenchmen, you are too intelligent to fail to sense that the new government will require new manners. That the citizens of a free state conduct themselves like a despotic king's slaves is unthinkable: the differences of their interests, of their duties, of their relations amongst one another essentially determine an entirely different manner of behaving in the world.[2]

With the French Revolution we arrive at the most thoroughgoing of these first cultural revolutions. The examples of the earlier revolutions, the nature of commercial and political life in the Old Regime, the influence of sensationalist philosophy on political theory and practice, and the revolutionary dynamic itself all contributed to the particularly extensive conceptualization and practice of France's revolutionary transformation of the everyday. Even in this case, however, the revolutionaries found themselves limited by contradictions in their vision, disagreements among themselves, and material conditions. Effectively "republicanizing everything" and producing "new manners" proved to be more difficult than anticipated. But the politically articulate also sometimes found that their efforts to politicize the everyday were more successful than they expected or thought appropriate. While the revolutionaries largely limited their intervention to the public sphere, artisans and consumers took the initiative in "revolutionizing" goods used within the home. Unintended consequences, or excesses, were not, of course, limited to the domestic sphere (nor to material culture); but each appropriation or re-use had its own logic and its own implications for the revolutionary present and the future. This chapter tells the story of what was and was not attempted, and what was accomplished, in France's revolutionary decade.

Throughout this period those involved in the events, like their predecessors in England and North America, argued that the aesthetic and the rhythms of everyday life required complete transformation.[3] The Revolution could not be made solely in political tracts, in legislative acts, in public meetings, or on the battlefield. To cite the historian Mona Ozouf, revolutionaries thought that: "The festival was an indispensable complement to the legislative system, for although the legislator makes the laws for the people, festivals make the people for the laws."[4] Because the Revolution could not be made by only a few, but needed to be lived by all, the music, street-names, food, clothing, language, theater, calendar, and architecture that shaped people's daily lives were to be republicanized. Contemporaries justified the position that a change in the *political* ordering of society required a refiguring of the mundane details of everyday life by arguing for the extraordinary power of signs and symbols. As one Gastin put it: "The language of signs has always had a powerful effect on the spirit and the heart. Signs have a magical quality, which has, in all times, ruled men, leading them either into bondage or freedom."[5] Political discourse reached the mind; signs, bodily practices, and material things touched the heart. This position was echoed in contemporary Armand-Guy Kersaint's explanation of the need for republican architecture: "If I were to speak to men chosen at random and in need of education ... I would focus on ... the need to strike the spirit of the multitude with the help of buildings and monuments, at the same time as I attempted to convince them by reason."[6]

In parallel to the months following the regicide of England's Charles I, the immediate task was to remove the monuments and statues that served to legitimize royal authority as well as that of the Church.[7] Given the saturation of the French land- and city-scapes in the period by royal and religious edifices, gardens, portraits, and insignia, a thorough eradication was impossible. It was, perhaps, the very omnipresence of the Old Regime, its insistent embodiedness and quotidian presence, that made those engaged in its overthrow so eager to create new forms.

Language, music, rituals, and objects both mundane and grandiose were understood to have a powerful pedagogic effect that could be harnessed either to the cause of reaction or to that of change. They could either freeze the world in the old ways of subservience to the king, or win people over to the new principles of rationality, liberty, fraternity, and equality. It was, therefore, vitally important that they be properly conceived and used so that they could "... win more people to independence than will battles."[8] Once people were engaged in the revolutionary effort, the stuff of everyday life could actually be used to regenerate the nation. In terms that echo English and American Puritan teachings of moral rectitude, but in a secular idiom, they argued that the old styles that "[u]nder the empire of despots, the useless class of unemployed rich people had determined ... blindly follow[ing] the vicissitudes of fashion" would be replaced by a style "dictated by reason and approved by good taste." Not only would the foolish "caprices of rich people's imagination" be replaced by a rational aesthetic form, but differences in "rank and fortune" would no longer be marked by style.[9]

Later in the Revolution, signs would come to be understood as filling the void left by the absence of the king. The people, now that they were no longer linked by their royal father, needed a new means of bonding with the abstraction called "France."

A sense of national belonging was to be created by "a common and distinctive sign of the French."[10] The judicious deployment of culture would, furthermore, help prevent political backsliding. A unified national clothing style, for example, would enable people to *feel* French and remind them of their commitment to republicanism. It was thought that "[a] national costume will accomplish the goal, a goal which is so important to a free people, to announce, or *to be reminded of oneself* everywhere and at all moments." Given the novelty of the experience of freedom and democratic representation, without this reminder one might "forget" oneself as a free citizen. But it was not only the transformation of domestic culture that was at stake, but the perception of the French abroad. "French citizens will no longer be confused with those of nations still languishing in the irons of slavery."[11] Thus the pedagogic power of culture was understood to have four possible effects: it could trap people in old ways, reinforcing the evils of monarchism and social differentiation; it could bring people into the revolutionary cause; it could, once they were engaged in the Revolution, help rid them of the last vestiges of their old ideas and selves; and, finally, it could help consolidate and represent the French nation.

Most people seem to have agreed with this proposition that cultural change could transform people's political positions. There was, however, considerable disagreement during the decade of the Revolution concerning just how revolutionary style and taste were to be created. The idea of the state's mandating the aesthetic of objects of everyday life was very familiar; it was what the monarchy had attempted to do through patronage, royal academies, regulation of the guilds, and sumptuary law since the fourteenth century. This strategy's very familiarity, however, because it identified the practice with the Old Regime, made it problematic. Intensive state involvement in what would come to be conceived of as private life was now highly controversial. Some were simply opposed to what they understood to be wasting time on trivialites; trivialities that they, furthermore, associated with the excessive and intrusive control of the Crown. For example, one critic writing in 1794 argued in a tract on the illegitimacy of regulating hairstyles: "It is only disarmed *Jacobins* who could be committed to such outmoded worries."[12] Others argued against it on practical grounds: state intervention in matters of everyday style was too difficult, too expensive, too artificial. Much more fundamental were the arguments of those opposed because they thought that aesthetics and everyday practices should be a space of individual liberty, free from state interference.

This lack of consensus concerning the nature and boundaries of the politicization of the everyday may be seen in the seeming paradox of the combination of a resounding discursive silence on the aesthetics of domestic life *and* the production and consumption of – an admittedly limited quantity of – explicitly revolutionary domestic goods. In a period when liberty bonnets were substituted for *fleurs-de-lis* on highway milestones, streets renamed, the calendar reconfigured, republican dress debated, contests for new buildings and monuments held, and new units of measurement devised, no laws were passed and no restrictions imposed on, and no calls for new visions of domestic interiors were made. And yet furniture, tapestries, porcelain, and *bibelots* (knickknacks) ornamented with the most explicit republican symbolism were made. It should be noted that there is some uncertainty concerning the precise dating of these objects. While it is clear from the historical record that some were produced during the revolutionary decade itself, others may have been made and purchased subsequently as commemorative objects.[13] Whether contemporary or made to keep the Revolution alive in people's minds, however, the existence of consumables with unmistakably revolutionary motifs made during or shortly after the revolutionary decade bears witness to the persuasiveness of the argument that it was important to be reminded of the Revolution at all moments. Without coercion, French artisans chose to make these objects and French citizens to have them in their homes.

These spontaneous, unmandated aesthetic innovations have generally been overlooked by art historians, who argue that there was no revolutionary style in furniture or the other decorative arts.[14] Many chronologies of furniture styles, for example, leap directly from Louis XVI to Empire, and even those that pause at the turn of the nineteenth century do so only long enough to note that the Directory and Consulate styles came between the two styles named for the two authoritarian regimes. A few disparaging sentences are generally offered concerning the relatively few extant pieces of furniture, porcelain, wallpaper, and tapestry decorated with revolutionary symbols or texts. These pieces are deemed aesthetically derivative and uninteresting. The explanation for an absence of a truly revolutionary form in the decorative arts is usually quite pragmatic: it is attributed to the brevity of the revolutionary period or to the destruction of the court system. The revolutionaries' definitively documented preoccupation with clothing style on the one hand and architecture on the other (among the many other projects), however, render these explanations unsatisfying. Why attempt to change clothing and the built environment and not furniture and the other arts of the home? Clothing and furniture were commodities with great symbolic potential; both were, as we have seen, in fact used by Crown and court in the *ancien régime* to augment their power. And historians have demonstrated the massive expansion of the market in consumer goods and of the non-courtly cultural world more broadly in the four decades before the Revolution.[15] One would, therefore, have expected the revolutionaries to have been concerned with *all* domains of the everyday aesthetic repertoire.

I will suggest in this chapter that this silence on the subject of interior decoration was as much a symptom of the revolutionaries' understanding of the relation between the public and the private as it was the result of the limited possibilities of the revolutionary moment or the constraints of the court system. But there was another question at stake beyond that of the appropriate role of the state and the role of individual initiative: how did the cultural practices actually work? Were revolutionary clothing, songs, paintings, and language the outward signs of a regenerated soul? Or, rather, was the soul to be regenerated *through* the use of revolutionary rituals and objects? To put it another way, was culture largely a sign of regeneration or the pedagogic means to regeneration?

In the regime that was in the process of being overthrown, culture was supposed to be revelatory, not pedagogic. As we have seen in Chapter 2, possessions ideally matched one's rank and station: they revealed to onlookers who one was, socially and politically; and thus sumptuary laws were passed to prevent people from seeming to be what they were not. This system was breaking down in practice in the half-century before the Revolution, but it remained, nonetheless, a powerful model. Ironically, some of those most passionately engaged in overturning the Old Regime were also the most convinced by this conception of goods inherited from that regime. According to this view, only those already committed, heart and soul, to the Revolution should possess the signs of the Revolution, and *all* of those committed to the Revolution were obliged to show their loyalty outwardly. There was to be no barrier between seeming and being, no difference between outside and inside. Others disagreed, arguing that it was by being surrounded by revolutionary icons, by having every element of one's everyday life transformed, that one would unlearn all the bad lessons of the past and *be* regenerated. Adherence to a revolutionary aesthetic thus revealed a person desiring re-birth, rather than a hypocrite pretending to be something they were not. This issue remained unresolved for the length of the revolutionary decade (and one could argue that we still struggle with it today).

In these debates over what form even the most minute details of everyday life should take were crystallized what was perhaps the central dilemma of the Revolution: How were the demands of liberty and equality to be reconciled? It soon became clear that, even in the midst of revolutionary upheaval, many people – whatever their political position – continued to favor the songs, plays, and clothing of pre-revolutionary days, in which social differentiation was inscribed. Should the government require that certain furniture, porcelain, or hats be purchased and used? Should the government censor plays, operas, and newspapers? When should the goal of social equality impinge on the liberty of the individual? When should the dignity of office – of judges or legislators, for example – take precedence over the likeness of all inhabitants of the nation? And, since not only was a new order, but a new nation being created by means of goods, morals, and social practices, should foreigners be allowed, or even forced, to adopt French styles when in France? Finally, what, in fact, was an appropriate "republican" style? What did it look like? Even more particularly, what was a "republican *French* style"? Would such an aesthetic emerge spontaneously from the people once they were free of the chains of monarchy?

No experiments in revolutionary cultural forms were created *ex nihilo* during the revolutionary years – but then they never are. Whether in music, theater, interior decoration, or clothing styles, the new forms were hybrids. Revolutionaries turned primarily to three sources for inspiration for their new aesthetic: the classical world, French "popular" culture, and in some domains, the courtly culture they were trying to abolish. Extensive borrowings were made from the Greek, Roman, and Etruscan worlds. One such symbol was the modification of the *pilleus*, the conical hat placed on the heads of emancipated slaves by their Roman masters, as a sign of their freedom.[16] It became widespread in the fall of 1792 among the *sans-culottes* (see Figure 5.2 and 5.7 below).[17] The red cap became one of the most widely recognized – and contested – symbols of the Revolution. The borrowing as well as exact reproductions of motifs and objects from the Greek and Roman republics as well as Etruscan-inspired motifs can be seen in the furniture produced during the Revolution as well as the clothing.[18] This theme was carried to considerable lengths, as is made clear by the production during the Revolution of an entire (700-piece!) ensemble of accurate, historically specific, Greek furniture.[19] But goods could also change meanings through use. Thus the *pilleus*, once it was used by the radical *sans-culottes* movement, gained a French name – *bonnet rouge* – and a new association. A reference to the contemporary popular classes was thus layered onto that to the liberated slaves of the classical world.[20]

The second major source was style identified as popularly, indigenously, "French," sometimes in opposition to the foreign and sometimes in distinction from the court culture of the monarchs. In the *Opéra*, for example, during the early years of the Revolution, themes from French history dominated, although they did share the stage with classical tales. The emphasis was on producing heroic examples – with a strong emphasis on self-sacrifice and collective endeavor – for people to follow.[21] Another – and much more contested – referent were forms and styles understood to be "popular" in origin. The most famous of these is, of course, the "uniform" of the *sans-culottes* depicted in idealized form in the 1792 painting by Louis-Léopold Boilly in Figure 5.1.

In addition to the long trousers rather than knee-breeches (*culottes*) from which the group derived its name, the style was characterized by other elements of working-class dress, including the short jacket or *carmagnole*. Some historians have argued that this outfit had far more presence representationally, whether satirically or admiringly – in paintings, drawings, and prints – than on the street.[22] Given that the term *sans-culottes* referred to an actually existing sartorial practice, this seems likely to be both true and false. There were surely very substantial numbers of men participating in the Revolution while wearing full-length pants rather than knee-breeches, just as there were, no doubt, many poor participants in the American Revolution dressed in domestically produced fabric.[23] How many of those who wore rough fabric in the American context and how many of those wearing trousers in the French did so as an explicitly political gesture is of course harder to say. What is clear is that the term *sans-culottes*, and the style associated with it, like homespun, had strong signifying power. People associated that style with the popular revolutionary movement.

The *sans-culottes* style is both reminiscent of and very different from that of the homespun-wearing gentleman of the American Revolution, however. Both outfits gained *political* meaning when they were worn by those who did not normally

Figure 5.1 *The Singer Chenard, as a Sans-Culotte*, 1792 (oil on panel) by Louis-Leopold Boilly (1761–1845). ©Musées de la ville de Paris, Musée Carnavalet, Paris, France/Lauros/Giraudon/The Bridgeman Art Library.

wear them – elites in both cases, since both homespun and the garb of the *sans-culottes* were generally worn by those who could not afford better. This meaning was underscored by the fact that in both cases the clothing carried connotations of independence and labor. Servants and slaves were dressed by their masters, in livery, in cast-offs, or, in the American case, in cheap foreign fabric.[24] But then the stories diverge; the meaning of homespun lay precisely in the fact that it had been made *at home*, understood both socially (within the household) and politically (in America). What mattered was its locus of production, whereas it was consumption that created meaning in the case of the *sans-culottes*. The significance of the trousers was that they were normally only worn by working men. The fact that the *sans-culottes* has a necessarily masculine referent also marks an important distinction to the American case. While homespun was ungendered in use and gendered feminine in its making, the icon of the French movement was a man, doing masculine, productive labor. There was, of course, a working-class woman's equivalent to the *sans-culottes* outfit; but it was much less codified, and went unnamed. This would, as will be seen in further detail below, be emblematic of important differences in the gendering of the two revolutionary moments and the post-revolutionary nation-states to follow.

Both homespun and the *sans-culottes*, by contrast, were alike in their distance from the Puritan dress of the seventeenth century. Both homespun and the *sans-culottes* were, of course, political rather than religious in their origin, and both were appropriated and had their meanings altered as a result of the revolutionary dynamic. Some American and French revolutionaries hoped, furthermore, that people would be transformed by their wearing of revolutionary garb, while others shared the Puritan belief that their appearance was (and should be) the outward sign of their inward state (either saved or republican, depending on the case). In all three instances, dress was mobilized for representational use, quite apart from its capacity to either change or reflect its wearer's inner state.

The third source for revolutionary forms, the styles developed during the Old Regime, was, of course, the most problematic. Their usage was seen particularly strongly in genres in which production happened slowly and stylistic changes were technically complicated. Furniture is a good example. In the case of furniture, *ancien régime* structures (skeletons) were re-used, but given a republican skin. The furniture was rather hastily made, and most often built with cheaper indigenous woods (rather than the exotic wood used in courtly furniture of the eighteenth century). In addition to revolutionary symbols, cabinet-makers inscribed patriotic and revolutionary phrases in the surfaces of the furniture and bronze-makers turned their talents to decorative pikes.[25] Finally, depictions of major events – the Declaration of the Rights of Man, the Tennis Court Oath, the storming of the Bastille – were very common[26] (see Figure 5.8 below).

Neither cultural forms, then, nor cultural policy remained static over the revolutionary decade. The logic of cultural policy from the fall of the Bastille to the ascent of Napoleon was marked by three rather distinct periods. During the early years of the Revolution, the dominant preoccupation was with breaking free of constraints inherited from the Old Regime and spreading the revolutionary word. The stress was very much on liberty, liberty to dress as one pleased, buy the furniture one liked, see the plays one enjoyed and say what one meant. The next period, the Jacobin, involved a different balance between equality and liberty, characterized by much greater state involvement in aesthetic form. It was also in this middle period that the entire structure of society, polity, and Church were transformed. The final period was, not surprisingly perhaps, typified by a refusal of the thorough politicization of private life, and involved many returns to what were thought of as Old Regime practices, but within a republican context.

The Early Years: Inventing Revolutionary Forms

The first three years of the Revolution were marked by the undoing of the perceived injustices and abuses of the Old Regime, and an attempt to construct a viable constitutional monarchy. Nonetheless, revolutionary legislators – who were also busy abolishing the feudal system, passing the Declaration of the Rights of Man, creating a new constitution, turning the clergy into civil employees of the state, and arresting the king – also took time to structure the aesthetic education of the nation and its symbolic repertoire. Initially, the enjoyment of freedom, the coexistence of Old Regime and quickly-produced revolutionary forms, and generally a rather playful attitude towards the forms and practices of everyday life were the dominant themes. Most participants and bystanders assumed that the Revolution would come to a quick end with a constitutional monarchy and a set of political and economic reforms. This view was reinforced by the creation of narratives describing Louis XVI as having struggled to be a good king, only to discover that "prejudices were too deeply rooted and abuses too powerfully protected, for the nation to be able to enjoy the good intentions of its king."[27] No one, of course, could predict the far more dramatic course the Revolution would take.

That one of the first acts of the National Assembly was to reject the official costumes that distinguished one Estate from the other as well as to seek designs for a new building with an aesthetic form appropriate to the new political vision attests to the importance of symbolic representation during the early years of the Revolution.[28] Plans were also quickly drawn up for new monuments to commemorate the taking of the Bastille or to honor Louis XVI.[29] These transformations of the built environment were not only to enable those alive at the moment of political upheaval to internalize new values, but also to serve to remind future generations of the importance of freedom. Events caused the architectural projects to remain only on paper; but even if few monuments were built, the Revolution made its presence felt in public squares through the "liberty tree" campaign of the spring of 1792. During March and April, thousands of trees were planted in villages, towns and cities throughout France, some of which, fulfilling their planters' hopes, still tower over town squares today. Reinforcing the pedagogic project of the liberty trees was the diffusion of smaller, portable, revolutionary objects across the realm.[30] For example, miniature sculptures of the Bastille (made out of stones of the fortress) were sent to municipalities in the rest of France as a symbol of the victory over despotism and to help render what had been a Parisian moment, national.[31] Even the food one ate and rituals of conviviality were to be republicanized.[32] Alongside the officially sponsored projects were those of more commercial initiative: very shortly following the taking of the Bastille on July 14, 1789, a whole series of commemorative objects appeared – buttons, china, iron rings adorned with fragments from the Bastille, watches illustrating the taking of the prison or adorned with revolutionary slogans[33] (see for example Figure 5.2). While some historians have interpreted this as a cynical move to make some quick

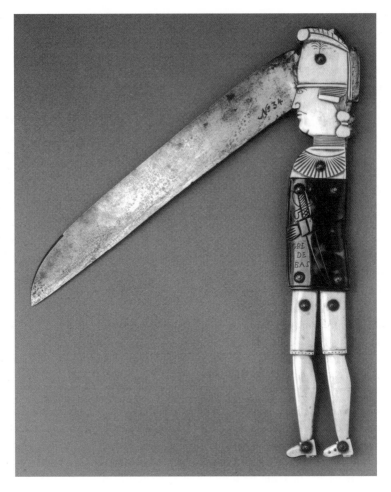

Figure 5.2 *Canif de la Bastille,* Musée Carnavalet, Paris. ©Photo by Musées de la ville de Paris/Denis Svartz.

money out of a sensational event, I think it at least as likely that those designing, producing and distributing such objects understood themselves to be doing politics.[34] The dream was that people all over France would quickly have some sign of the Revolution in the intimacy of their homes, and even on their person, as well as the opportunity to witness monuments to liberty and equality in their everyday lives.

Everyday goods, *objets d'art*, and plans for monuments produced early in the Revolution employed a variety of self-consciously republican iconography – clasped hands (the symbol of fraternity), triangles with an eye in the middle (the symbol of reason), Phrygian hats.[35] Many of these objects, like a penknife whose hinge was composed of the head of a man wearing a Phrygian cap, used the reproduction of clothing already dubbed "revolutionary" to convey their meaning.

It was not considered enough simply to remove royal symbolism, nor to produce simpler, more popular, furniture, clothing, pottery or watches (although that was also done). People would come to believe in liberty, equality and fraternity through touching, using, and seeing the symbols and allegories associated with those principles. This theme is even more marked in the architectural projects.

The architect Etienne-Louis Boullée's 1792 design for the Palais national (probably drawn up in response to a call from the Academy of Architecture), for example, was characterized by sharply drawn geometric forms, embellished and softened with revolutionary emblems and texts (Figure 5.3). Its basic shape was delineated by a square, at the center of which stood a sphere forming an amphitheatre in which the deputies would meet. The façade was unbroken by windows, but relieved by a massive inscription of the Declaration of the Rights of Man and the Citizen. The Palais national thus melded symmetrical two- and three-dimensional geometric forms – squares and spheres – representing the principle of the equality of all representatives of the nation, the pedagogic literalness of revolutionary text, and the allegories of republican virtues.[36] While full of references to the classical world, the design is wholly forward-looking and original; it was a new building for a new form of government.

The Palais national was never built and the years of revolutionary upheaval were generally not propitious for actually creating these visions in stone and mortar. And, while the demands of the decorative arts were lighter than those of the building trades, there were significant barriers to production – as opposed to planning – in those trades as well.

Particularly in the domain of furniture, the nature of the production process itself limited the extent of transformation in these years. High-quality furniture required wood seasoned over years, the collaboration of many artisans and workshops, and thousands of hours of labor. Radical changes in furniture's structure necessitated

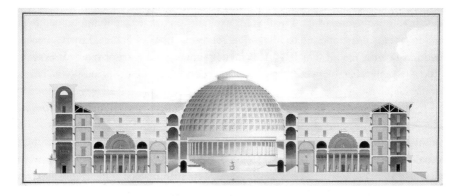

Figure 5.3 Etienne-Louis Boullée's 1792 design for the Palais national no. 3, "Coupe passant par la salle d'Assemblée." Bibliothèque Nationale de France.

extensive reflection and experimentation. Thus, while changes in clothing practices could happen from one month to the next and architectural innovations were matters of decades and great capital investment, alterations in furniture were a matter of years. At the time the Bastille was taken, Parisian furniture-makers were engaged in work that would take months (and in some cases far longer) to finish, and had a backlog of orders from the Crown, the court, and urban elites. One of the ironies, therefore, of French furniture history, as noted by Pierre Arizzioli-Clémentel, is that some of the finest representations of Louis XVI-style furniture were finished during the revolutionary period.[37] Georges Jacob, Bernard Molitor, Adam Weisweiler, and other celebrated furniture-makers continued delivering pieces to Marie Antoinette, Louis XVI and Monsieur the comte de Provence and others until 1792.[38] This royal and noble clientele even commissioned some new pieces in this period.

While some of this furniture continued to display the ornateness and ostentatious luxury of court furniture, much of it, like the architecture of the time, even when made for noble or royal clients, embodied a seemingly austere form of neoclassicism. Neoclassicism was not, of course, a novelty at the end of the eighteenth century; it had been gradually gaining influence since the discoveries of Pompeii and Herculaneum at mid-century.[39] But while most of the furnishings inspired by neoclassicism earlier in the century had combined angularity with rich ormolu mounts and even Japanese lacquer, by the 1790s the ormolu had been reduced to a minimum (if present at all), and large surfaces were covered with single sheets of veneer.[40] As the historian Ulrich Leben points out, given the expense of mahogany veneer, such pieces could easily cost as much as their most ornate competition. Just as in the dress of the wealthy Puritans, at stake was not economy, but rather the representation of sobriety and seriousness. Thus, just as furniture with revolutionary motifs was necessarily based upon *ancien régime* forms, even courtly furniture produced during the Revolution was influenced by revolutionary aesthetic norms.

A similar overlapping of courtly and republican culture may be seen in the plans for monuments during the first years, which continued to honor the king.[41] A project celebrating the taking of the Bastille, for example, envisaged a column topped by a statue of the king, supported by allegorical representations of France, Liberty, Peace, and Law. At the feet of the allegorical statues would run the major rivers of France, "the most natural emblem of the proportional contribution of all citizens to the needs of the state."[42]

Clothing, as the commodity that had already been most freed from the constraints of court life and regulation, seems to have been the site of the greatest variation in this early period.[43] While most French women and men continued to wear their usual clothing, some took advantage of a new freedom of consumption. They were liberated from the few remnants of sumptuary law still in place at the end of the Old Regime – red-heeled shoes, for example, had been reserved for the king until the fall of the monarchy – but, more importantly, they used clothing to mark their political positions. Many of those who were opposed to the upheaval took to wearing black as a sign of mourning, while those in favor wore military uniforms even when not on duty (or not even in the military), while still others donated their silver and gold shoe-buckles to the revolutionary cause.[44]

This sartorial battle was matched by a vocal contest. At the onset of the Revolution, after the taking of the Bastille, what had suddenly become Old Regime songs were reworked. The first completely new song of the Revolution – "Ça ira" – was born during the preparation of the first festival of the Federation, July 1790. "Ça ira" – having no fixed lyric or tune – could be, and was, adapted to different political occasions and audiences. It even inspired the royalists to adopt a song of their own – an aria from the opera *Richard the Lion-hearted*.[45] In the theater, too, the repertoire balanced explicitly political and traditional plays, although before 1793 audiences were rather critical of officially patriotic theater.[46] In this period of the Revolution, then, people felt free to express a wide range of political opinion through their dress, furnishings, watches, singing, and theater attendance. They could imagine the most extraordinary of building forms. Everything – from the responsibilities of the king, to women's political rights, to slavery – seemed open to question. Goods and speech remained highly politicized, as they had been before the fall of the Bastille, but the field was open. People could wear what they chose and say what they pleased, fearing a shouting match at most. Furthermore, anyone could, and did, speak. It was a period of great political engagement of women. Whether in the March on Versailles on October 5, 1789 in which market women confronted the king and the queen over the price of bread and forced their move to Paris, or participation in political clubs and public debate, or in formal texts like *The Declaration of the Rights of Woman*, women both seized a political place and were allowed, even encouraged, by many radicalized men to do so. Thus, those usually most distant from politics – women, the poor, the young, those of French nationality and those born abroad – all claimed both a political voice and access to politicized goods.[47]

In all domains of expression – words, goods, and performance – this openness was facilitated by the commercial society and public sphere that had developed in Paris in the last forty or so years of the Old Regime. Coffee houses, theaters, salons, music halls, public gardens, even shops, had become sites for philosophical and political discussion. At times the merging of commercial and political culture produced some startling effects. Despite its royalist leanings, the first French fashion magazine, known during the first year of the Revolution as the *Magasin des Modes Nouvelles*, quickly published illustrations of clothing with revolutionary motifs and designs of hats, buckles and other clothing. By early fall of 1789 they had started including images of the Bastille or representations of the Third Estate pictured on their wares. In February 1790, the magazine's owner hired a new editor, Le Brun, who was known for his revolutionary sympathies. Under his leadership the magazine changed title, being now called the *Journal de la Mode et du Goût*, and became more consistent in its effort to advance the revolutionary cause by persuading people to change their taste. For example the issue of February 25, 1790 included a plate showing

"A man dressed in a suit of black fabric '*à la Révolution*'" and the next opined that while "the beginning of the Revolution did give birth to many new fashions, a fact to which most women seemed more or less indifferent, today, their taste has begun to wake and many of them are showing themselves to be patriots, adopting the colors of the nation."[48] This combining of revolutionary and commercial interests was short-lived; by November 1790, the magazine had changed editors again and reverted to its openly monarchist stance.[49]

By 1791 and early 1792 a greater emphasis was being placed on the need for political and aesthetic pedagogy at the same time as the Revolution's commitment to freedom of expression was underscored by the abolition of theatrical censorship in 1791. This move to free the theater from constraint is especially striking in the context of the English and American revolutions. One of the first moves of the English revolutionaries had been to ban the theater, while the Americans remained deeply suspicious of it. Those engaged in the French Revolution put more weight both on freedom and on their faith that theater could be harnessed to the revolutionary process rather than necessarily serving the interests of monarchy. The importance of the theater in political critique in eighteenth-century France no doubt accounts, at least in part, for this confidence. This period saw the invention of new theatrical forms, including melodrama and an expansion of the audiences for the theater.[50] The complex possibilities for using theater to work through the meanings of representation, sincerity, and authenticity would be further elaborated in the later years of the Revolution.

With the opening of the Louvre as a national museum in 1792 and the "The Muséum Français" the following year, the explicit goal of consolidating the Revolution through education implied that there was a limit to the trust the revolutionary leadership had in the spontaneous good political sense of the people.[51] This period saw no moves towards cultural coercion, but the idea became widespread that if the polity and society were to be truly regenerated, education was needed. More and more cultural interventions – typified by the replacement of "Ça ira," which had no written tune or lyric, with the composed battle cry, "la Marseillaise" as the official song of the republicans – demonstrated an increasing formalization and regimentation of the Revolution. Not only was the "Marseillaise" a fixed song, but its lyrics were nationalist rather than revolutionary, whereas many of the variants "Ça ira" explicitly advocated radical social and economic change.

The elements of this triple commitment – to liberty of expression, to political pedagogy, and to homogeneity of revolutionary culture – might appear, in hindsight, to have been in tension or even in contradiction, but they were seen as complementary at the time. Proponents of the law abolishing theatrical censorship assumed that uncensored theater would "purify morals, give lessons in citizenship … and be schools of patriotism and virtue."[52] And the opera, which had changed its name from the "Académie Royale de Musique" to "the Opéra National," voluntarily adopted a self-consciously pedagogic mission (while also taking advantage of its new freedom from censorship). In a petition to the Committee of Public Safety for funds, advocates argued: "The Opéra will always be a school of patriotism. The Greeks used to gather to celebrate their Olympic Games and to see the magnificent eras of their history revived in the verses of dramatic poets. It is time for the French to enjoy with enthusiasm the pleasure of admiring their own exploits and to see staged their own glory."[53]

As the Revolution became more radical during the summer of 1792, the emphasis in cultural policy shifted towards national homogeneity and the obligation to demonstrate one's adherence to the nation through one's clothes and other practices. The earliest legislation concerned the cockade. The cockade was a rosette made out of ribbon or fabric, worn on a hat or coat, or sometimes pinned in women's hair. It was not an invention of the Revolution, but rather had a long history as a means of indicating political affiliation or military rank, notably in both the English Restoration and in the American revolutionary army. On July 5, 1792, a law passed requiring all adult men to wear the tricolored cockade (this obligation was extended to women the following April). The complexity of the implications of this law have been highlighted by the historian Jennifer Heuer. On the one hand the law, by requiring that all mark their appearance in the same way, limited their individual freedom of expression and forced at least the façade of adherence to the revolutionary project. On the other hand, the law was very inclusive. It specified that all adult men (and then adult women) living or traveling through France were required to wear the national cockade.[54] Just as the Protectorate had both enabled and coerced all adult men to join the polity by swearing an oath, all adults – whether French or foreign, servant or master, rich or poor, sane or mad – were *constrained* by this law, but they were also *enabled* by it. All were put on the same plane of equality and likeness within the nation. This law marked an important transition in the Revolution, from a focus on liberty, to a focus on equality. It demonstrated the universalizing hopes of the Revolution at this date as well: it was not just French citizens, or those born in France, who could and were obliged, to wear the sign of the Revolution, but all who found themselves on the territory. This law expressed the hope that even those who passed through France only briefly would pick up from the cockade the magic of liberty, equality, and fraternity.

Jacobin Cultural Revolution

The years following the fall of the monarchy were characterized by a deepening of the Revolution. This was a period of direct democracy, involving a distrust of representation, political and otherwise. The tensions already visible during the first three years between liberty and equality and between liberty and uniformity increased, with a tendency towards equality and uniformity at the expense of liberty. With the European war and the domestic counter-revolutionary movement, fears of a regression to older political forms intensified and willingness to enforce revolutionary principles by coercion increased. As one author put it, in the context of making an argument for a republican calendar: "The best way to attack superstition is no doubt ridicule; but if it is a question of abuses destructive to the government and to the social order and one limits oneself to these means, the evil will grow with leaps and bounds. The need to employ force and proactive measures, in such circumstances, is even more critical in time of revolution."[55] The question of confidence in "the people" was also unresolved. At moments, it was assumed that the people's political sense was to be trusted, at others it was thought rather that they were in need of radical re-education. Likewise the ambiguity concerning the signs and symbols of everyday life intensified. The absence of consensus, however, did not impede the radical transformation of the entire culture and society during these years. "The unity of the Republic requires unity in weights and measures, like unity in language, unity in legislation, unity in the government... How could the friends of equality tolerate a *bigarrure* as embarrassing as units of measurement that preserve the memory of the shameful feudal serfdom; and what a contradiction for republicans to measure the fields with the royal *arpent,* or to measure a length of fabric with a foot of the king..."[56] Thus, weights and measures were rendered uniform, the calendar, the names of streets and towns were altered, certain clothing became obligatory, certain plays and musical compositions were censored, and linguistic reforms were implemented.

Language reform – that is the teaching of French – was understood to be an especially urgent issue since, at the beginning of the Revolution, of a population of 26 million, 12 million either did not know French or understood it poorly.[57] After January 1794, French was to be the language for all public documents and plans were set in place for the teaching of the language throughout the nation. In fact, like most of the architectural projects, the schools were not built during the Revolution, and the ultimate Frenchification of the territory would have to await the Third Republic. Some people did nonetheless learn French through political participation and, especially men, through service in the army. Certainly more spoke the language at the end of the Revolution than at its beginning. Crucial here was that this sharing of the language by *all* the French, so that all could participate in the polity, was considered an essential political project.

To the standardization of language was added an effort to do the same to weights and measures across the French territory. As of August 1793, the enormous diversity of units of measure were replaced by the gram and kilo for weight and the centimeter, meter and kilometer for distance.[58] This was not the first effort to do so. As early as 1790, Bureaux de Pusy had eloquently declared that "...we should fear that the *départements* will tend to isolate themselves, to perceive themselves as independent units of the collectivity ... given that, what better way to bring together diverse spirits and interests, and to produce unity ... than a common language, common signs, and identical rules for all the objects that individuals find useful or necessary in their everyday lives and how much the uniformity of measures would not help fulfill this!"[59] The change took three years, but the principles behind it remained the same. And, unlike many of the other revolutionary innovations, these were not only to prove durable, but in fact became global standards.

Less successful in the long term, but even more dramatic at the time, was the rationalization of the calendar. In October 1793, the French calendar started over again. Year I, marked by the declaration of the Republic, had started on September 22, 1792. A new starting date for the French nation, a new way of reckoning time, and new names for the units of the calendar were needed because: "[t]he Revolution has reformed the souls of the French; it trains them day after day in revolutionary virtues. Time opens a new book in history and in its new unfolding, as simple and full of majesty as equality, it should engrave with a new and vigorous burr the annals of regenerated France."[60] The French were thus able to accomplish, even if only briefly, the vision imagined by the English revolutionaries a century earlier – the restarting of time (and of history) itself.[61] The new year was divided into twelve months of equal length, which were renamed after the climactic conditions appropriate to the season. The months were divided into three weeks of ten days each, and days were ten hours long.

This rational recalibration of the clock required the production of new time-pieces. While some were simply decenal, others were pedagogic in two senses – providing both instruction in the new mode of telling time and in republican principles. The watch pictured on the cover of the original English edition of this book (Berg, 2008) provides a vivid example. It had four faces – two showing the hour and minute in the old time and two in the new – so that people could adapt less painfully to the new mode of telling the time. Between the two pairs stood an allegorical figure combining a number of republican symbols – the scales of justice, a phyrgian cap, and a pike. It thereby also served to remind the wearer about the *purpose* of the new mode each time he or she consulted the watch.

Consistent with the other transformations was the recreation of holidays.[62] Those venerating saints were replaced by days in honor of plants and animals, and other elements of the natural world. This last provision underscores the fundamental place of the new calendar in the dechristianization project of the Revolution. An attempt was made to efface the birth of Christ from memory, as well as Sunday and all Christian holidays. They were all replaced with rational, secular, national festivals. Furthermore, children born during the twelve years the republican calendar lasted were given names either of plants or of flowers, or named after republican virtues or revolutionary or classical heroes.[63]

In a regime ready and willing to attempt to republicanize the names of plants and seasons, it is not surprising that attention, as in the other two revolutionary moments, was turned to coinage. Augustin Dupré, the General Coin Engraver, created the first French republican coin following the decree of 28 Thermidor, Year III (1795), that: "the bronze coins will bear the figure of Liberty with the legend

'French Republic'."[64] The historian Patrick Laurens argues that this was, in fact, the first appearance of the official figure of the Republic. The allegory appears, in profile just as the king had before, coiffed not with the classical *pilleus* but the more popular *bonnet rouge*. Coinage represented, until the first use of the postage stamp in 1848, the best means of everyday circulation of the new vision of the political order.

Within the space of a few years, in sum, French citizens saw all aspects of their everyday lives utterly transformed. They were to speak a different language, their Sundays were not to be spent in church, their roads and towns had unfamiliar names, the boundaries of their *départements* were redrawn, their weeks had ten days, their months different names, their food novel weights. They, furthermore, belonged to the *nation* in a new way. Although France had been administratively unified for a very long time, that administrative unity did not have much meaning for any but a very small fraction of the elite. After the Revolution that, too, was to change.

Many of these issues can, once again, be seen clearly through an analysis of clothing. The advent of new fabric at lower prices on a relatively open market had made clothing subject to frequent replacement, and to fashion among urban elites (and those perhaps not so elite) from the mid-eighteenth century on.[65] This commodification of clothing enabled French men and women to use it to express social desires and to contest the political order. The sartorial commemoration of significant political events – like the American Revolution – clearly demonstrates this transformation in the use of clothing in the pre-revolutionary period. Those changes cohabited, however, with a continued use of clothing by the court to reinforce its prestige, an enduring ideology that dress should follow station, and a heritage of state regulation of clothing.

Revolutionaries' efforts to regulate or at least influence the clothing styles worn in France can thus be understood to be building on an inherited tradition and practice, and also intervening where intervention was possible. Clothing design was relatively easy, its production relatively quick, and the cloth, thread and findings (including ribbons and buttons) of which it was made required, unlike the wood from which furniture was crafted, no seasoning period before use. Revolutionaries thus once again built on the old and the new, the discursive and the material, in their efforts to turn monarchists into republicans through dress. The idea of legislating clothing they drew from the days when the Crown (and Church) could impose style, the idea of changing clothing quickly they drew from the much newer world of fashion, and they counted on the organization of production actually to produce the clothing.

Early in the Jacobin period (in December 1792) a recommendation was made that "...it shall be determined by the legislative body what mode of dress should be given to children of different ages from birth to adolescence. The form of dress worn by all citizens, their arms, their exercises, the festival paraphernalia and all things of common concern should likewise be determined by the legislature."[66] This proposal was not made law at the time, but it was taken seriously. At this juncture in the revolutionary dynamic, it was considered possible to regulate "all things of common concern," despite the violence such regulation would necessarily have done individual liberty and the lack of trust it expressed in the good sense of the people. With the further radicalization of the Revolution – from the regicide of Louis XVI on January 21, 1793 through the Terror inaugurated on September 5, 1793 until the overthrow of the Jacobins in late July 1794 (Thermidor Year II) – efforts to create and to enforce a civilian uniform continued. In many ways, these attempts to create a national uniform recalled the sumptuary laws of the Old Regime, with one fundamental difference. These outfits were to mark differences of gender, age, and service to the Republic, not hereditary rank or purchased office. Echoes may also be heard here of the sumptuary law passed under Cromwell's Protectorate, in which service, not birth, was to give rank and rights, although the French, unconstrained by Puritanism and enabled by the more highly developed fashion system, went much further in the creation of new forms.

In the spring of 1793, another side of Jacobin ideology emerged in the invitation of the *Société populaire et républicaine des arts* to all French citizens to submit ideas for a republican costume. By making this a contest in which *all* citizens could participate (even if the results were to be judged by a few) the task of defining the Republic, being put in the hands of the many, was democratized (perhaps emulating the American call for designs for the Capitol building in 1782). The terms of the contest underscored the valorization of unity and equality above liberty, because the *Société populaire* tended to favor one uniform for all, with no distinction between the military and civilian, nor between the holders of political office and ordinary citizens. None of the designs submitted was considered adequate, and the *Société* later forwarded a document, entitled *Considérations sur les avantages de changer le costume français*, to the Convention. The Committee of Public Safety responded by inviting the painter Jean-Louis David to present "…his views and suggestions on the means of improving national costume and of rendering it more appropriate to republican morals and to the character of the Revolution."[67] David's sketches (like those of the respondents to the original contest) displayed very strong classical influences, and differentiated only faintly among civilians, soldiers, and office-holders. As can be seen in the following popularization of his ideas through their use on a fan (Figure 5.4), David did, however, make a marked effort to avoid the popular dress of the *sans-culottes*.[68]

As the historian Lynn Hunt has powerfully argued, David's work exemplified a contradiction: "On the one hand, the deputies or representatives of the people were supposed to be simply a transparent reflection of the people, that is, just like them, because part of them. For this reason, everyone was supposed to wear a new national uniform that would efface differences. On the other hand, the representatives were obviously other, different, not like the people exactly because they were the teachers, the governors, the guides of the people. Accordingly, the uniforms of officials were to be just distinct enough to permit recognition."[69] Contemporaries argued, however, that political service should be more clearly marked: "…a national clothing style

Figure 5.4 *Eventail aux costumes des membres du Directoire*. Musée Carnavalet, Paris. ©Photo by Musées de la ville de Paris/Andreani.

would offer an easy way to show the age and diverse public functions of citizens, without changing the sacred foundations of equality."[70]

David's outfits were never produced, and this was the last effort to advocate a civil uniform for the French people. Part of why these efforts failed was that there was no consensus on the legitimacy of the state's imposing a civilian uniform; freedom of attire had been, after much heated debate, declared a right by the Convention on 9 Brumaire, Year II (29 October 1793). Nor was there consensus on whether equality and sameness would carry the day, or social differentiation, or if, in fact, it was possible to reconcile equality with difference.

Revolutionary legislators discovered, in other words, that they could not reach agreement even among themselves concerning a new "sumptuary" system. They, therefore, limited their regulatory efforts to accoutrements (like the cockade) for all, or complete uniforms for official representatives of the state. While there were considerable political constraints on efforts to create a new republican style of dress, there were few material constraints; if the legislators could have found accord and persuaded the public, the clothing industry could have rapidly produced and distributed the clothing.[71] Another domain of intervention, architecture, posed a different set of challenges.

Architecture lies at the other pole – in both temporal and material terms – from clothing. Designing new buildings is a lengthy process; their actual construction is even more so, and one that requires massive capital investment. 'Revolutionary' architectural forms built on and modified earlier designs and, in fact, the *oeuvres* of many of the most celebrated architects of the Revolution were characterized by considerable continuity between their royal and their republican projects. Architecture also, of course, had a very different relation to the market. While guild artisans theoretically had a monopoly on clothing production and distribution before the Revolution abolished the corporations, they had been competing with 'free' labor for at least a century. Architecture, even for private use, had been much more successfully policed (even if the labor in the building trades, too, was less so). When revolutionary legislators and theorists turned their attention to the pedagogic and representational potential of the built environment, therefore, they saw different possibilities and constraints than in the case of dress. The state's power was far less disputed; but so too was its capacity. And, like the English Civil War, the Revolution's impact on French cityscapes was generally negative rather than positive. That is, the Revolution succeeded in destroying a great many ecclesiastical, monastic, royal, and noble sculptures, edifices and monuments. The Revolution constructed very little, however, and certainly did not create a republican built environment.

Despite the failure actually to erect structures, however, a great deal of energy and thought went into imagining what they should look like throughout the Revolution. Architecture was understood as an especially effective means of public education; buildings and monuments were to promote virtue. Their materiality and scale were understood to give them particular powers. As the architect Étienne-Louis Boullée, whose design for the new Palais national has been discussed above, put it: "The images that they [buildings] offer to our senses should arouse in us feelings analogous to the use to which the building is put."[72] The built environment had the capacity, therefore, to change how people felt: a properly built lawcourt would inspire sentiments of justice, or a school a desire for learning. Revolutionary leaders were eager to encourage reflection on republican architecture. In Years II and III of the revolutionary epoch alone, the government sponsored at least fourteen architectural or monumental competitions intended either to generate designs for the commemoration of important events or the renovation of buildings, or to provide space for activities considered important.[73] These *concours* attracted a great deal of attention from laypeople and architects alike.

Three architects dominated the architectonic vision of the new revolutionary everyday: Étienne-Louis Boullée (1728–1799), Claude-Nicolas Ledoux (1736–1796) and Jean-Jacques Lequeu (1757–1824).[74] Although the three had quite distinct visions, they all show a marked influence of the Greek and Roman worlds, but at the same time a desire to adapt those aesthetic norms rather than simply to reproduce them. Their hundreds of drawings were also almost all characterized by utopianism, as if they had known, which they may well have, that these projects would only ever exist on paper. We have already discussed Boullée's design for the Palais national; Lequeu's 'Temple de l'égalité' of the Year II, demonstrates a later effort to embody the political principles of the Revolution in architecture.

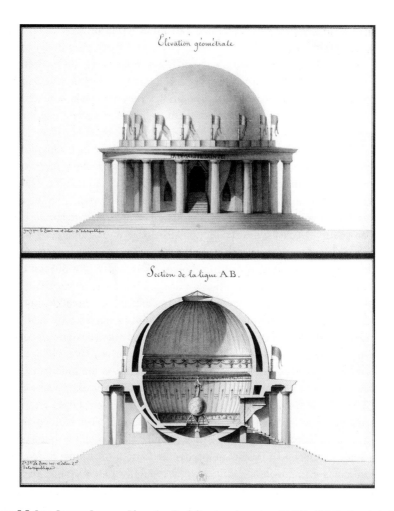

Figure 5.5 Jean-Jacques Lequeu, *Plan géométral d'un temple consacré à l'Egalité*. Section de la ligne AB, 1793–1794, Bibliothèque Nationale de France.

Lequeu's *Temple de l'égalité* was, emphatically, based on the sphere. Lequeu chose, furthermore, triply to underscore the theme. Not only was the sphere contained within the circular portico, but he inscribed a smaller sphere within the sphere. As visitors penetrated the temple, they would find themselves before a small figure, *Egalité*, balancing precariously on the contained sphere gazing out at walls ornamented with classical motifs. The unrelenting roundness – even the round columns were deprived of their conventional square bases and capitals – is destabilizing, perhaps as destabilizing as entering into a political and social system based on equality from a society of orders. The exterior of the globe was, however, both nationalized and rendered less abstract by a parade of tri-colored flags set into the top of the portico. The flags humanized the temple, bringing it back to earth, and grounding it in the French nation.

While it would be a radical over-simplification of a massive production of diverse projects during the revolutionary decade (and particularly during Years II and III) to claim a status of "typical" for either Boullée's *Palais national* or Lequeu's *Temple de l'égalité*, many of the projects produced in response to the government's calls for designs shared some fundamental characteristics with these two buildings: form, proportion, and decorative elements were borrowed from the classical world, but altered to create something new; austere geometric forms were combined with allegory; there was a melding of universalist and national tropes; and an effort was systematically made to evoke nature and nature's beauty.

Equally important was their very public nature. With one exception – a competition to design the ideal rural building – all the government's calls were for buildings or monuments either to represent fundamental republican principles (like Lequeu's temple), to provide appropriate space for a crucial political or cultural function (like Boullée's palace), or to commemorate a hero or a crucial revolutionary victory. Although the vast majority of the architects active during the Revolution had extensive experience in domestic architecture, that expertise was not called upon by pamphleteers or legislators, who were far more preoccupied with the pedagogic possibilities of the public than the private sphere. This same focus on the public rather than the domestic may be seen in revolutionary discourses on furniture.

The only effort to shape the aesthetics of interior design during the period of the First Republic (from 1792 to 1795) was in 1792 as plans were being made to convene the National Convention, when it was realized that the legislative body would not be able to do its work without chairs in which to sit and tables at which to write. A star cast was assembled to imagine appropriate furnishings for this new political space: Jean-Louis David proffered a sketch for the armchair of the president, the architects Charles Percier and Pierre-François-Léonard Fontaine provided the celebrated *menuisier* Georges Jacob with drawings for the rest of the furnishings.[75] These pieces followed the already-established model of luxurious simplicity, but with different references. Thus, the two winged griffins supporting the president's desk indicate that Jacob probably turned to Greece for inspiration,[76] and the front-legs of the representatives' chairs in the form of winged lions (carved out of mahogany) appear to have been borrowed from the Republic of Venice.[77]

Although new furnishings were commissioned for the new republican political space, the problem of furnishing the new representative political body did not provoke anything like as much interest as the problem of clothing the literal bodies of the Republic's citizens. Neither in 1792 nor during the years following was there any discussion of mandating appropriate furnishings for the homes of French citizens. A parallel may be seen in another decorative art – porcelain. During the Revolution the director of the Sèvres porcelain manufactory, Antoine Régnier, was ordered to destroy the *ancien régime* molds and drawings, but not given a positive

Figure 5.6 *Théière semée de coquelicots et bleuets à motif de bonnet phrygien*, 1795–1796. Musée Carnavalet, Paris. © Photo by Musées de la ville de Paris/Pierrain.

program to follow.[78] It is fascinating that nonetheless the teapot shown in Figure 5.6, with a *bonnet rouge* in pride of place, was only one of a number of revolutionary-themed objects produced there during these years.

No national competitions were held for styles or forms of furniture, ceramics, or tapestry appropriate to the Republic, nor was there debate on the topic. Once the National Convention was furnished, the issue seems to have faded from official concern, never to reappear. Production rhythms and the loss of markets may go a long way to explain both the continued construction of monarchical-style furniture and limits on how much republican furniture was made in this period, but it does little to explain the absence of discourse on the subject. At first glance one might think that the explanation for the revolutionaries' unusual silence lies in the material conditions of the trade; why waste time discussing something one cannot change? The massive debate on architecture, particularly monumental architecture, however, belies that hypothesis. The examples need not be limited to architecture; revolutionary legislators, journalists and pamphleteers were voluble on a fantastic array of topics concerning republican design and everyday life, whether practicable or not.

I would like to suggest that the lack of engagement of thinkers and legislators who were obsessed by the minutiae of everyday life with domestic interiors may be explained by the conjuncture of two phenomena. First of all, it was only in the second half of the nineteenth century that the domestic space of ordinary citizens (as opposed to elites in the *ancien régime*) would take on political meaning.[79] While Jules Michelet and his fellow nineteenth-century republicans wrote extensively about the implications of domestic style for political identity and position, their eighteenth-century forebears did not. Part of that change had to do with the market – by the end of the nineteenth century more people could make more choices about the appearance of their home – but much of it had to do with changing understandings of both republicanism and the nation.[80]

A second and related factor was that a shared characteristic of all the topics of intensive revolutionary debate was that they could be understood primarily to concern the *public* world, the world outside the home. Clothing, of course, moved between the private and the public, and architectural innovation would change the lives people lived inside as well as what they perceived from the outside. In the revolutionary-era discussions of these two critical elements of everyday life, however, it was their public meaning that was of the greatest concern. Discourses on republican clothing had very little to say about how it might influence familial relations, either between wives and husbands or between parents and children. And, unlike the feminist dress-reform efforts of the next century, there was no interest expressed in an increase in individual freedom of movement or practicality.[81] Clothing was to be republicanized in the interests of promoting – at different moments of the Revolution – freedom of choice or collective identification or political values. This exclusion of the material culture of the private sphere from official efforts at politicization comes in significant contrast to both the understanding of the place of the home in the American Revolution and laws within the French Revolution regulating marriage and other seemingly domestic issues. As we saw in Chapter 4, American revolutionaries took the need and possibility of the politicization and nationalization of the home, and women's emotional, pedagogic, and physical labor within it, very seriously. The French First Republic, furthermore, took radical steps in equalizing the relation of men and women within marriage.[82] The French Revolution enacted John Milton's blueprint for divorce (without, of course, making use of any of the religious language). Divorce was made legal in September 1792 through a particularly liberal law in which either party could sue for divorce or couples could divorce by mutual consent. And yet, at this, the arguably most radical point in the cultural revolution, no serious attention was paid to the home.

Likewise, unless they concerned buildings to which the public would have access, Revolutionary-era architectural projects were largely preoccupied with the façades, and the exteriors more generally. Texts did not discuss, again as later ones would, how living in a dwelling in which space was differently allocated or with a different relation to the outside world might help form republican subjects or inculcate a sense of national belonging. This was not only a textual omission; in the thousands of extant architectural drawings, little attention is paid to conveying a detailed and powerful sense of the experience of dwelling in a building. The built environment, like clothing, largely mattered in so far as it shaped people's public, collective experience.

It is, therefore, no accident that the only furnishings actually commissioned by the revolutionary government were for public buildings, ranging from legislative bodies, to schools, city halls, and libraries. The furnishing of citizens' everyday life was of little concern both because of the liberal separation between a public sphere of state intervention and a private sphere of individual liberty, and because it was not understood to matter politically. The elaboration of a model of a solidaristic public polity resting on a culturally unified nation would happen gradually over the course of the nineteenth century. The grandchild of the Revolution – the Third Republic – would therefore come to take a great interest in the political and social signification of all of its inhabitants' dwellings; but that was a century later.

Given the lack of official engagement and the crisis of the decorative arts trades from Year IV of the Revolution onwards, it is remarkable that any innovation occurred at all, but some did. This "republican" furniture was characterized by natural, solid wood (rather than veneer), indigenous and relatively inexpensive materials (instead of exotic woods, and precious stones and metals), and marquetry inlays of Phrygian caps, pikes and revolutionary texts.[83] In these pieces, not only did indigenous wood replace imported, but it was often left in something close to its natural state. While this was in part no doubt due to the constraints posed by wartime austerity, it was consistent with the revolutionaries' valorization of nature. Even if inlays of gemstones or exotic woods or bronzes were both too closely associated with court and Crown and too costly for the period, the nakedness and humbleness of the wood could have been hidden under paint or colored varnish – neither of them expensive techniques. In parallel, while carved and turned elements became relatively rare, the surfaces of many of the desks, *armoires*, and tables were ornamented with marquetry depicting revolutionary scenes and emblems, and reproducing revolutionary texts.

Thus, for example, the anonymous *secrétaire* shown in Figure 5.7 was constructed from what would appear to be indigenous walnut, finished only with a wax polish. Its legs are sawn and devoid of ornamental detail. Aside from a minimalist softening of the bottom edge of the desk, its only departure from radical austerity is a simple marquetry motif: a pike overlaid with a Phrygian cap in an oval medallion on the front, framed by a rectangle in fine baguettes.

Almost equally plain is a small three-drawer side-table also most probably in French walnut (but it could even be pine), ornamented with marquetry muskets, pikes, Phrygian caps and chains.[84] It is a slightly more complex piece of furniture; the legs bear the gentle curves characteristic of the period between Louis XV and

Figure 5.7 *Secrétaire en pente.* Musée Carnavalet, Paris. ©Photo by Musées de la ville de Paris/ Joffre.

Louis XVI, and it has an elegant bronze lock on each of its drawers. Both pieces are held by the Musée Carnavalet – the museum devoted to the history of the city of Paris – and no doubt owe the honor of their home in that collection to their historical rather than their artistic interest. In neither case would the design or the quality of the artisanry earn them a place in a decorative arts (as opposed to historical) museum. But their very simplicity contributes to their interest and importance.

Modest people would not have commissioned new furniture – however simple – during these terribly difficult and uncertain times. These pieces must, therefore, be of an intentional austerity, an austerity intended to express in the most thorough manner possible the republican sentiments of their owners.

Two other pieces, from the same period and held in the same museum, underscore that argument. The *meuble à deux corps* is thoroughly revolutionary in its motifs.[85] Each of its six figures includes a text with a revolutionary theme, surrounded by revolutionary and patriotic symbols ranging from the cock (*le coq gaulois*) to pikes and flags, while an overseeing eye of reason coifs the entire piece. Unlike the other two objects, however, this chest is entirely covered with an elegant veneer, the marquetry is quite elaborate, and the piece is very carefully finished. The materials remain modest – it is made of French wood and there is no use of precious metal – but the artisanry is relatively complex. Thus although close inspection reveals that the marquetry was cruder than that of the court pieces earlier in the century, this was an expensive and luxurious piece of furniture. Likewise, a revolutionary *coiffeuse* is crafted of less elegant solid wood, but conveys its revolutionary message in careful and quite intricate bas-relief sculpture.[86]

The range of furniture inscribed with revolutionary images or texts, or bearing republican motifs is very wide, including beds, bed-side tables, *coiffeuses*, desks, and *armoires*. They could, therefore, have been found in all rooms of the dwelling, indicating that those who chose to purchase them were not merely concerned with appearing republican in the most public rooms of the private sphere (the dining-room and the *salon*) nor in simply reflecting their political sentiments back to themselves in the most intimate space of the bedroom.

A parallel set of changes may be seen in the other decorative arts: from the porcelain teapot decorated with a Phrygian cap (illustrated above)[87] or a more plebeian ceramic plate showing a cock standing on a canon, under which is written: "Je veille pour la nation,"[88] to wallpaper depicting Liberty and Equality as two young women in classical dress, decorative elements were drawn from the repertoire of revolutionary symbols, events, and texts.[89] The red and white valance in Figure 5.8 designed by the celebrated Jean-Baptiste Huet, for example, would have provided its owners a quotidian reminder of two key events of the Revolution – the taking of the Bastille and Confirmation of the Constitution. Window draperies, furthermore, bridged the domestic and public worlds. The depiction of a political scene on a curtain thus propelled those inside to go out, to leave the comfort of home for the streets.

These goods are somewhat puzzling. As noted above, there was no requirement, nor even explicit encouragement for their consumption or production by revolutionary governments or pamphleteers. In the absence of such exhortation and given their cost, who would have made or bought them and why? The motivation for their production – generally anonymous – is difficult to establish with certainty. It is likely, however, given the very high rates of revolutionary participation by artisans

Figure 5.8 Jean-Baptiste Huet, Valance, *Fall of the Bastille and the Confirmation of the Constitution*, 1792. Plate-printed cotton, Jouy, France. (Victoria and Albert Museum, London. Museum number 1682-1899.)

in the decorative arts industries, that many of these objects reflect the convictions of their makers. They did not necessarily have the time or the resources to engage in a thorough redesign of their goods, but wanted, nonetheless, to make them conform to republican principles. One of the styles they had mastered in the last years of the *ancien régime*, the more austere form of neoclassicism, was, in its references to the Roman republic and Greek democracy, perfectly compatible with current political views. When those forms were inscribed with revolutionary emblems they became even more appropriate for politically-active producers. Artisans would not, however, have made these goods if no one wanted to buy them. But who would want such things? Although far less luxurious than many furnishings and decorative items from the late *ancien régime* or the *Directoire*, the purchase of such durable and encumbering yet fragile items in the middle of revolutionary upheaval, or even after the Revolution as a commemorative act – if these do, indeed, post-date the Revolution – suggests both means and a very powerful commitment to republican principles. One would imagine that some of those who had bought the more sober of neoclassical furniture and other decorative goods in the late *ancien régime* were now buying explicitly revolutionary-style items. Although detailed evidence is lacking, it would seem likely that the clientele for furnishings ornamented with Phrygian caps and pikes would be republican elites who sought to display, affirm, or be reminded of their political rights and obligations. The existence of these objects, therefore, bears witness to the power of the discourse of cultural revolution; some French artisans and consumers appear to have taken the mandate to *live* the Revolution even more seriously than those debating and legislating the contours of legitimate state intervention into the private lives of French citizens.

Related dilemmas of liberty and regulation, as well as different issues of represent-ation and transparency, can be seen in the case of musical and theatrical performances during these years. On August 4, 1793, theatrical censorship was reinstated, with scripts to be reviewed by the Committee on Public Safety.[90] The historian James Johnson has argued that in the process of the general critique of representation and the climate of suspicion reigning during these years, the suspension of disbelief necessary to dramatic performance had become untenable. Rather, "[i]n the service of revolutionary fraternity, which united performer and spectator in the higher unity of citizenship, stage fiction gradually disappeared and 'drama' became the public re-creation of everyday scenes."[91] The new standard for plays became that they be true to life. Furthermore, with the rule of the general will as the dominant paradigm, "privacy was superfluous."[92] All were to share the same experiences, and to share them openly; in a fascinating echo of Charles I's participation as his own allegory in court masques, actors performed in street clothes and the audience also joined in the spectacle.[93] As the work of Johnson, the historian Laura Mason and others have shown, the same dynamic and the same timing held for music. Mason persuasively argues that: "Song culture did more than simply express a politics that had prior existence: singing helped to create the political life of the nation."[94] The reigning concern was for collective participation in musical production.[95] For example, "[i]n preparation for the *Festival de l'Être Suprème*, music teachers from the Institut National de Musique fanned out across Paris, with violins, to teach the city Gossec's *Hymne à l'Être Suprême*."[96] Furthermore there was a sense that common participation in song could banish differences among citizens and reinforce the national community. Not surprisingly, in this context, the chorus gained a new importance.[97] The chorus *was* the people, as opposed to the soloists, who were only the *representatives* of the people.[98] Not only was the choral emphasized, but the music was simplified and polyphony greatly reduced, because, as Johnson argues, it: "…implied a divided social body. Dramatically, it signified protagonists at cross purposes; experientially, it made transparency between stage and spectator difficult; musically, it promoted dangerously personal experience. In short, polyphony was the musical equivalent of dissent."[99]

This particular manifestation of cultural revolution came to an end with the fall of the Jacobins. The seemingly complete eradication of the distinction between public and private, the demand for complete transparency of motive and belief, the imposition of national unity by force, all proved to be more than the French people could bear. The effort, however, to regenerate the nation by means of the radical transformation of the aesthetic and rituals of their everyday life remains an intriguing experiment.

Separating the Public and the Private, the French and the Foreign

The long five years from the execution of Robespierre through to Napoleon Bonaparte's coup of the 18th Brumaire were characterized, first of all, by an end to the experiment with direct democracy and a corresponding rethinking of the principles of political representation. This relegitimation of the idea of representation – and the separation of political and social life – made a turn to a different kind of culture possible, and perhaps necessary.[100] The fall of the Jacobins was also followed by a counter-response, especially by the young, to the strictures and limitations of their cultural revolution. Thus the period was marked by a turn to exaggerated versions of pre-revolutionary style and taste, producing in turn its own counter-reaction in the Directory.

In the midst of these challenges to the previous three years' cultural policy, revolutionary thinkers continued nonetheless to engage the problem of how to mold the taste of the nation, how to instill in people's bones a new way of doing things and a new way of being. The abandonment of both the idea of government imposition of a single, unified culture on all – as an expression of the general will – and of the idea of merging private and public life made this task all the more difficult. It was a moment of the acknowledgement of conflict and difference within the French people. How could one ensure solidarity and regeneration in a context of difference, of privacy, of mediated relations between the people and its government? This period was therefore marked as well by a renewed and intense preoccupation with defining the French nation and especially distinguishing, for the first time, between those who inhabited the territory and those who had political rights as citizens.

These issues emerged starkly in the last public debate on the regulation of clothing in the Council of Five Hundred that started in December 1798 and continued into the following spring. At this time the wearing of the national cockade was still required by law, but compliance with the law was poor. Many of those who still had a cockade attached to their clothing, hid it under scarves or other garments, while others not only refused to display it, but tore off the cockades of others when they had the chance. Therefore, the debate turned first around whether the state should resort to punitive measures to force the daily display of the national symbol.[101]

The debate rapidly became a means of tackling the whole question of national belonging and citizenship. While earlier legislation concerning the cockade had imposed it on *all* adults present on French territory – including women, servants, and foreigners – the suggestion was now made that all three of these groups should be prohibited from marking their identification with the Revolution and with the nation by means of a cockade. Those urging these exclusions argued that it was only those who possessed full political rights who should be allowed to wear the cockade. Those opposed said that facilitating the social cohesion of the nation mattered more, and that therefore all those who were of French nationality, regardless of their political status, should be allowed to wear this symbol.[102] The idea that foreigners should be included in the community of the Revolution and the nation was no longer discussable at this date; some even suggested that foreigners should be marked with an identifying sign.

The debate on women's exclusion focused on whether or not women were really part of the nation-state. Those opposed to women's right to wear the cockade argued that Frenchness was something one earned on the battlefield. Women were not capable of defending the nation, and therefore not fully part of that nation. The importance of military service was underscored by the argument of some that only those men who had done military service should be allowed to wear the cockade, attributing great emotional power to it: "...it is ... the sign of our attachment to the republican government, and of the precious title of 'Frenchman' which we should take on in the cradle and abandon only when we descend into the tomb."[103] Furthermore, in a reprise of the trope of expressing political disquiet in gendered terms, it was argued that were women to wear the cockade it would no longer be possible to tell men and women apart. English and American critics of court (and in the American case European) culture hoped to persuade by saying that luxurious dress effeminized men. Critics of women's participation in the French Republic now argued that if women were, by the wearing of the cockade, to be fully incorporated into that polity, they would, since the Republic was definitively masculine, *become* men. Those arguing the opposite position emphasized the need to retain women within the republican cause not because they were equal to men or entitled to full participation but because their particular frailties and domains of power made them especially important: "Their influence is especially in need of guidance, because the empire of fashion is entirely theirs. Let us teach them the colors of liberty ... in repeatedly emphasizing the meaning of these honorable emblems we will form a national spirit, which will quietly become the most powerful tool of the republican government."[104] Women were powerful, but needed education in political principles. There was, then, movement toward a position articulated much earlier in the Revolution by Olympe de Gouges in her *Declaration of the Rights of Woman* and very present in the American Revolution's "republican motherhood" – that of women's special contribution to the nation-building project.

Indicative of the latency of this position was that despite the extraordinary profusion of commercially and artisanally produced objects of everyday revolutionary culture and a very long tradition of domestic needlework of all kinds, French women do not appear, unlike Americans, either in the revolutionary moment itself or in the next century, to have produced any politicized textiles. Women's participation and the home would ultimately be politicized, because the nation needed women's emotional labor to complement men's contribution of productive work, the sword, and reason to the state. Servants posed yet further different challenges and possibilities.

The debate over whether or not servants should wear the cockade turned on definitions of freedom, equality, national belonging, and citizenship. Those opposed insisted that it was independence and property ownership that had made the role of citizen so honored in Rome. Granting citizenship to those who were in the service of others would tarnish the very concept. Those in favor argued that such reasoning reinforced the evils of pride and social differentiation.[105] They argued that the cockade was a sign of Frenchness, of belonging to the nation, not of political citizenship *per se*; therefore all should be allowed to wear it.[106] Servants were still French, and still essentially free. To mark them off in any way would go against the very principles of the equality of all before the law.[107] Limitations on who could wear the cockade "...would weaken the very foundations of an order of things whose stability is essentially based on the emotions/attachment of its citizens."[108] Even more seriously, depriving servants of the right to wear the symbol of France would be divisive of the nation itself: "In a republican state, one must have but one single body, one single spirit; anything that divides it will inevitably lead to altering it in a manner more or less fatal for general tranquility."[109]

The final resolution was to restrict the wearing of the cockade to adult men who were not servants, had not been convicted of a crime and were not mentally ill. The preceding debate had focused on entitlements rather than obligations, however, thus seeking a sense of unity through exclusions rather than through likenesses, while also shifting the place of law in constituting the state and the very nature of that nation-state. With this law, "the national cockade was no longer an obligation, a 'strict requirement,' but rather a right guaranteed by a constitutional act that assumes obligation."[110] In this modern nation-state, the law was to guarantee rights, not impose obligations. It was to be minimalist, rather than maximalist. The emphasis was to be put on liberty, rather than equality, and the state was to remove itself from the now private world of signs.

As important as were regulation and debate, practices were equally significant. In the domain of furniture – where there continued to be no public discussion of state intervention – styles changed with the *Directoire* (November 1795–November 1799). That period was characterized by a return of both ostentatious luxury and a new version of neoclassicism deeply marked by Napoleon's 1798 Egyptian campaign. A daybed produced sometime between 1795 and 1803 by François H. G. Desmalter (1770–1841) and Georges II Jacob (1786–1803) shows the change very clearly. This piece is crafted of solid mahogany, mahogany veneered on beech wood, and gilt bronze. And, while the style is reminiscent of the neoclassicism of Louis XVI, the armrests are composed of two winged sphinx-like creatures, and the feet protected with bronze castings resembling palm leaves. The object itself – a daybed, which became popular in this period in part because of its reference to Roman forms – was indicative of the return to a melding of luxury and neoclassicism (albeit that of a now expanded classical world). Thus, just as elegant, visibly extravagant clothes were favored by the *jeunesse dorée* in this period, their elders commissioned exotic and sensual versions of neoclassicism to mark a transformation in the revolutionary dynamic, a transformation presaging the return of court culture under the First Empire. This same trajectory may also be seen in other social practices in what is called the "Thermidorian Reaction."

During the Thermidorian Reaction, that is the period of rebellion against the austerity and literalism of the Jacobins, the revolutionary regime was faced with a people who had suffered a long period of deprivation, lived through the Terror, and were now rebelling against constraint, even though still deeply involved in revolutionary culture and politics. Thus, even when people fought against constraint they often used the strategies and forms of the preceding revolutionary years. Even the *jeunesse dorée*, for example, perceived to be the emblem of reaction against Jacobinism, used its tactics. The *jeunesse dorée* were bands of wealthy youth who roamed Paris, luxuriously dressed, enjoying themselves ostentatiously but also informally policing theaters, music halls, and public spaces. They forced actors and musicians with Jacobin pasts to recant publicly before allowing them to perform. They were associated with interrupting performances of which they disapproved by singing a song, the *Réveil du peuple*, that criticized the Terror. The song was quickly adopted into the revolutionary canon, to be played in Parisian theaters and by the National Guard in alternation with the Marseillaise.[111]

While the Thermidorian Reaction is perhaps best known for this turning of the strategies of the revolutionary crowd against the Revolution (and its subsequent taming by officialization), James Johnson has persuasively argued that it was both the end of the direct democracy and the effort under Thermidor and the Directory to redefine politics and to recreate a separation between public and private, between official culture and private culture, that had the most dramatic effect on cultural forms (at least in theater and music).[112] With the separation of official, state culture and private culture, and with the lessening of regulation, people both reverted to Old Regime cultural forms, and, more commonly in fact, created cultural hybrids – like the *jeunesse dorée*. Thus women and men of all ages started wearing very extravagant clothing and, by 1798–1799, women turned to essentially transparent forms of "classical dress."[113] Women – and those designing for them – took a form that, while certainly present under the Old Regime, had gained far more popularity during the Revolution – classicism – and turned it to a completely different use. Under the Revolution, classicism had stood for democracy and austerity; women in the late 1790s used it to flirt.

Another reaction, as the government made an effort to regulate and control political action – like singing in the streets – and channel it in particular directions was simply to withdraw. Laura Mason has argued that in 1795 and 1796, people turned away from revolutionary political culture and returned either to traditional popular song or to Old Regime repertories.[114] While song, and, as will be seen in a moment, clothing, became divided into official and private forms, Johnson argues that the theater, by contrast, simply became privatized:

> Thermidor … changed the relationship between the people and the government. By imposing its own authority over that of the revolutionary sections, the Convention substituted the principle of representation for the immanent and indivisible sovereignty

of the 'nation assembled.' To recognize the Convention's authority was to recognize the state and society as separate entities and to reject the former politicization of private life ... The theater ceased ... to be a microcosm of the national will.[115]

With this came a renewed willingness to suspend disbelief, to believe that actors were actors playing roles and the audience was composed of many individuals each reacting privately as well as collectively to the drama before them. Far, conceptually if not temporally, from the moment of Jacobin cultural revolution, this is a tableau for a liberal democratic society in which substantial portions of the lifeworld are deemed to be outside politics and the space of collective action limited.

Both the rebellion against government control and the government's own sense of the need to limit its intervention in cultural life provoked continued reflection on what the government's role in song and other cultural forms should be. Clothing also continued to be a major preoccupation of those committed to the continuation of the Revolution. In September 1795 [Vendémaire Year IV], the celebrated Abbé Grégoire published a report on clothing. He argued that the wearing of uniforms specific to office would enhance the dignity of the office at the same time as it would remind the office-holders that their social recognition depended entirely on their office.[116] Unlike many of his predecessors, however, he argued that one cannot regulate the clothing or behavior of everybody, but would have to count on people seeking to emulate the officials. Grégoire's arguments were apparently convincing, and one of the last acts of the Convention in October was to pass a law prescribing clothing for officials. As Lynn Hunt has argued, costumes for legislators were "a means of enhancing the perception of natural truths."[117] The political order was to be both revealed and produced by the difference in the clothing of the politicians and the citizenry.

The decade of the Revolution saw an extraordinary production of cultural forms and an extraordinary range of positions on the relation between politics and culture, the public and the private, equality and liberty. In the domain of music, for example, during the "...period between 1790 and 1800, no fewer than fifty works of revolutionary inspiration were performed at the Opéra and the Opéra-Comique."[118] This during a period in which, among a myriad other changes, a monarchy was replaced by a republic; the Catholic Church was replaced by the cult of the Supreme Being; a new calendar and a new system of weights and measures were put into place; the administrative map of France was redrawn; the tax system was transformed; and a war was fought. Many of these innovations had but short lives: the revolutionary calendar is remembered only by historians and French schoolchildren; many of the first names invented during these years would later provoke only bemused pity for those forced to bear them; and furniture with carefully crafted marquetry slogans quickly entered the domain of the "curiosity" rather than the antique. Many contributions have been more enduring, however: the Marseillaise is still the French national anthem; most of the world continues to use the metric system of weights and measures; the Louvre is still the nation's premier museum; and the *départements* demarcated during the Revolution are still used to administer France. Even more significant historically than these specific contributions, however, is the heritage of a linkage of everyday aesthetics and practices with political participation and belonging.

Those involved at virtually all moments of the Revolution were convinced that culture was not apolitical. They were all, however, preoccupied with the problem of balancing the need for national solidarity and political transformation through culture against individuals' right to freedom from state interference in their lives at work and at home. The ending of the corporate system meant that production was far freer of government regulation than it had been; creating national solidarity through a shared style produced in state workshops was not, therefore, an option. The politicization of the home was viewed with, perhaps, even greater distrust, so that even at the height of the Jacobin cultural revolution no one was talking about republican furniture or wallpaper, even if people were actually making and buying it. The Directory confirmed that state cultural policy would henceforth affirm liberty over equality and fraternity, although Napoleon would attempt to recreate a style of state.

These cultural revolutions left the modern nation-state with a fundamental conundrum. Even the strongest parliamentary monarchies, democracies, and republics cannot, because of their liberal commitments, mandate national cultural forms or practices. And yet modern nation-states need the affective bonds that are most effectively made through culture. This is, to complicate the story further, also a profoundly gendered conundrum. Ultimately, all these states were forced to admit women to full political participation. And yet, all of them also continued to define women and the home as the site of the nation's affective bonding. The question of who would build the nation, once women joined the state, was unresolved. All of them really believed, in other words, that if women also wore the cockade, the brothers would cease to love each other.

–6–

Legacies
Culture in the Modern Nation-state

Much united nineteenth-century Britain, France and the United States, and a good deal of that common experience was a result of their interlocking revolutionary experiences.[1] Much, of course, also divided them; and many of those differences may be attributed to how each of their revolutions played out. What they had in common were their efforts to create patriotic sentiment through the iconography and ritual of state and the active construction of national solidarity. Those efforts were complicated, however, by their commitment in principle, if not always in practice, to *laissez-faire* policies; the exclusion of women from suffrage and the elaboration of a cult of domesticity, while at the same time expanding towards white manhood suffrage; a radical intensification of industrialization, commercialization, mobility, and urbanization; territorial and/or colonial expansion; slavery and its abolition; domestic social conflict; religious toleration; and a material world of combined plenty and penury. They differed in their forms of governance; conceptions of legitimate government power (particularly that of the national state); relations between Church and State; understandings of the relation among individuals, collectivities, and the State; and the boundaries of the domestic sphere and the corresponding limitations and possibilities for women's political engagement.

All three nations used cultural institutions to try to create a national aesthetic adequate to emotionally binding their citizens to the nation. They all faced challenges from the commercialized, commodity culture, with its tendencies towards fragmentation and the internationalization of late nineteenth-century capitalism. Each nation faced that challenge differently, however, in ways shaped by its history of revolution and national consolidation in the seventeenth and eighteenth centuries. This chapter will analyze, first, the common histories and shared revolutionary legacies, and then the equally significant differences, before concluding with a discussion of the implications of both for the present.

Common Legacies: State Cultural Intervention

The first half of the nineteenth century was the period of early nation-formation in the United States, while in France imperial, monarchical, and republican regimes alternated and sometimes overlapped, and Britain continued to be governed by a parliamentary monarchy. For each the problem of creating national solidarity was different than it had been in the revolutionary age. The United States was already struggling with growing sectional tensions over slavery that tested how closely united the states would be now that they were independent from England, and there was equally great disagreement over defining the appropriate powers of the national government. Successive French governments were extremely unstable, and largely concerned with political survival, with economic development, and with renewed colonial expansion. Although Britain was emerging as the dominant economic power in the Atlantic world, it was faced with how to deal with slavery, and with a rebellious colonial empire, at the same time as the working classes at home were protesting against their political exclusions and economic hardships. Even though the *nation* and national belonging were, to some extent, taken for granted, the *state* was a matter of much greater preoccupation. Each polity's particular revolutionary experience shaped people's imaginaries of the state by which they hoped to be governed but, in all three cases, in the attempt to determine the appropriate functions and boundaries of the state, an ideological divide between public and private, political and domestic, and sites of production and sites of consumption emerged.

They all, within the limits each of their state structures imposed, maintained and elaborated the repertoires inherited from their revolutionary moments: the celebration of national holidays; keeping the memory of events and heroes alive by naming streets and buildings after them; coinage and paper money inscribed with key principles and figures of the nation's history; continual reworking of national flags; the writing and teaching of national anthems and auxiliary songs. Each of these strategies were, in fact, not only maintained but in most cases elaborated, facilitated by a vastly improved post office, increasingly quick and reliable transportation services, and ameliorations in minting and printing technologies. The celebrations of major national historical events and the birthdays of national leaders often became more spectacular as those organizing the events borrowed techniques from the world of commercial entertainment. But there was the sense, as there had been during the revolutions, that these practices alone would not suffice to create and maintain affective linkages among the vast community of strangers that constituted modern nation-states. Another heritage from the three revolutions, particularly the American and the French, however, complicated the task of looking to material culture and everyday practices for that necessary work of nation-building.

All three nation-states had inherited from their moments of revolutionary rupture a powerful belief in the need to protect individuals and the economy from state intrusion. In Old Regime France, in pre-Civil War England, and in colonial North America, the national state, whether in the form of Crown or Parliament, had had the capacity for arbitrary intrusion into many domains of life (whether or not it had the actual will to do so). In each case, revolutionaries reacted to those limitations, ultimately arguing for the overwhelming importance of liberty, with powerful implications for the politics of the everyday. The nineteenth century was thus a world ostensibly governed by the principles of *laissez-faire*. Political thinking was dominated by the hope (or fantasy) of keeping the government out of workshops, out of homes, out of schools, out of people's lives. The ideal was an economy that would be self-regulating, with individuals freely selling their labor on the market without the mediation of collective organizations or of the State. Likewise, society and domestic life were to be detached from political interest. The State was not, therefore, to intervene directly in the shaping of national culture either through the market or through the home.

This was, correspondingly, the moment of the "cult of domesticity" in America and of its equivalent in France and Britain. The "domestic sphere" was, of course, a fantasy, but a powerful one; homes were to be refuges from the harshness of both modern politics and modern economics, and women were to be their guardians. This new split between public and private was to some extent fictive, and to some extent real.[2] Post-revolutionary regimes retreated quickly from even engaging in debates on gender equality. Instead they either retained or created legal systems that made women economically and legally dependent on their fathers or husbands, restricting their civil and as well as their political rights. Middle-class women were, in fact, more limited (or more protected, depending on one's viewpoint) from their fathers', husbands' or brothers' businesses than they had ever been. Working-class women continued to work for wages both at home and in workshops and factories. That labor was, however, more and more often rendered invisible or judged unnatural. In theory, then, all women were to be at home, protected from an economy and polity understood to be increasingly savage. Not only were production and distribution now to be banned from the home, but so was politics. In fact, political interests were to retire from all aspects of the private – that is, economic and social – world. This was, of course, a paradox. Middle-class homes were to be protected from the rigors of politics and the sordidness of business, yet they depended upon the profits of a capitalist political economy for their very existence.

This goal of a non-intrusive state was ultimately thwarted by yet another revolutionary heritage – the expectation of political participation. Although the time-frames varied, all three governments expanded their suffrage to include all adult white men by the end of the century. This enlargement of the voting polity did not happen without struggle; all three societies witnessed dramatic conflict between working and middle classes throughout the century. Workers fought for a voice as full members of the state, for wages adequate to buy the new goods available, and for working hours short enough to enjoy them. Questions of political representation and representation through goods took on new acuteness in this context. Over the course of the struggle, and particularly once the vote was won, many argued that working-class men now needed to be educated in citizenship. One strategy was to educate them directly in schools, museums, expositions, and libraries. An equally important strategy was to educate their women, so that as mothers and wives they could instill a love of nation in their menfolk and children. That domestic pedagogy was to happen through appropriate consumption and everyday practices. Education in national solidarity for both sexes was viewed as all the more necessary because the rapid expansion of capitalism in the nineteenth century was perceived to undermine all kinds of solidarities, including those of the nation.

Wage differentials created class conflict; women's labor outside the home left most women unavailable to do the necessary emotional work of maintaining the nation; and a profusion of new goods fractured the material culture of the nation. As consumer industries developed and advertising techniques became more sophisticated, people were understood to have more means to differentiate themselves from their fellow citizens than ever before. And, by the end of the nineteenth century, advertising was especially potent in this regard.[3] It told people that by their acquisitions, by their lifestyle, they would demonstrate their uniqueness, their individuality, their particular virtues. The goal was the paradox of "appropriate uniqueness." This possibility of social differentiation through consumption was made all the more problematic by the influx of immigrants.

The 1880s saw massive immigration into France and the United States and, to a lesser extent, into England. People fleeing economic crises, overpopulation, and political repression in Italy, Eastern Europe, and China, among other places, made new lives for themselves in new homelands. In all three nation-states, the law made the acquisition of citizenship by most white immigrants relatively easy. The polities were therefore faced with the question of how one turned foreigners into nationals, that is, how one enabled them to connect emotionally to the people whose polity had become their own. This task seemed even harder given the fragmentation of society through conflict over production, and through the power of consumption. It was not, therefore, only foreigners who were perceived as needing transformation into nationally-minded Frenchmen and women, Englishwomen and men, or Americans. Even the native-born were perceived to be lacking national, as opposed to regional or local, affect and solidarity. This lack was all the more worrying because of the removal of the property qualification for manhood suffrage and the creation of mass armies. It was feared that men who were insufficiently attached to the nation would be incompetent voters and unreliable soldiers.

One hope was to harness the power of the same forces perceived to be so destructive. It was hoped that the improvement of the infrastructure and the development of a mass press and chain stores within each nation-state would help build ties among the nation's citizens.[4] They could travel more easily, they could read the same magazines, they could visit each others' towns and regions, and they could buy standardized goods. People from very different parts of the country and regional cultures lived side by side when they migrated to cities. It was argued, wishfully perhaps, that national solidarity through differentiation from those of other nationalities was something that could be accomplished through responsible consumerism: "You are too good a Frenchwoman to think that you've fulfilled your duty by simply giving a lot of money and a free hand to a decorator," wrote a taste professional in a guide to women, "American women do that willingly – it's so convenient! But you are certainly enough behind the times to prefer your home [in English in the text] to the most luxurious of furnished hotels."[5] Or, as the great French republican and historian Jules Michelet put it: "In this great body of a nation ... [a]certain idea enters by the eyes (fashion, shops, museums, etc.)... All receive the thinking of all, perhaps without analyzing it, but they nonetheless receive it."[6] This point was further emphasized by the French social theorist Charles Fonsegrive: "Living on the same soil, subject to the same climate, hearing the same voices, having the same examples before one's eyes, receiving a common education from things and from men ... we gradually form a common manner of feeling and reacting. Out of all these common things, we constitute an image or idea of the *patrie*."[7] But this was wishful thinking, and known to be wishful thinking at the time it was articulated. Political commentators remained anxious, therefore, that the fundamental effects of the market were divisive, and the state needed to provide a counter-weight to them; but the question was, how?

Despite an increasing perception of the need for state intervention, a powerful sense remained, in all three polities, that the state could not actually *dictate* a national style, any more than it could actually *own* or *run* most businesses. The market had to be allowed to function relatively freely. People were to be permitted to buy whatever they wanted without the constraint of sumptuary law. Artisans and artists had to be enabled to create what forms they chose, without state-mandated limitations on materials. Even as patron, the bourgeois state of the late nineteenth century had a much more limited role than the monarchies of the Old Regime. The state could regulate production, the state could create institutions in which taste was taught, the state could impose tariffs on goods coming in from abroad, but the state could not actually create a national style. Yet they were all worried about not only the social strife that industrial capitalism created through conditions of production, but about the political fragmentation created through the multiplication of goods and styles within one nation that market forces inevitably generated. Manufacturers, whose priority was selling, invented new and different versions of the same object, for different seasons, different places, different ages, different genders, and different classes, thereby encouraging increased consumption. But those stylistic differences of everyday life were perceived to be potentially fragmenting of the unified nation-state. There was something close to consensus that the symbols of state, everyday icons, and holidays needed reinforcement from other domains if the national culture and national solidarity were to resist the centrifugal force of the market.

All three countries used the same five institutions as the building-blocks of their cultural policy – national monuments, universal exhibitions, museums, libraries, and schools. Witnessing their country's contemporary achievements at the universal exhibitions, viewing the national cultural patrimony in a museum, reading the national literature in a library, learning about the nation's past in school, they all assumed, would instill a sense of likeness, of common identity, of mutual responsibility into the inhabitants of the nation. But while all three nations created and used these same institutions, they did so in significantly different ways. Just as the likenesses are extraordinarily informative of similarities among modern nation-states, the differences reveal the importance of particular historical trajectories.

It is in the context of international universal exhibitions, known in England as great exhibitions, in France as *expositions universelles*, and in the United States, as world's fairs, that the commonalities of modern nation-states' cultural policy are most apparent. During the first half of the nineteenth century both France and England sponsored national trade fairs, designed to display and thereby encourage technological innovation. The intended public for these fairs were largely manufacturers. Starting with 1851 Crystal Palace Exhibition in London, the fairs became international rather than national, and generally much more ambitious in scope, adding political to economic goals.

These exhibitions, held in major cities throughout Europe and North America, between 1850 and 1950, were giant events, covering many acres, in major cities throughout Europe and North America, to which each nation sent examples of what it considered its finest accomplishments. These fairs were intended to educate the middle classes, to moralize the working classes, and to display the technical and artistic prowess of the exhibiting nations. Especially towards the end of the nineteenth century, the fairs became a means both of harnessing competition among nations and of fostering national sentiment within each nation. Exhibitions became ubiquitous in the industrial world during the nineteenth century, occurring as often as twice a decade. They were marked by their cosmopolitanism and their efforts at comprehensiveness, as well as their founders' hopes of effecting social change through the expos. Paris hosted universal exhibitions in 1855, 1867, 1878, 1889 and 1900, and two specialized exhibits – a decorative arts exposition in 1925 and a Colonial Exposition in 1930. After 1851, the English sponsored Great Exhibitions in 1862, 1871–1874, 1883–1886 and into the twentieth century, as well as a variety of colonial exhibitions in the period from the 1890s through to the 1920s. The United States entered the competition with the New York World's Fair in 1853, followed by the Philadelphia Centennial Exposition in 1876, Chicago's Columbian Exposition of 1893, the St. Louis World's Fair of 1904, and a variety of others into the late twentieth century. The expositions grew enormously in size from the mid-century to the *fin-de-siècle*, with vast increases in exhibitors, attendance, and space. In France, the official time of preparation went from two to eight years between 1855 and 1900; the number of displays quadrupled from 24,000 to 83,000; and the approximate number of visitors grew from 4 million in 1855 to 48 million in 1937.[8]

Planners of the expositions used strategies of both identification and differentiation in their attempts to contribute to building national solidarity. They hoped to instill a sense of national pride and of patriotism through the display of national prowess and through mass participation in a shared experience. Thus as people came together to witness the technological and artistic achievement of their country, they would come to identify with it and with each other. To this end, colonialism and imperialism were also highlighted at most universal exhibitions from the 1890s through to the 1930s. Even the United States, which did not have formal colonies (although it did acquire various forms of over-rule of the Philippines, Cuba, Hawaii, and Puerto Rico after its victory in the Spanish–American war in 1898), had large ethnographic exhibits. Colonial and ethnographic exhibits were created in the hope of connecting people through their shared pride in their countries' power and through the construction of a shared sense of likeness and superiority compared to the "primitive." That likeness was to be constituted through a common "national," "modern" taste.

National governments competed among themselves for the honor of hosting fairs, and they invested hugely in them. In addition, in the US context, the competition between cities was fierce. Both national and state-level involvement ran deep: the Columbian Exposition (Chicago 1893) was established by an act of Congress in 1890, and world's fair boards were appointed by state legislatures.[9] The fact that there was so little effort to hold French expositions outside Paris (only two were held elsewhere) or English fairs outside London, while American fairs moved around the country, is indicative of the decentralization and weakness of the national government in the United States.[10]

Thus the task of constructing national identity through these events varied in its difficulty from country to country. It was easiest for the English, who had a very strong state and a monarchy that could be mobilized to symbolize the nation. In fact, the presence of royalty at the fairs was considered essential for their success. At the end of the century, in the face of economic difficulties and increasing challenges in sustaining the colonial project, more was invested in the effort to exude Englishness.[11] The French occupied a middle ground: the French state was very powerful and highly centralized, but it was also widely resented, and political differences were profound. The cultural politics of unification through linguistic uniformity and the eradication of regional difference sparked a counter-reaction. French regions, in fact, maintained powerful identities through this period. The problem was most difficult in the United States, where suspicions of the federal state ran deepest. Another limit on the expositions' potential for nation-building was their combined commercial and nationalist purpose. Goods were, after all, for sale at the expositions, and prizes won there were vital marketing aids.

Less ambiguous in their purpose were the museums, libraries, schools, and national monuments in which the state also invested in this period.[12] In some ways, museums – permanent collections of objects regularly displayed to the public in a systematic way – could be conceptualized as merely the rendering permanent of the transitory fairs. They were also a site of the display of goods, of peoples, and of customs. A few, like the Museum of Manufacturers in London, founded in 1852, did emerge from an exhibition, in this case that of 1851. It quickly grew and moved to new quarters becoming the South Kensington Museum (in 1857), and at the turn of the twentieth century was the foundation for the celebrated Victoria and Albert Museum, dedicated to the decorative arts. Most museums, however, found their origin in a different location and universal exhibitions and museums generally had complementary, not competitive, functions in the implementing of national cultural policy. While the exhibitions of the nineteenth century grew out of the tradition of annual national and international markets whose purpose was the exchange of goods, museums grew out of a tradition of noble and royal, collecting, although their history goes back as far as the Museum of Alexandria. Private collections proliferated in Europe in the sixteenth and seventeenth centuries. *Museums*, in this sense, were private spaces within houses devoted to the categorization and study of objects, most often of the natural world.[13] It was only at the cusp of the eighteenth century (in 1683) that the Ashmolean became the first of these to grant some limited public access. This trend continued and spread in the eighteenth century. In 1750, a selection of pictures from the French royal collection was displayed to the public for three hours, two days a week in the Luxembourg Palace. And, as was discussed in Chapter 5, an attempt was made actually to implement the plan that had originated with the Crown of turning the royal palace of the Louvre into a museum. Revolutionary events slowed that effort; but it came to fruition under the first Empire. In England, the British Museum – actually a library and museum – founded on the private collections of Hans Sloane, Harley and Cotton – opened its doors in 1759, albeit with very limited hours and tightly controlled access. The first public exhibition of English art was held in 1760, the Royal Academy was founded in 1769, and the National Gallery in London opened in 1828. The pattern was similar in the American colonies and in the United States of the early national period. The first museum, in this case like the British Museum a collection devoted to natural history, was the Charleston Museum, begun in 1773. In 1786, Charles Willson Peale opened his collection of portraits of revolutionary heroes to the public, and this became the basis of the Pennsylvania Academy of Fine Arts. In the late nineteenth century, a notion of museums as a means of improving the taste of the nation, and thus consolidating that nation as well as aiding in competition with Britain and other industrialized countries, was added to the more traditional idea of museums as a place where the patrimony of the country could be preserved.

By the 1870s in England and the 1890s in France, municipalities and the state were also creating museums specifically for a working-class public. In Paris, for example, the first "evening museum" opened its doors in 1895. Just after its inauguration, it was written up in the press in the following terms: "All of those who are interested in the development of popular education and in the rapid development of thought leading towards a peaceful future, will turn their eyes on the city of Paris. The evening museum can unite scattered good will, can put into contact those who know and those who want to learn – the artist and the artisan."[14] It was assumed that workers were a kind of raw talent, "natively" possessing good taste, but in need of education: "Certainly, we are not unaware that there exists an aesthetic instinct in the world of workers, ready to be moved by the manifestations of beauty in all of its forms. But these instincts need to be developed, and we will take the initiative in providing the education necessary to fully taste artistic pleasures."[15] That education was important not just to improve people's skills as workers, but also to increase their sense of national belonging.

The relation between both state and society and art museums was more complicated in the United States than in England or France, because of the long-standing American suspicion of the arts and the relative poverty of American production throughout the nineteenth century. Most American artists were trained in Europe and identified with a European tradition. There was the question of what, given the absence of a national artistic tradition, exactly, should an American collection contain to help train its viewers in national identity and national pride? Despite this difficulty, the 1870s were the boom decade for starting museums in the United States. The Museum of Fine Arts in Boston and the Metropolitan Museum of Art in New York were both chartered in 1870, Philadelphia Museum in 1876, the Art Institute of Chicago in 1879, and the Art Institute of Detroit in 1885.

By the 1880s, therefore, all three nations were investing heavily in creating permanent local, regional and national patrimonies, with the hopes that citizens of all classes would learn how to negotiate the relation of the local and the national and to *feel* part of a national collectivity. Art museums in particular also helped define the nation in relation to other countries in a way somewhat different from the world's fairs. While the fairs encouraged competitive comparison, museums emphasized both distinctions among national traditions and the interconnections among them. Thus all European and American museums had sections on classical art, emphasizing their common link to the republics of Greece and Rome. Museums conveyed a complex message of local, regional and national uniqueness, but a uniqueness that composed first a national, then a civilizational whole. In this, libraries did similar cultural work, although starting from an earlier date.

While museums were comparatively late to arrive in the United States, library construction was relatively precocious. The Boston Public Library, when it opened in 1852, became the first public library in the country. There had, of course, been subscription libraries as early as the eighteenth century, and the renowned Boston Athenaeum was incorporated in 1807. These, however, were private institutions, serving only those who could afford to pay their membership fees and rental costs. A very similar pattern obtained in England and France (although, in the French case, slightly later). In France, for example, the main library specializing in the decorative arts, the Bibliothèque des Arts Décoratifs, was founded as a private library in 1866, and then became a publicly (nationally rather than municipally) owned library twenty years later. Likewise the Bibliothèque Forney, a technical library, was founded in 1886, with money from the legacy, ten years earlier, of the industrialist Charles Forney.

The only national-state level intervention in libraries was in the domain of deposit libraries; but it was an important and enduring one. All three countries built national deposit libraries – the Library of Congress, the Bibliothèque Nationale, and the British Museum – as storehouses of the national printed heritage. All books published in the nation-state were to be held in these libraries, and they would thereby provide the resources for the writing of the nation's history. The task here was much easier than for national museums, because their purpose was well-defined and finite. It was obviously impossible to collect *all* of the paintings done within the national boundaries, and it would have been absurd to attempt to do so. Paintings and other hand-crafted objects were obviously unique; creating a national collection therefore necessarily required a selection process. Acquiring a copy of every book published with a nation-state was an automatic process and it did not entail depriving private individuals of access to ownership of those books. Thus, the nature of the object itself structured the kind of institutional home appropriate to it and its place in the task of constituting the nation. Schools were yet a different site in which this task was carried out.

Schools were considered, perhaps, the key institutions for creating loyal citizens. By the late nineteenth century, elementary schooling was free and obligatory in France, England, and the United States. Although the location of control of public schools varied – in France they were a matter for the national state, in England a combination of the municipality and the nation, and in the United States, municipalities and the various states – in all three countries they were understood to have a doubled obligation of producing good workers and good citizens. Seconding these schools providing a general education were, from as early as the 1830s in Britain, followed later in the century in the United States and France, institutions designed specifically to improve the nation's taste. The motivation here was both international and domestic, driven on the one hand by fear of competition in the decorative arts' market, and on the other by a sense that market forces were fragmenting the nation's taste and thereby endangering its very being.

A final means by which the state attempted to have an emotional presence was through public monuments. Creating an everyday instantiation of the nation and the state through monuments was not a novelty in the late nineteenth century. As we have seen, in Europe monarchs had erected statues of themselves since the Renaissance, and the French Revolution saw a multitude of plans for permanent, public commemorations of its events. But the late nineteenth century saw a radical increase in the pace of monument construction as well as a new density of monuments throughout the territories of all three nations.

The French Third Republic set about a systematic installation of statues of the allegory of the Republic, Marianne, in towns all across the country. The *exposition universelle* of 1889, celebrating the centennial of the Revolution, was the occasion for a competition for an appropriate new symbol for the new Republic and the new century. The outcome of that competition was the Eiffel Tower, a sharp break with France's tendencies in the nineteenth century to that date to build historicist monumental architecture. Whether small statues of Marianne across from the church in a village square, or the enormous, iron, Eiffel Tower on the banks of the Seine, all of these projects were initiated, and paid for, by the central government.

The state's role was very different in the United States, where in the 1880s and 1890s there was an explosion of patriotic monuments, especially to American war heroes. These monuments and the ceremonies that accompanied them were intended, as the historian Neil Harris has argued, to be "a material basis for nationality, a check to the country's cultural contrasts in a defined and ritualized religion of patriotism." The monuments ranged from a statue of Nathan Hale in Central Park, to a memorial of Mary Washington. Strikingly, these monuments were not commissioned, erected, or paid for by local, state or federal government, but by organized groups of citizens. The statue of Nathan Hale was the work of the Sons of the American Revolution, while that of Mary Washington was the work of the Daughters of the American Revolution. The Statue of Liberty, donated by the French government, rested on a pedestal for which America's private citizens had paid – through a subscription, not through taxes. In addition to these statues, this was a period of attentiveness to the historical patrimony of the nation as a whole. Historical sites and battlefields were marked and restored. Preservation necessary for this restoration and to tell the story of the events behind the battlefields, historic houses and famous churches, was guaranteed by the creation of archives.[16] This example of local, philanthropic, and volunteer participation in the celebration of the nation, in contrast to the French centralized model, brings us to the question of the differing legacies of each revolutionary moment.

Diverging Paths

The governments of all three nation-states inherited from their respective revolutions, therefore, the problematic of fostering their citizens' consciousness of national identity in a putatively democratic republic. By the 1880s that task had become even more complicated, especially given the pace and challenges of industrialization and the expansion of the suffrage. Their respective historical trajectories diverged quite sharply during the nineteenth century, and given the differences in their logics of governance so did their cultural policies. In France, the first seventy years of the century saw two empires, two monarchies, and one republic, before the definitive arrival of representative government with the Third Republic. In the United States, regional and state affiliations remained very strong, and the federal government weak, until after the Civil War. That conflict, and its very difficult aftermath, made clear the need for national cultural as well as political integration. Finally, the English state had little interest – for the opposite reason – in attempting to create a national culture. Despite a series of political scandals, and social conflict in the metropole and the colonies, there was little sense that the state was fragile or in need of cultural reinforcement. Each country resolved both the political and the social issues differently. These nineteenth-century trajectories, along with differences in each of their revolutionary legacies, created three fundamental divergences in how the relation between politics and culture came to be understood: (1) the power of the national state; (2) the location of the division between the public and private, and its corollary of the relation of the individual and collectivities to the state; and (3) the place of religion.

Of the three, Americans were the most reluctant by far to grant powers to their federal government in the linked domain of cultural policy or practice. This was not because nineteenth-century Americans did not think that national identities had to be consciously instilled, but because they either lacked confidence that the national government could do so or did not believe that it should. Debates that had raged following the Declaration of Independence and in the very early national period concerning the relationship between the states and the nation were not resolved, but simply compromised. Tensions between the national government and the states were exacerbated, particularly in the ante-bellum period, by terribly deep divisions among the states. Even after the Civil War created a more truly United States, the national government was viewed with deep suspicion and understood to be alien, while local and state government were still conceived as forms of self-governance.[17] Until the Progressive Era, then, the dominant position was that nation-building should be done through private initiative, or municipal or state government. It was only the pressures of an economy that refused to pay attention to political boundaries that forced Americans to be willing to give greater power to their national state.

The French present the starkest contrast. The French state was already highly centralized before the Revolution, and the revolutionary and Napoleonic periods only further consolidated that process. While regional identifications remained very strong, and regionalism as a political movement arose in opposition to the Third Republic's energetic efforts at cultural homogenization in the last thirty years of the century, there was no conception of "states' rights" as such. The major source of contestation of the national state's cultural powers came not from the regions, but from the Catholic Church. France was also the only one of three polities with a truly national school system, the only one in which local governments depended so directly and so heavily on the national state. It was also the polity that demanded the greatest degree of cultural uniformity from its inhabitants. Centralization was aided, of course, by the pre-eminent place of Paris. In both England and France, the identity between the largest commercial center and the political capital was reinforcing. Washington, DC, by contrast, was an artificial city, itself the outcome of the impossibility of settling the nation's capital in any existing colonial city or state.

The English situation fell between the other two polities. There had been a strong national state in England for several centuries, but regional polities and regional affiliations remained very powerful throughout the nineteenth century. Until late in the century, the national state made little effort to impose itself, perhaps because it was so strong it did not need to.

These differences in conceptions of the appropriate power of the national state were mirrored in the relation between individual, community, and nation. France retained from the Revolution a conception of the indivisibility of the nation. Rather than the idea that representative political bodies existed, in part at least, to adjudicate conflicts between different geographically-based interests, representatives were to speak for all the French. The United States, with its very strong states' rights tradition, lay at the other end of the spectrum. Congress was acknowledged to be the site of struggle among different constituencies with different needs and different desires. Protection of the rights of both individuals and states was considered paramount. The English state occupied a middle ground between these two. Districts were understood to differ, and municipal governments were relatively powerful; but much of everyday life was under the control of the central government. These differences had crucial implications for the place of taste in the constitution of these modern nation-states.

The gendering of nation-making and, correspondingly, the nature of women's political participation also differed in significant ways in the three polities. As we saw in the last chapter, French revolutionaries, unlike their English and American predecessors, were silent about the aesthetics of domesticity, both because of the liberal separation between a public sphere of state intervention and a private sphere of individual liberty, and because it was not understood to matter politically. It is crucial, therefore, not to conflate the everyday, the embodied, the ritualized, and the domestic. American and French revolutionaries shared a preoccupation with the first three; but they parted ways on the fourth. And this parting of ways had crucial implications for both the gendering of politics and the concrete manifestations of the abstract divide between the public and private.

Women in post-revolutionary England, America and France found themselves excluded from formal politics; but that exclusion worked in different ways. Although American revolutionaries and early nationals, and English political thinkers, were much shyer about state power and state intervention than the French, one could argue that the American politicization of the home was actually far more extensive and intensive than the French, leaving women, even when denied formal political participation, a sense of themselves as actors on the national stage. In France, the politicization of the public was absolute, but the Revolution's commitment to, and definition of, liberty excluded the home, and the women that homes were understood to shelter from politics.

In the United States, women in the nineteenth century translated principles of "republican motherhood" and their experience in the homespun movement, spinning bees, and quilting parties into the creation of both women's clubs and participation in the Abolitionist movements.[18] Out of those, in turn, later grew other social movements, including the struggle for suffrage. In France, by contrast, when

Frenchwomen were forced out of the political sphere, first within the Revolution and then by the Napoleonic Code, the domestic world to which they returned was depoliticized, radically privatized, and individualized. There were no quilting bees, no women's clubs (one should, however, note the revival of salon culture); and although there were some brilliant feminist theorists, there was no substantial women's movement until very late. Britain, in this case, looks more like its former colony than its neighbor across the channel. Although women's participation in the English revolution was very different from that in the American, the combined moralizing-politicizing of the home, in combination with the possibilities for independent reflection, writing and speech offered by radical Protestantism, provided women a foundation upon which their claims to a political voice would be made.

The revolutions that ushered in the modern age did not invent a new world *ex nihilo*; they each built upon their inherited repertoires of political and cultural forms. But something radical did, indeed, happen. Modern nation-states are fundamentally different from those that preceded them in their commitment to capitalism, to mass suffrage, to mass armies, to freedom from excessive state intrusion, and to the principle of equality before the law. They all, therefore, faced, and continue to this day to face, the problem of creating loyalty in a polity in which people do not know each other, often do not come from shared cultures, and are not emotionally compelled by love for a paternal monarch, and in which they are divided by the inequities and heterogeneity of market-driven economies. Nation-states continue, in fact, to create national culture, well beyond the world of monuments, national holidays, postage stamps and coins. There continue to be distinctive national modes of dressing, moving, talking, and eating. Those are, however, fading rapidly, challenged by transnational forces, particularly those of religion and mass culture. The differing reactions of each of the three nation-states discussed here demonstrate the continued power of each nation's revolutionary heritage.

The French state very actively pursues a policy of national cultural hegemony. State subsidies are provided only for publications in French; a minimum percentage of songs played on national radio stations must be in French; the school curriculum remains national and uniform; the state invests heavily in museums and theaters; and recent French presidents have chosen to leave a cultural institution as their legacy. It is important to underscore here that the state has the power to shape culture because it invests in it. The United States presents a different picture. The decentralization and privatization of cultural production in the United States remains very great. Questions of language use are decided locally, not nationally, as are virtually all matters of education. Because the very definition of "the public" is different, most cultural institutions rely on private donations and philanthropy. Thus "National Public Radio" in the United States spends substantial air time, volunteer and staff labor, and money on fund-raising, while in France public radio is paid for by tax revenues. Britain, until the end of the twentieth century, had a hybrid model, with strong state cultural provision combined with both private philanthropy and local control. In recent decades the national state's share has been systematically shrinking. The seeming paradox of this situation is that, despite the very weak state presence in the production of culture in the United States, there is a very definable and tangible "American culture"; and despite the very strong presence of the state in the production of "French culture," that culture seems to be far more fragile. The paradox, of course, is easy to explain: the rapid movement of goods and people in the contemporary world, combined with economies of scale, means that "national" cultures in polities the size of France are virtually impossible to protect from hybridization. But, as the example of the recent controversy over Muslim headscarves in all three polities indicates, national differences in the definition of the "public" and the "private" persist, and powerfully shape national cultural policy.

A significant number of girls and women in France, Britain and the United States have chosen, in recent years, to cover their heads in public. The forms of the headcoverings have varied, as have the explanations given for why they are being worn. More dramatic, however, is the range of reaction. In the United States and Britain the general stance has been that headcovering is a matter of individual choice, a question of private behavior, and a domain where, in addition, freedom of religion must govern. Even when headcoverings are worn "in public" – that is, in schools, government offices, on the street, or at the mall – they are private because they are a matter of individual choice. In France, by contrast, headcoverings are "private" only when they are at home, in a bus, in a park, or in a shop. All governmentally subsidized institutions – schools, hospitals, post offices, universities, etc. – are by definition "public," and therefore a terrain in which behavior must conform to the state's definition of appropriate French behavior. In the twenty-first century neither the French, nor any other modern state, including China, can effectively control culture; all, however continue to struggle with the complex legacies of the cultural revolutions that opened the modern era.

Notes

Chapter 1   The First Cultural Revolutions

1. I acknowledge that some scholars argue that it is precisely in those preoccupations with culture that the dark side of modernity lay, presaging the excesses of later revolutionary moments. See for example, Dorinda Outram, *The Body and the French Revolution: Sex, Class and Political Culture* (New Haven, CT: Yale University Press, 1988) and Zygmunt Bauman, *Modernity and the Holocaust* (Ithaca, NY: Cornell University Press, 1989).
2. For crucial conceptual work on the relation of politics, emotion, and nation see Lauren Berlant, *The Anatomy of National Fantasy: Hawthorne, Utopia, and Everyday Life* (Chicago: Chicago University Press, 1991) and Lauren Berlant (ed.), *Intimacy* (Chicago: Chicago University Press, 2000).
3. There is little scholarship that conceptualizes the place of culture in the English, American or French revolutions as "cultural revolution." On this point see Lynn Hunt, "Introduction: The French Revolution in Culture: New Approaches and Perspectives," *Eighteenth Century Studies* 22, no. 3 (Spring 1989): 293–301. There are, however, a few important texts that do: Philip Corrigan and Derek Sayer, *The Great Arch: English State Formation as Cultural Revolution* (Oxford and New York: Basil Blackwell, 1985); Dror Wahrman and Colin Jones (eds), *The Age of Cultural Revolutions: Britain and France, 1750–1820* (Berkeley, CA: University of California Press, 2002). Cissie Fairchild does not frame her intervention precisely in those terms, but that is the point of "Fashion and Freedom in the French Revolution," *Continuity and Change* 18, no. 3 (2000): 419–33. Key on the cognate, but very different, concept of political culture are: Keith Michael Baker, *Inventing the French Revolution: Essays on French Political Culture in the Eighteenth Century* (Cambridge: Cambridge University Press, 1990) and Keith Michael Baker *et al.*, *The French Revolution and the Creation of Modern Political Culture* (Oxford: Pergamon Press, 1987–94). Important comparatively and conceptually is the work in the Russian context: Katerina Clark, *Petersburg, Crucible of Cultural Revolution* (Cambridge, MA: Harvard University Press, 1995); Sheila Fitzpatrick (ed.), *Cultural Revolution in Russia, 1928–1931* (Bloomington, IN: Indiana University Press, 1977); Sheila Fitzpatrick, *The Cultural Front: Power and Culture in Revolutionary Russia* (Ithaca, NY: Cornell University Press, 1992); Richard Stites, "Russian Revolutionary Culture: Its Place in the History of Cultural Revolutions," in *Culture and Revolution,* ed.

Paul Dukes and John Dunkley (London: Pinter Publishers, 1990); Richard Stites, *Revolutionary Dreams: Utopian Vision and Experimental Life in the Russian Revolution* (Oxford: Oxford University Press, 1989).

4. Ernest Renan, "What is a Nation?" in *Nations and Identities*, ed. Vincent P. Pecora (London: Blackwell, 2001), pp. 162–77. Also see Benedict Anderson, *Imagined Communities: Reflections on the Origin and Spread of Nationalism* (London: Verso, 1983).

5. Fairchild's "Fashion and Freedom" provides a concise and incisive intervention.

6. Deborah Gould, *Feeling Activism: Emotions and Reason in ACT UP's Fight Against AIDS* (Chicago: University of Chicago Press, 2007); William M. Reddy, *The Navigation of Feeling: A Framework for the History of Emotions* (New York: Cambridge University Press, 2001). Jeff Goodwin, James Jasper, and Francesca Polletta (eds), *Passionate Politics: Emotions and Social Movements* (Chicago: University of Chicago Press, 2001).

7. Pierre Bourdieu, *Distinction: A Social Critique of the Judgment of Taste*, trans. Richard Nice (Cambridge, MA: Harvard University Press, 1984); Mihaly Csikszentmihalyi and Eugene Rochberg-Halton, *The Meaning of Things: Domestic Symbols and the Self* (Cambridge: Cambridge University Press, 1981); and Serge Tisseron, *Comment l'esprit vient aux objets* (Paris: Aubier, 1999).

8. Given parallels between the English and the Dutch economic, political and religious transformations in the seventeenth century, it is arguable that the book should also have included that story. See, particularly: Simon Schama, *The Embarrassment of Riches: An Interpretation of Dutch Culture in the Golden Age* (Berkeley: University of California Press, 1988) and Jonathan I. Israel, *The Dutch Republic: Its Rise, Greatness and Fall 1477–1806* (New York: Oxford University Press, 1995). It was, however, simply more than could be taken on here.

9. For an insightful discussion of the different ways the concept of culture has been invoked even by anthropologists, see William H. Sewell, "The Concept(s) of Culture," in *Beyond the Cultural Turn: New Directions in the Study of Society and Culture*, ed. Lynn Hunt and Victoria Bonnell (Berkeley, CA: University of California Press, 1999), pp. 35–61.

10. For England see Christopher Hill (ed.), *The English Revolution of 1640: Three Essays* (London: Lawrence and Wishart, 1940), and his *The World Turned Upside Down: Radical Ideas in the English Revolution* (New York: Viking, 1972); R. H. Tawney, "The Rise of the Gentry," *Economic History Review* 11, no. 1 (1941): 1–38. The classics on the French Revolution are Ernest Labrousse, *La crise de l'économie française à la fin de l'ancien régime et au début de la Révolution* (Paris: Presses Universitaires de France, 1944); Georges Lefebvre, *Quatre-vingt-neuf* (Paris: Maison du Livre Français, 1939); and Albert Soboul, *Les Sans-Culottes de l'an II* (Paris: Librairie Clavreuil, 1958). A useful review

is Geoffrey Ellis, "The 'Marxist Interpretation' of the French Revolution," *English Historical Review* 93, no. 367 (April 1978): 353–76. The historiography of the American Revolution has used the synonymous language of "propertied men" rather than bourgeois: see Gordon S. Wood, *The Creation of the American Republic, 1776–1787* (Chapel Hill, NC: University of North Carolina Press, 1969).

11. For England, an elegant summary is Lawrence Stone, "The Bourgeois Revolution of Seventeenth-Century England Revisited," *Past and Present* 109 (November 1985): 44–54. For a sympathetic critique of Hill in particular, see David Underdown, "Puritanism, Revolution, and Christopher Hill," *The History Teacher* 22, no. 1 (November 1988): 67–75. For the French Revolution see Alfred Cobban, *Social Interpretation of the French Revolution* (Cambridge: Cambridge University Press, 1964); François Furet, *Interpreting the French Revolution*, trans. Elborg Forster (Cambridge: Cambridge University Press, 1981); David Garrioch, *The Formation of the Parisian Bourgeoisie, 1690–1830* (Cambridge: Cambridge University Press, 1996); George Taylor, "Non-Capitalist Wealth and the Origins of the French Revolution," *American Historical Review* 72 (1967): 469–96.

12. Colin Jones, "Bourgeois Revolution Revivified: 1789 and Social Change," in *Re-writing the French Revolution*, ed. Colin Lucas (Oxford: Oxford University Press, 1991), pp. 69–118; Colin Jones, "The Great Chain of Buying: Medical Advertisement, The Bourgeois Public Sphere, and the Origins of the French Revolution," *American Historical Review* 101 (February 1996): 13–40; Cissie Fairchilds, "The Production and Marketing of Populuxe Goods in Eighteenth-century Paris," in *Consumption and the World of Goods*, ed. John Brewer and Roy Porter (London: Routledge, 1993), pp. 228–48; Robert Forster, *Merchants, Landlords, Magistrates: The Depont Family in the Eighteenth Century* (Baltimore, MD: Johns Hopkins University Press, 1980).

13. Sarah Maza, *The Myth of the French Bourgeoisie: An Essay on the Social Imaginary, 1750–1850* (Cambridge, MA: Harvard University Press, 2003).

14. References to historiography on particular aspects of this may be found in Chapter 5. The key theoretical text is Jürgen Habermas, *The Structural Transformation of the Public Sphere: An Inquiry into a Category of Bourgeois Society*, trans. Thomas Burger (Cambridge, MA: MIT Press, 1989). T. C. W. Blanning, *The Culture of Power and the Power of Culture: Old Regime Europe 1660–1789* (Oxford: Oxford University Press, 2002) provides a broad historical analysis.

15. T. H. Breen, *The Marketplace of Revolution: How Consumer Politics Shaped American Independence* (Oxford: Oxford University Press, 2004).

16. For the importance of sensationalism in France see Jan Goldstein, *The Post-Revolutionary Self: Politics and Psyche in France, 1750–1850* (Cambridge, MA: Harvard University Press, 2005); John C. O'Neal, *The Authority of*

Experience: Sensationalist Theory in the French Enlightenment (University Park, PA: Pennsylvania State University Press, 1996).

17. See, however, the essays in Geoff Eley and William Hunt (eds), *Reviving the English Revolution: Reflections and Elaborations on the Work of Christopher Hill* (London and New York: Verso, 1988). The literary critic James Holstun has written a Marxist analysis of the revolution, focusing on the poor: *Ehud's Dagger: Class Struggle in the English Revolution* (London: Verso, 2000); and although not defining itself explicitly as such, see also Robert Brenner, *Merchants and Revolution: Commercial Change, Political Conflict, and London's Overseas Traders 1550–1653* (Princeton, NJ: Princeton University Press, 1993).

18. Joan Thirsk, *Economic Policy and Projects: The Development of a Consumer Society in Early Modern England* (Oxford: Clarendon Press, 1978), especially Chapter 8; Linda Levy Peck, *Consuming Splendour: Society and Culture in Seventeenth-Century England* (Cambridge: Cambridge University Press, 2005); Carole Shammas, "Changes in English and Anglo-American Consumption from 1550 to 1800," in *Consumption and the World of Goods*, ed. John Brewer and Roy Porter (London: Routledge, 1993), pp. 179–80. Robert Brenner also supports the argument for an expanded market in seventeenth-century England, but does not argue that it resulted in a consumer society: Brenner, *Merchants and Revolution*. The argument for the later dating may be found in Neil McKendrick, John Brewer and J. H. Plumb (eds), *The Birth of a Consumer Society: The Commercialization of Eighteenth-Century England* (London: Europa Publications Limited, 1982); Carole Shammas, *The Pre-Industrial Consumer in England and America* (Oxford: Oxford University Press, 1991); Beverly Lemire, "'A Good Stock of Cloaths': The Changing Market for Cotton Clothing in Britain, 1750–1800," *Textile History* 22, no. 2 (1991): 311–28; Peter N. Stearns, "Stages of Consumerism: Recent Work on the Issues of Periodization," *Journal of Modern History* 69 (March 1997): 102–17.

19. Joan B. Landes, *Women and the Public Sphere in the Age of the French Revolution* (Ithaca, NY: Cornell University Press, 1988); Carole Pateman, *The Sexual Contract* (Stanford, CA: Stanford University Press, 1988); Lynn Hunt, *The Family Romance of the French Revolution* (Berkeley, CA: University of California Press, 1992); Joan Wallach Scott, *Only Paradoxes to Offer: French Feminists and the Rights of Man* (Cambridge, MA: Harvard University Press, 1996); Geneviève Fraisse, *Reason's Muse: Sexual Difference and the Birth of Democracy*, trans. Jean Marie Todd (Chicago: University of Chicago Press, 1994); Linda Kerber, *Women of the Republic: Intellect and Ideology in Revolutionary America* (Chapel Hill, NC: University of North Carolina Press, 1980); Linda Kerber, *No Constitutional Right To Be Ladies: Women and the Obligations of Citizenship* (New York: Hill and Wang, 1998), Chapter 1; Ruth Bloch, *Gender and Morality in Anglo-American Culture* (Berkeley, CA: University of California Press, 2001), Chapters 3, 7 and 8.

20. Michael Walzer, *The Revolution of the Saints: A Study in the Origins of Radical Politics* (New York: Atheneum, 1965), p. 14.

21. Leora Auslander, *Taste and Power: Furnishing Modern France* (Berkeley: University of California Press, 1996), part III; Leora Auslander, "Women's Suffrage, Citizenship Law and National Identity: Gendering the Nation-State in France and Germany, 1871–1918," in Patricia Grimshaw, Katie Holmes and Marilyn Lake, eds. *Women's Rights and Human Rights: International Historical Perspectives* (London: Macmillan, 2001), pp. 138–152.

22. Although the "Atlantic world" of *Cultural Revolutions* often diverges from the interpretations in the following, they have provided essential inspiration: Carla Pestana, *The English Atlantic in an Age of Revolution, 1640–1661* (Cambridge, MA: Harvard University Press, 2004); Nicholas Canny and Anthony Padgen (eds), *Colonial Identity in the Atlantic World, 1500–1800* (Princeton, NJ: Princeton University Press, 1987); Nicholas Canny, "The British Atlantic World: Working Towards a Definition," *The Historical Journal* 33, no. 2 (1990): 479–97; Peter Linebaugh and Marcus Rediker, *The Many-Headed Hydra: Sailors, Slaves and Commoners, and the Hidden History of the Revolutionary Atlantic* (Boston: Beacon Press, 2000); David Armitage, "Making the Empire British: Scotland in the Atlantic World, 1542–1707," *Past and Present* 155 (May 1997): 34–63; David Geggus, *The Impact of the Haitian Revolution in the Atlantic World* (Columbia, SC: University of South Carolina Press, 2001); David Hancock, "The British Atlantic World: Coordination, Complexity, and the Emergence of the Atlantic Market Economy, 1651–1815," *Itinerario* (Autumn 1999): 107–26.

23. In thinking about the problems and possibilities of writing a history that compares, juxtaposes and entangles I have found the following particularly useful: Michael Werner and Bénédicte Zimmermann, "Penser l'histoire croisée: entre empirie et réflexivité," *Annales: HSS* 1 (janvier–février 2003): 7–36; Marcel Detienne, *Comparer l'incomparable* (Paris: Editions du Seuil, 2000); Eric Fassin, "Fearful Symmetry: Culturalism and Cultural Comparison after Tocqueville," *French Historical Studies* 19, no. 2 (Autumn 1995): 451–60; Deborah Cohen and M. O'Connor (eds), *Comparison and History* (New York: Routledge, 2004).

24. For the full elaboration of this argument (and theoretical references) see Leora Auslander, "Beyond Words," *American Historical Review* 110 no. 4 (October 2005): 1015–45.

Chapter 2 Ermine and Buckskins: Culture and Politics in Early Modern Courtly and Colonial Society

1. My analysis here has been influenced by Norbert Elias, *The Court Society*, trans. Edmund Jephcott (New York: Pantheon, 1983).

2. Roger Chartier, "Introduction to Part II," in *A History of Private Life III: Passions of the Renaissance*, ed. Roger Chartier, trans. Arthur Goldhammer (Cambridge, MA: Harvard University Press, 1989), p. 163.

3. Although England had a larger immigrant population than did France in this period, and the movement of people within the archipelago greatly complicates the story, as do the dynamics among England, Ireland, Scotland, and Wales. For England on this issue see Laura Hunt Yungblut, S*trangers Settled Here Amongst Us – Policies, Perceptions and the Presence of Aliens in Elizabethan England* (London: Routledge, 1996). For France see Peter Sahlins, *Unnaturally French: Foreign Citizens in the Old Regime and After* (Ithaca, NY: Cornell University Press, 2004).

4. Louis de Rouvroy de Saint-Simon, *The Memoirs of the Duke de Saint-Simon: Volume V*, trans. Francis Arkwright (New York: Brentano's, 1915), pp. 276–8.

5. For bibliography and analysis of the recent literature on governance in Old Regime France see Peter R. Campbell, "Review: New Light on Old Regime Politics," *The Historical Journal* 40, no. 3 (September 1997): 835–43, and Colin Jones, "Political Styles and Power in *Ancien Régime* France," *The Historical Journal* 41, no. 4 (December 1998): 1173–82.

6. For French finance see Michael Kwass, *Privilege and the Politics of Taxation: Liberté, Égalité, Fiscalité* (Cambridge: Cambridge University Press, 2000); for a succinct overview see Richard Bonney, "What's New about the New French Fiscal History," *Journal of Modern History* 70, no. 3 (September 1998): 639–67. For venal office see William Doyle, *Venality: The Sale of Offices in Eighteenth-Century France* (Oxford: Clarendon Press, 1996); Hilton Root, *The Fountain of Privilege: Political Foundations of Markets in Old Regime France and England* (Berkeley, CA: University of California, 1994).

7. For court culture and patronage systems in seventeenth-century England and France see Linda Levy Peck, *Court Patronage and Corruption in Early Stuart England* (London and Boston: Unwin Hyman, 1990); R. Malcolm Smuts, *Court Culture and the Origins of a Royalist Tradition in Early Stuart England* (Philadelphia: University of Pennsylvania Press, 1987); Eveline Cruickshanks (ed.), *The Stuart Courts* (Stroud: Sutton, 2000). A helpful review essay of some of the literature of the previous decade is Martin Butler, "Early Court Culture: Compliment or Criticism?" *The Historical Journal* 32, no. 2 (June 1989): 425–35. Also see Sharon Kettering, *Patrons, Brokers, and Clients in Seventeenth-century France* (New York: Oxford University Press, 1986); Sara E. Chapman, *Private Ambition and Political Alliances. The Phélypeaux de Pontchartrain Family and Louis XIV's Government, 1650–1715* (Rochester, NY and Woodbridge, Suffolk, UK: University of Rochester Press, 2004); William Beik, *Absolutism and Society in Seventeenth-Century France: State Power and Provincial Aristocracy in Languedoc* (Cambridge: Cambridge University Press, 1988); Jay M. Smith (ed.), *The French Nobility in the Eighteenth Century: Reassessments and*

Reinterpretations (University Park, PA: Pennsylvania State University Press, 2006).

8. David L. Smith, "The Impact on Government," in *The Impact of the English Civil War*, ed. John Morrill (London: Collins and Brown, 1991), p. 32.

9. Although Glenn Burgess has argued that it came very close. See his *Absolute Monarchy and the Stuart Constitution* (New Haven, CT: Yale University Press, 1996).

10. Nicholas Henshall, *The Myth of Absolutism: Change and Continuity in Early Modern European Monarchy* (London and New York: Longman, 1992); Jay M. Smith, *The Culture of Merit: Nobility, Royal Service and the Making of Absolute Monarchy in France* (Ann Arbor, MI: University of Michigan Press, 1996); Bernard Vonglis, *L'Etat c'etait bien lui: essai sur la monarchie absolue* (Paris: Cujas, 1997).

11. Sarah Hanley, *The Lit de Justice of the Kings of France: Constitutional Ideology in Legend, Ritual and Discourse* (Princeton, NJ: Princeton University Press, 1983).

12. Jeffrey Merrick, *Order and Disorder under the Ancien Régime* (Newcastle on Tyne: Scholars Publishing, 2007); Katherine Crawford, *Perilous Performances: Gender and Regency in Early Modern France* (Cambridge, MA: Harvard University Press, 2004); Louis A. Montrose, *The Subject of Elizabeth: Authority, Gender, and Representation* (Chicago: University of Chicago Press, 2006).

13. Ralph Giesey, *Rulership in France 15th–17th Centuries* (Aldershot: Ashgate, 2004); Roy C. Strong, *Coronation: A History of Kingship and the English Monarchy* (London: HarperCollins, 2005), and his *Tudor and Stuart Monarchy: Painting, Pageantry, Iconography*, Vol. 3 (Woodbridge UK, Rochester USA: Boydell Press, 1997); David Bergeron, *English Civic Pageantry 1558–1642* (London: Edward Arnold, 1971); David Cressy, *Bonfires and Bells: National Memory and the Protestant Calendar in Elizabethan and Stuart England* (Stroud: Sutton, 2004).

14. Jeffrey Merrick, "The Body Politics of French Absolutism," in *From the Royal to the Republican Body: Incorporating the Political in Seventeenth and Eighteenth-century France,* ed. Sara E. Melzer and Kathryn Norberg (Berkeley, CA: University of California Press, 1998), p. 19; and his *The Desacralization of the French Monarchy in the Eighteenth Century* (Baton Rouge, LA: Louisiana State University Press, 1990).

15. Roger D. Abrahams, "Antick Dispositions and the Perilous Politics of Culture: Costume and Culture in Jacobean England and America," *The Journal of American Folklore* 111, no. 440 (Spring 1998): 119–20. These masques could also provide contexts for negotiation between the aristocracy and the Crown: see David Lindley, "Courtly Play: The Politics of Chapman's *The Memorable Masque,*" in *The Stuart Courts,* ed. Eveline Cruickshanks (Stroud: Sutton, 2000), pp. 42–58.

16. Richard A. Burt, "'Licensed by Authority': Ben Jonson and the Politics of Early Stuart Theater," *English Literary History* 54, no. 3 (Autumn 1987): 529–60, esp. 529–31 and 540; Jennifer Woodward, *The Theater of Death: The Ritual Management of Royal Funerals in Renaissance England, 1570–1625* (Rochester, NY: Boydell Press, 1997).

17. Merrick, "The Body Politics of French Absolutism," p. 19. See also Jean-Claude Daufresne, *Le Louvre et les Tuileries: Architectures de fêtes et d'apparat: Architectures ephémères* (Paris: Mengès, 1994).

18. Images of many Stuart and Bourbon coins are available online: "Charles I gold crown – 1632–1641" and "Charles I shilling 1635–1639" (www.predecimal. com/p6stuart.php); "Charles I farthing – Richmond issue 1625–1634" and "Charles I halfcrown 1625–1642" (www.kenelks.co.uk/coins/stuart/stuart.htm); "Seventeenth-century trade token" (http://witneyblanketstory.org.uk/WBP. asp?navigationPage=Brief%20history); "Silver coin of Louis XIV, dated 1674," (http://en.wikipedia.org/wiki/Image:Louis_XIV_Coin.jpg). They may also be seen in the collections of the Louvre and the British Museum.

19. Image of "James I gold unite – Second coinage 1604–1619" available online: (http://www.predecimal.com/p6stuart.htm).

20. H. Hoffmann, *Les monnaies royales de France depuis Hugues Capet jusqu'à Louis XVI* (Paris: H. Hoffmann, 1878), planche 102; Victor Gadoury, *Les monnaies royales françaises de Louis XIII à Louis XVI: 1610–1792* (Monte Carlo: V. Gadoury, 1978).

21. Gay L. Gullickson, *Spinners and Weavers of Auffay: Rural Industry and the Sexual Division of Labor in a French Village, 1750–1850* (Cambridge: Cambridge University Press, 1986).

22. See for example: *By the King a Proclamation Concerning the Execution of the Lawes against Recusants* (London: Bonham Norton and Iohn Bill, Printers to the Kings most Excellent Maiestie [*sic*], 1626–1627) M.DC.XXVI; *By the King: A Proclamation Concerning the Trade of Ginney, and Binney, in the Parts of Africa* (London: Robert Barker, printer to the Kings most excellent Maiestie and by the assignes of Iohn Bill [*sic*], 1631). These and hundreds more may be viewed on the Early English Books website.

23. Frederick Siebert, *Freedom of the Press in England 1476–1776* (Urbana, IL: University of Illinois Press, 1952); Tim Harris "Propaganda and Public Opinion in Seventeenth-Century England," in *Media and Revolution*, ed. Jeremy D. Popkin (Lexington, KY: University Press of Kentucky, 1995); Barbara de Negroni, *Lectures interdites: Le travail des censures au XVIIIe siècle, 1723–1774* (Paris: Albin Michel, 1995).

24. Jenny Andersen and Elizabeth Sauer (eds), *Books and Readers in Early Modern England: Material Studies* (Philadelphia: University of Pennsylvania Press, 2002); Tessa Watt, *Cheap Print and Popular Piety, 1550–1640* (Cambridge: Cambridge University Press, 1991).

25. Adam Fox, "Rumour, News and Popular Political Opinion in Elizabeth and Early Stuart England," *The Historical Journal* 40, no. 3 (September 1997): 597–620.

26. Robert Darnton, *The Forbidden Best-Sellers of Pre-Revolutionary France* (New York: W. W. Norton, 1995); Robert Darnton, *The Literary Underground of the Old Regime* (Cambridge, MA: Harvard University Press, 1982); Thierry Rigogne, *Between State and Market: Printing and Bookselling in Eighteenth-Century France* (Oxford: Voltaire Foundation, 2007).

27. David Bell has persuasively demonstrated that both national sentiment and nationalism predated the Revolution in France, but that the source of those feelings was the Church rather than the State: David A. Bell, *The Cult of the Nation in France: Inventing Nationalism, 1680–1800* (Cambridge, MA: Harvard University Press, 2001). See also Colette Beaune, *The Birth of an Ideology: Myths and Symbols of Nation in Late-medieval France*, trans. Susan Ross Huston (Berkeley: University of California Press, 1991).

28. See Yungblut, S*trangers Settled Here Amongst Us.* On French regional diversity in the eighteenth century see Alan Forrest, *Paris, the Provinces, and the French Revolution* (London: Arnold, 2004), Chapters 2 and 3.

29. Paula Blank, *Broken English: Dialects and the Politics of Language in Renaissance Writings* (New York: Routledge, 1996).

30. John Morrill, "The British Problem, c.1534–1707," in *The British Problem c. 1534–1707: State Formation in the Atlantic Archipelago,* ed. Brandan Bradshaw and John Morrill (New York: Palgrave, 1996), p. 3.

31. Michel de Certeau *et al.*, *Une politique de la langue: La Révolution française et les patois* (Paris: Editions Gallimard, 1975).

32. Ronald Edward Zupko, *French Weights and Measures before the Revolution: A Dictionary of Provincial and Local Units* (Bloomington, IN: Indiana University Press, 1978); Ronald Edward Zupko, *British Weights & Measures: A History from Antiquity to the Seventeenth Century (*Madison, WI: University of Wisconsin Press, 1977).

33. Keith M. Brown, "The Scottish Aristocracy, Anglicization and the Court, 1603–38," *The Historical Journal* 36, no. 3 (September 1993): 543–76.

34. William Weber, "*La musique ancienne* in the Waning of the *Ancien Régime*," *Journal of Modern History* 56 (March 1984): 58; William Weber, *La musique ancienne in the Waning of the Ancien Régime* (Chicago: University of Chicago Press, 1984).

35. Chandra Mukerji, *Territorial Ambition and the Gardens of Versailles* (Cambridge: Cambridge University Press, 1997), p. 48. See also Elizabeth Hyde, *Cultivated Power: Flowers, Culture and Politics in the Age of Louis XIV* (Philadelphia: University of Pennsylvania Press, 2005).

36. Roy Strong, *The Renaissance Garden in England* (London: Thames and Hudson, 1979), pp. 200–20.

37. Joan B. Landes, *Women and the Public Sphere in the Age of the French Revolution* (Ithaca, NY: Cornell University Press, 1988); Carole Pateman, *The Sexual Contract*, Stanford, CA: Stanford University Press, 1988. The importance in France of salons led by women as a site of debate outside the court is further evidence. For the early period, see Carolyn Lougee, *Le Paradis des Femmes: Women, the Salon and Social Stratification in Seventeenth-Century France* (Princeton, NJ: Princeton University Press, 1976). For the eighteenth century see Dena Goodman, *The Republic of Letters: A Cultural History of the Enlightenment* (Ithaca, NY: Cornell University Press, 2004).

38. Crawford, *Perilous Performances*.

39. Linda Levy Peck, "The Language of Patronage: A Discourse of Connection," in her *Court Patronage and Corruption in Early Stuart England* (London: Unwin Hyman, 1990), pp. 12–29.

40. Robert Brenner, *Merchants and Revolution: Commercial Change, Political Conflict, and London's Overseas Traders 1550–1653* (Princeton, NJ: Princeton University Press, 1993), pp. 199–200.

41. R. Malcolm Smuts, "Art and the Material Culture of Majesty in Early Stuart England," in *The Stuart Court and Europe*, ed. R. Malcolm Smuts (New York: Cambridge University Press, 1996), p. 93; Smuts, *Court Culture*, p. 5.

42. James H. Johnson, "Musical Experience and the Formation of a French Musical Public," *Journal of Modern History* (June 1992): 201–202. See also, James H. Johnson, *Listening in Paris: A Cultural History* (Berkeley, CA: University of California Press, 1995).

43. Weber, *"La musique ancienne,"* p. 59.

44. Richard Ollard, *The Image of the King: Charles I and Charles II* (New York: Atheneum, 1979), p. 33.

45. Hart Vaughan, "On Inigo Jones and the Stuart Legal Body: Justice and Equity … and Proportions Appertaining," in *Body and Building: Essays on the Changing Relation of Body and Architecture*, ed. George Dodds and Robert Tavernor (Cambridge, MA: MIT Press, 2002), p. 145. I am grateful to Meredith Ries for bringing this to my attention.

46. For an example of a tapestry that was moved with Charles I as the court migrated from palace to palace see Mortlake Tapestry Factory, *Tapestry from the story of Vulcan*, 1620–1625 (Victoria and Albert Museum, London), Museum number T.170-1978. Online at http://images.vam.ac.uk.

47. Alan Hunt, *Governance of the Consuming Passions: A History of Sumptuary Law* (New York: St. Martins Press, 1996), pp. 90–1; Philip Mansell, *Dressed to Rule: Royal and Court Costume from Louis XIV to Elizabeth II* (New Haven, CT: Yale University Press, 2005); Jennifer M. Jones, *Sexing La Mode: Gender, Fashion and Commercial Culture in Old Regime France* (Oxford: Berg, 2004), Part I; Caroline Weber, *Queen of Fashion: What Marie Antoinette Wore to the Revolution* (New York: H. Holt, 2006).

48. For quote see *The Lord Keeper's seal cup,* 1626–1627 (Victoria and Albert Museum, London), museum number M.59:1,2-1993. Online at http://images.vam.ac.uk. See also the museum's *Cup and cover,* REPRO.1888B/1,2-635. For royal miniatures viewable at the Victoria and Albert museum website, see Sr. Balthazar Gerbier, *Portrait miniature of Charles I*, ca. 1618–1620, museum number: P.47.1935; Isaac Oliver, *Portrait miniature of Henry Frederick Prince of Wales, ca. 1612,* museum number P.149-1910. For engraved silver medallions see Simon de Passe, *Medallion of Charles, Prince of Wales,* 1616, museum number 961-1904; Simon de Passe, *Medallion of King James I, Anne of Denmark, and Charles Prince of Wales,* 1616–1620, museum number 062-1904. For a commemorative object, see the clock made by David Ramsay, which showed James I with his two sons holding the Pope's nose to a grindstone, c.1610–1615, museum number M.7-1931. For France see Antoine-François Callet, *Louis XVI*, oil on canvas, 1789 (Collection du musée d'art Roger-Quilliot, Ville de Clermont-Ferrand, photo: Musée Roger-Quilliot, Clermont-Ferrand). May be seen on the web site of the Royal Academy of Arts: http://www.royalacademy.org.uk/exhibitions/citizensandkings/portraits-of-sovereigns-and-heads-of-state,318,AR.html. For an engraved print (that would have existed in multiple copies and could have been diffused) see *Portrait of Louis XVI,* 1790, engraving by Charles Clément Balvay, after a painting by Antoine-François Callet), May be seen at http://commons.wikimedia.org. For examples of furniture see the collections in the Louvre and the Musée des Arts Décoratifs in Paris as well as the furnishings in Versailles. Many examples may be seen online. For example: *Guéridon,* 1669: Philippe Caffiéri, sculptor and La Baronnière may be seen on the website of the Louvre. http://www.louvre.fr/llv/oeuvres/alaune.jsp?bmLocale=en; An example of a diplomatic gift is the gold enameled snuff box depicting Louis XV and Maria Leckzinska made by Daniel Govaers (known as Gouvers before 1754) and Jean-Baptiste Massé (The Louvre, Paris), museum number 1725l. © R.M.N. Online at http://www.louvre.fr/llv/oeuvres. Also see David Howarth, *Images of Rule: Art and Politics in the English Renaissance, 1485–1640* (Berkeley, CA: University of California Press, 1997); Thomas N. Corns (ed.), *The Royal Image: Representations of Charles I* (Cambridge: Cambridge University Press, 1999), p. 49. See for example, Hubert le Sueur, *Bust of Charles I,* Marble, 1631 (Victoria and Albert Museum, London), Museum number A. 35-1910. Online at http://images.vam.ac.uk.

50. Peck, *Court Patronage,* pp. 12–29; Valerie Cumming, *Royal Dress: The Image and Reality 1580 to the Present Day* (New York: Holmes and Meier, 1989), pp. 15–26.

51. For examples of luxurious seventeenth-century English court dress see *Portrait of Captain Smart,* 1639 (Victoria and Albert Museum, London), museum number 534-1892. Online at http://images.vam.ac.uk; *Portrait of Dudley, Third Baron North,* c.1615 (Victoria and Albert Museum, London), museum number:

P.4&:1-1948. Online at http://images.vam.ac.uk; Marcus Gheeraerts, *Portrait of Margaret Laton, c.*1620 (Victoria and Albert Museum, London), museum number E. 214-1994. For parallel examples for France, see the online collections at the Louvre.

52. Jonathan Brown, *Kings and Connoisseurs: Collecting Art in Seventeenth-century Europe* (Princeton, NJ: Princeton University Press, 1995); Martin Warnke, *The Court Artist: On the Ancestry of the Modern Artist*, trans. David McLintock (Cambridge: Cambridge University Press, 1993).

53. Smuts, "Art and the Material Culture of Majesty," pp. 92–3, 110.

54. André Castelot, *Queen of France* (New York: Harper & Brothers, 1957), p. 220.

55. Alexandre Pradère, *French Furniture Makers: The Art of the Ebéniste from Louis XIV to the Revolution*, trans. Perran Wood (London: Sotheby's, 1989), p. 26.

56. Orest Ranum, *Paris in the Age of Absolutism* (Bloomington, IN and London: Indiana University Press, 1979), Chapter 5.

57. Simon Thurley, *Whitehall Palace: An Architectural History of the Royal Apartments, 1240–1698* (New Haven, CT: Yale University Press, 1999).

58. J. Newman, "Inigo Jones and the Politics of Architecture," in *Culture and Politics in Early Stuart England*, ed. Kevin Sharpe and Peter Lake (Stanford, CA: Stanford University Press, 1993), pp. 229–57.

59. That said, the Crown was not entirely able to control London's growth, any more than it was completely able to regulate theatrical productions or the press: R. Malcolm Smuts, "The Court and Its Neighborhood: Royal Policy and Urban Growth in the Early Stuart West End," *Journal of British Studies* 30 (April 1991): 117–49.

60. Edouard Pommier, "Versailles, l'image du souverain," in *Les lieux de mémoire Vol. 2: La Nation,* ed. Pierre Nora (Paris: Gallimard, 1986), p. 193.

61. Mukerji, *Territorial Ambition.*

62. Guy Walton, *Louis XIV's Versailles* (Chicago: University of Chicago Press, 1986); Vincent Maroteaux, *Versailles: Le roi et son domaine* (Paris: Picard, 2000), and Gérard Sabatier, *Versailles ou la figure du roi* (Paris: Albin Michel, 1999).

63. Anne-Marie Lecoq, "La symbolique de l'Etat: Les images de la monarchie des premiers Valois à Louis XIV," in *Les lieux de mémoire Vol. 2: La Nation*, ed. Pierre Nora (Paris: Gallimard, 1986), p. 201.

64. Natacha Coquery, *L'espace de pouvoir: de la demeure privé à l'edifice public, Paris 1700–1790* (Paris: Seli Arslan, 2000) and Katie Scott, *The Rococo Interior: Decoration and Social Spaces in early Eighteenth-century Paris* (New Haven, CT: Yale University Press, 1995).

65. For the French part of this story, see Pradère, *French Furniture Makers.*

66. Roland E. Mousnier, *The Institutions of France under the Absolute Monarchy 1598–1789: Society and the State*, trans. Brian Pearce (Chicago: University of Chicago Press, 1979), pp. 153–90.

67. Lecoq, "La symbolique de l'Etat," pp. 156–8.

68. This issue will be further discussed in Chapter 5. See, however, in addition to the salon literature cited above and that in Chapter 1, Daniel Gordon, *Citizens without Sovereignty: Equality and Sociability in French Thought, 1670–1789* (Princeton, NJ: Princeton University Press, 1994); John Shovlin, *The Political Economy of Virtue: Luxury, Patriotism, and the Origins of the French Revolution* (Ithaca, NY: Cornell University Press, 2006).

69. Margaret Spufford, *The Great Reclothing of Rural England: Petty Chapmen and their Wares in Seventeenth-Century England* (London: Hambledon Press, 1984); see also the references in Chapter 1.

70. Gullickson, *Spinners and Weavers*, p. 35.

71. Daniel Roche, *The People of Paris,* trans. Marie Evans (Berkeley, CA: University of California Press, 1987), pp. 150–1.

72. Cissie Fairchilds, "Fashion and Freedom in the French Revolution," *Continuity and Change* 18, no. 3 (2000): 419–33.

73. For the latter point see: David Starkey, "Representation through Intimacy," in *Symbols and Sentiments: Cross-cultural Studies in Symbolism*, ed. Joan Lewis, (London: Academic Press, 1977). For political pornography see Lynn Hunt, ed., *Eroticism and the Body Politic* (Baltimore, MD: Johns Hopkins University Press, 1990) and Antoine de Baecque, *La caricature révolutionnaire* (Paris: Editions du CNRS, 1988), and his *The Body Politic: Corporeal Metaphor in Revolutionary France, 1770–1800*, trans. Charlotte Mandell (Stanford, CA: Stanford University Press, 1997).

74. "Edit sur la réforme des habits (1): Paris, 12 juillet, 1549," in *Recueil générale des anciennes lois françaises*, vol. 13 (Paris: Belin-le-prieur, 1828), p. 102.

75. Sarah Maza, *Servants and Masters in Eighteenth-century France: The Uses of Loyalty* (Princeton, NJ: Princeton University Press, 1983).

76. "Edit sur la réforme des habits," pp. 103–4.

77. N. B. Harte, "State Control of Dress and Social Change in Pre-Industrial England," in *Trade, Government, and Economy in Pre-Industrial England*, ed. D. C. Coleman and A. H. John (London: Weidenfeld and Nicolson, 1976).

78. For quotation and illustration, see the website of the Victoria and Albert Museum (http://images.vam.ac.uk), museum number T.7-1922.

79. Steven L. Kaplan, *Bread, Politics and Political Economy in the Reign of Louis XV*: Vol. 1 (The Hague: Martinus Nijhoff, 1976), p. xxvi.

80. Jean-Yves Bercé, *Revolt and Revolution in Early Modern Europe: An Essay on the History of Political Violence*, trans. Joseph Bergin (New York: St. Martins, 1987).

81. "Déclaration portant règlement pour les habits, et défenses de porter aucuns passemens d'or et d'argent: Paris, 31 mai 1644," in *Receuil générale des anciennes lois françaises*, vol. 17 (Paris: Belin-le-prieur, 1829), p. 41.

82. Cited in Harte, "State Control of Dress," p. 139.

83. Michael Curtin, "A Question of Manners: Status and Gender in Etiquette and Courtesy Books," *Journal of Modern History* 57 (September 1985): 395–423.

84. Roger Chartier, *The Cultural Uses of Print in Early Modern France*, trans. Lydia G. Cochrane (Princeton, NJ: Princeton University Press, 1987), pp. 86–7.

85. Chartier, *The Cultural Use of Print*, p. 96.

86. Jean-Christophe Agnew, *Worlds Apart: The Market and the Theater in Anglo-American Thought, 1550–1750* (Cambridge: Cambridge University Press, 1986), p. 11.

87. On granting of monopoly privileges see: Brenner, *Merchants and Revolution*, p. 48 and passim. Sale of office was also not unknown in England: Charles R. Mayes, "The Sale of Peerages in Early Stuart England," *Journal of Modern History* 29, no. 1 (March 1957): 21–37. For France see Doyle, *Venality.*

88. Recent exponents of this position are Jon Butler, *Becoming America: The Revolution before 1776* (Cambridge, MA: Harvard University Press, 2000), and T. H. Breen, *The Marketplace of Revolution: How Consumer Politics Shaped American Independence* (New York: Oxford University Press, 2004).

89. Richard L. Bushman, *The Refinement of America: Persons, Houses, Cities* (New York: Vintage, 1992). Very different in focus but also stressing the Englishness of the colonists is Eliga H. Gould, *The Persistence of Empire: British Political Culture in the Age of Revolution* (Chapel Hill, NC: University of North Carolina Press, 2000).

90. See the following discussion for relevant citations.

91. David Hackett Fischer, *Albion's Seed: Four British Folkways in America* (New York: Oxford University Press, 1989) is the clearest statement of this argument, although neither I nor many others agree that those "folkways" remained stable in America. It is also the foundation of Bushman's *The Refinement of America.* For a critique of Fischer see Jack P. Greene *et al.*, "Albion's Seed: Four British Folkways in America – A Symposium," *William and Mary Quarterly* 48, no. 2 (April 1991): 224–308. Robert Blair St. George also suggests the instability, both in England and New England, of that division in his *Conversing by Signs: Poetics of Implication in Colonial New England Culture* (Chapel Hill, NC: University of North Carolina Press, 1998), Chapter 1. Also see Henry Glassie, *Pattern in the Material Folk Culture of the Eastern United States* (Philadelphia: University of Pennsylvania Press, 1968).

92. Jack P. Greene, *Peripheries and Center: Constitutional Development in the Extended Polities of the British Empire and the United States, 1607–1788* (Athens, GA: University of Georgia Press, 1986), Chapter 1.

93. For example, Barney Cohn, "Cloth, Clothes and Colonialism: India in the nineteenth century," in *Cloth and the Human Experience*, ed. Annette B. Weiner and Jane Schneider (Washington, DC: Smithsonian Institution Press, 1989); Jean and John Comaroff, "Homemade Hegemony," in their *Ethnography and the Historical Imagination* (Boulder, CO: Westview Press, 1992).

94. Clifford Zink, "Dutch Framed Houses in New York and New Jersey," *Winterthur Portfolio* 22 (1987): 265–94.

95. Roderic H. Blackburn and Ruth Piwonka, *Remembrance of Patria: Dutch Arts and Culture in Colonial America, 1609–1776* (New York: Albany Institute of History and Art, 1988), pp. 36–40; Joyce D. Goodfriend, *Before the Melting Pot: Society and Culture in Colonial New York City, 1664–1730* (Princeton, NJ: Princeton University Press, 1992), p. 213.

96. Neil D. Kamil, "Hidden in Plain Sight: Disappearance and Material Life in Colonial New York," in *American Furniture 1995*, ed. Luke Becherdite and William Hosley (Milwaukee, WI: Distributed by University Press of New England, 1995), pp. 191– 249; Neil P. Kamil, *Fortress of the Soul: Violence, Metaphysics, and Material Life in the New World, 1517–1751* (Baltimore, MD: Johns Hopkins University Press, 2005); Joseph Downs, "The de Forest Collection of Work by Pennsylvania German Craftsmen," *The Metropolitan Museum of Art Bulletin* 29, no. 10 (October 1934): 161, 163–9.

97. Frances Lichten, *Pennsylvania-German Folk Art*, in *The Concise Encyclopedia of American Antiquities*, ed. Helen Comstock (New York: Hawthorn Books, 1965), p. 401.

98. Mark M. Smith, "Culture, Commerce, and Calendar Reform in Colonial America," *The William and Mary Quarterly* 55, no. 4 (1998): 571.

99. Ira Berlin, *Many Thousands Gone: The First Two Centuries of Slavery in America* (Cambridge, MA: Belknap, 1998).

100. E.g. Stanley Elkins, *Slavery: A Problem in American Institutional and Intellectual Life* (Chicago: University of Chicago Press, 1959).

101. Robert E. Desrochers, "'Not Fade Away': The Narrative of Venture Smith, an African American in the Early Republic," *The Journal of American History* 84, no. 1 (1997): 40–66.

102. Shane White, "A Question of Style: Blacks in and around New York City in the Late 18th Century," *The Journal of American Folklore* 102, no. 403 (1989): 30.

103. Harryette Mullen, "African Signs and Spirit Writing," *Callaloo* 19, no. 3 (1995): 672; for the general argument, see 670–89.

104. For architecture, see Leland Ferguson, *Uncommon Ground: Archaeology and Early African America, 1650–1800* (Washington, DC: Smithsonian Institution Press, 1992); John Vlach, *Back of the Big House: The Architecture of Plantation Slavery* (Chapel Hill, NC: University of North Carolina Press, 1993); Thomas R. Wheaton *et al.*, *Yaughan and Curriboo Plantations: Studies*

in Afro-American Archaeology (Atlanta, NJ: National Park Service, 1983). For baskets, see Dale Rosengarten, *Row upon Row: Sea Grass Baskets of the South Carolina Lowcountry* (Columbia, SC: McKissick Museum, University of South Carolina, 1986). For crafts more generally, see Judith Wragg Chase, *Afro-American Art and Craft* (New York: Van Nostrand Reinhold, 1971). For a very helpful survey of the literature, see Theodore C. Landsmark, "Comments on African American Contributions to American Material Life," *Winterthur Portfolio* 33, no. 4 (1998): 261–82.

105. Mullen, "African Signs and Spirit Writing," p. 672.

106. Patricia Samford, "The Archaeology of African-American Slavery and Material Culture," *The William and Mary Quarterly* 53, no. 1 (1996): 107.

107. Shane White, *Somewhat More Independent: The End of Slavery in New York City, 1770–1810* (Athens, GA: University of Georgia Press, 1991), p. xx, Chapter 8.

108. Linda Baumgarten, *What Clothes Reveal: The Language of Clothing in Colonial and Federal America: The Colonial Williamsburg Collection* (Williamsburg, VA: The Colonial Williamsburg Foundation, 2002), p. 136.

109. Ibid., p. 133.

110. Nicholas Cresswell, *The Journal of Nicholas Cresswell, 1774–1777* (Port Washington, NY: Kennikat Press, 1968), p. 19, cited in John Michael Vlach, "Afro-American Domestic Artifacts in Eighteenth-Century Virginia," *Material Culture* 19 (1987): 13.

111. Cecelia Conway, *African Banjo Echoes in Appalachia: A Study of Folk Traditions* (Knoxville, TN: University of Tennessee Press, 1995).

112. Jay D. Edwards, "The Origins of Creole Architecture," *Winterthur Portfolio* 29, no. 2/3 (Summer–Autumn 1994): 155–89.

113. Mechal Sobel, *The World They Made Together: Black and White Values in Eighteenth-Century Virginia* (Princeton, NJ: Princeton University Press, 1987), p. 119.

114. John Michael Vlach, *The AfroAmerican Tradition in Decorative Design* (Athens, GA: University of Georgia Press, 1990), Chapter 8, especially pp. 136–8.

115. Mechal Sobel, *Teach Me Dreams: The Search for Self in the Revolutionary Era* (Princeton, NJ: Princeton University Press, 2000), particularly Chapters 2 and 3.

116. E. Brooks Holifield, "Peace, Conflict, and Ritual in Puritan Congregations," *Journal of Interdisciplinary History* 23 (Winter 1993): 551–70.

117. For details and charters, see The Avalon Project at the Yale Law School, online at http://www.yale.edu/lawweb/avalon. A key analysis of this is Greene, *Peripheries and Center.*

118. Richard R. Beeman, "Deference, Republicanism, and the Emergence of Popular Politics in Eighteenth-Century America," *The William and Mary Quarterly* 49, no. 3 (1992): 412.

119. Ibid., 419.

120. Daniel J. Hulsebosch, *"Imperia in Imperio*: The Multiple Constitutions of Empire in New York, 1750–1777," *Law and History Review* 16, no. 2 (1998): 319–79.

121. T. H. Breen, "English Origins and New World Development: The Case of the Covenanted Militia in Seventeenth-Century Massachusetts," *Past and Present* 57 (November 1972): 74–96.

122. Smith, "Culture, Commerce, and Calendar," p. 577.

123. Elizabeth E. Dunn, "'Grasping at the Shadow': The Massachusetts Currency Debate, 1690–1751," *The New England Quarterly* 71, no. 1 (1998): 54–76.

124. For an interesting discussion of this point, see Hulseboch, *"Imperia in Imperium."*

125. Peter H. Wood, "The Changing Population of the American South: An Overview by Race and Region," in *Powhatan's Mantle: Indians in the Colonial Southeast,* ed. Peter H. Wood, Gregory A. Waselkov and M. Thomas Hatley (Lincoln, NB: University of Nebraska Press, 1999), p. 90.

126. James H. Merrell, "Some Thoughts on Colonial Historians and American Indians," *William and Mary Quarterly* 46, no. 1 (January 1989): 94–119.

127. Fernando Ortiz, *Cuban Counterpoint: Tobacco and Sugar* (New York: Alfred A. Knopf, 1947), p. 102, cited in Charlotte Sussman, "Lismahago's Captivity: Transculturation in *Humphrey Clinker," English Literary History* 61, no. 3 (Autumn 1994): Note 3.

128. Cotton Mather, *India Christiana* (Boston, 1721), pp. 28–9, cited in James Axtell, "The White Indians of Colonial America," *The William and Mary Quarterly* 32, no. 1 (January 1975): 55–6.

129. J. F. D. Smyth, *A Tour of the United States of America* (London: G. Robinson, 1784), pp. 44–5, cited in Vlach, "Afro-American Domestic Artifacts," p. 6.

130. Colin G. Calloway, *New Worlds for Old: Indians, Europeans and the Remaking of Early America* (Baltimore, MD: Johns Hopkins University Press, 1988), p. 49.

131. Louis Martin Sear, "The Puritan and His Indian Ward," *American Journal of Sociology* 22 (July 1916): 80–93.

132. Sarah H. Hill, "Weaving History: Cherokee Baskets from the Springplace Mission," *The William and Mary Quarterly* 53, no. 1 (1996): 115–36, esp. 131–3; William Cronon, *Changes in the Land: Indians, Colonists, and the Ecology of New England* (New York: Hill and Wang, 1983); Axtell, "The White Indians of Colonial America," pp. 55–88; James Axtell, "Colonial America without the Indians: Counterfactual Reflections," *Journal of American History* 73, no. 4 (1987): 981–96; James Axtell, *The Invasion Within: The Contest of Cultures in Colonial North America* (New York: Oxford University Press, 1985); James Axtell, *Natives and Newcomers: The Cultural Origins of North America* (New York: Oxford University Press, 2001).

133. Calloway, *New Worlds for Old*, p. 46, Chapter 3.

134. *Two Broad-Sides Against Tobacco: The First by King James of Famous Memory; his Counterblast to tobacco and the Second transcribed out of that learned Physician Dr. Everard Maynwaringe* (London: John Hancock, 1672), dedication.

135. Axtell, "Colonial America without the Indians."

136. Ibid., p. 982.

137. Ibid., p. 990.

138. Richard Slotkin, *Regeneration through Violence: The Mythology of the American Frontier, 1600–1800* (Middletown, CT: Wesleyan University Press, 1973); Jill Lepore, *The Name of War: King Philip's War and the Origins of American Identity* (New York: Knopf, 1998).

139. Axtell, "Colonial America without the Indians," p. 995.

140. Richard R. Johnson, "The Search for a Usable Indian: An Aspect of the Defence of Colonial New England," *The Journal of American History* 64, no. 3 (1977): 623–51, particularly 625 and 648.

141. James Axtell and William C. Sturtevant, "The Unkindest Cut, or Who Invented Scalping?" *William and Mary Quarterly* 37, no. 3 (July 1980): 451–72.

142. Lester C. Olson, *Emblems of American Community in the Revolutionary Era: A Study in Rhetorical Iconology* (Washington, DC: Smithsonian Institution Press, 1991), p. 109.

143. Philip J. Deloria, Introduction to *Playing Indian* (New Haven, CT: Yale University Press, 1998).

144. Timothy D. Hall, *Contested Boundaries: Itinerancy and the Shaping of the Colonial American Religious World* (Durham, NC: Duke University Press, 1994). This is not an uncontested position; see for example Jon Butler, "Enthusiasms Described and Decried: The Great Awakening as Interpretive Fiction," *Journal of American History* 69, no. 2 (September 1982): 305–25.

145. For a case study in the early period, see Martin H. Quitt, "Immigrant Origins of the Virginia Gentry: A Study of Cultural Transmission and Innovation," *The William and Mary Quarterly* 45, no. 4 (1988): 629–55.

146. Jack P. Greene, "Political Mimesis: A Consideration of the Historical and Cultural Roots of Legislative Behaviour in the British Colonies in the Eighteenth Century," *American Historical Review* 75, no. 2 (1969): 337–60, and his *Peripheries and Center*, Chapter 1.

147. Silvio A. Bedini, "The Mace and the Gavel: Symbols of Government in America," *Transactions of the American Philosophical Society* 87, no. 4 (1997): Chapter 1.

148. T. H. Breen, "'Baubles of Britain'; The American and Consumer Revolutions of the Eighteenth Century," *Past and Present* 119 (1988): 73–104.

149. Bushman, *The Refinement of America*, p. xii and passim.

150. Baumgarten, *What Clothes Reveal*, p. 82.

151. Bushman, *The Refinement of America*, p. 296; Chapter 12.

152. See among others, Butler, *Becoming America*, pp. 5–6 and 133–4.

153. Brock Jobe, "The Boston Furniture Industry, 1720–1740," in *Boston Furniture of the Eighteenth Century*, ed. Walter Muir (Boston: Colonial Society of Massachusetts, 1974), pp. 3–48.

154. Michael N. Shute, "Furniture, the American Revolution and the Modern Antique," in *American Material Culture: The Shape of Things around Us*, ed. Edith Mayo (Bowling Green, OH: Bowling Green State University Press, 1984), p. 186.

155. E. McClurg Fleming, "Early American Decorative Arts as Social Documents," *The Mississippi Historical Review* 45, no. 2 (1958): 282.

156. Baumgarten, *What Clothes Reveal*.

157. For the argument for "Anglicization" see T. H. Breen, "An Empire of Goods: The Anglicization of Colonial America, 1690–1776," *Journal of British Studies* 25 (October 1986): 467–99.

158. Olson, *Emblems of American Community*, p. 2.

Chapter 3   England's Unfinished Revolution: Challenges to Monarchical Culture

1. The bibliography on the dynamics of the English Civil War is far too massive to engage with here. A useful, although far from neutral, short orientation may be provided by Ronald Hutton, *Debates in Stuart History* (London: Palgrave, 2004). On innovative forms of state culture see Sean Kelsey, *Inventing a Republic: The Political Culture of the English Commonwealth, 1649–1653* (Stanford, CA: Stanford University Press, 1997). For an effective summary of the dynamics of the moment in an Atlantic context, see Carla Pestana, *The English Atlantic in an Age of Revolution, 1640–1661* (Cambridge, MA: Harvard University Press, 2004).

2. Robert Zaller, "Breaking the Vessels: The Desacralization of the Monarchy in Early Modern England," *Sixteenth Century Journal* 29, no. 3 (1998): 757–78; John Brewer, "'The most polite age and the most vicious': Attitudes towards Culture as Commodity 1600–1800," in *The Consumption of Culture, 1600–1800*, ed. Ann Bermingham and John Brewer (London: Routledge, 1995), pp. 341–61; John Brewer, *The Pleasures of the Imagination: English Culture in the Eighteenth Century* (New York: Farrar, Straus, Giroux, 1997), especially the Introduction and Part I; Kevin Sharpe and Steven Zwicker (eds), *Refiguring Revolutions: Aesthetics and Politics from the English Revolution to the Romantic Revolution* (Berkeley and Los Angeles: University of California Press, 1998).

3. On the late sixteenth- and early seventeenth-century pre-history of this see Patrick Collinson, "Protestant Culture and the Cultural Revolution," in *Reformation to Revolution: Politics and Religion in Early Modern England*, ed. Margo Todd (London and New York: Routledge, 1995).

4. David Zaret, *Origins of Democratic Culture: Printing, Petitions and the Public Sphere in Seventeenth-Century England* (Princeton, NJ: Princeton University Press, 2000); Kate Gillespie, *Domesticity and Dissent in the Seventeenth Century: English Women Writers and the Public Sphere* (Cambridge: Cambridge University Press, 2006).

5. I obviously agree with those who argue that religious conflict played a crucial role in the revolutionary dynamic. See Glenn Burgess, "Was the English Civil War a War of Religion? The Evidence of Political Propaganda," *The Huntington Library Quarterly* 61, no. 2 (1998): 173–201, which includes a thorough historiographic guide.

6. For architecture see Timothy Mowl and Brian Earnshaw, *Architecture without Kings: The Rise of Puritan Classicism under Cromwell* (Manchester: Manchester University Press, 1995). For clothing, see below.

7. Nicolas Tayacke, *Anti-Calvinists: The Rise of English Arminianism 1590–1640* (Oxford: Clarendon Press, 1987).

8. Christopher Durston, *Charles I* (London: Routledge, 1998), p. 29; David Cressy, *Agnes Bowker's Cat: Travesties and Transgressions in Tudor and Stuart England* (Oxford: Oxford University Press, 2000), Chapter 12.

9. Julie Spraggon, *Puritan Iconoclasm during the English Civil War* (Rochester, NY: Boydell Press, 2003); Cressy, *Agnes Bowker's Cat*, Chapter 14.

10. John Walter, "The Impact on Society: A World Turned Upside Down?" in *The Impact of the English Civil War*, ed. John Morrill (London: Collins and Brown, 1991), p. 105.

11. Walter, "The Impact on Society," p. 107.

12. *The Actors Remonstrance or Complaint* (London: Edward Nickson, 1643), pp. 3, 5, 8.

13. John Milton, *The Doctrine and Discipline of Divorce: Restor'd to the Good of Both Sexes* (London: T.P. and M.S., 1643).

14. Phyllis Mack, *Visionary Women: Ecstatic Prophecy in Seventeenth-Century England* (Los Angeles: University of California Press, 1992); Keith Thomas, "Women and the Civil War Sects," in *Crisis in Europe, 1560–1660*, ed. Trevor Aston (New York: Basic Books, 1965), pp. 332–57. More recent are Patricia Higgins, "The Reactions of Women," in *Politics, Religion and the English Civil War*, ed. Brian Manning (London: Edward Arnold, 1973), pp. 179–224; Sharon Achinstein, "Women on Top in the Pamphlet Literature of the English Revolution," *Women's Studies* 1 (1994): 131–63; Patricia Crawford, "The Challenges to Patriarchalism: How Did the Revolution Affect Women?" in *Revolution and Restoration*, ed. John Morrill (London: Collins and Brown, 1992), pp. 112–28; Elaine Hobby, "'Discourse so Unsavoury': Women's Published Writings of the 1650s," in *Women Writing History: 1640–1740*, ed. Isobel Grundy and Susan Wiseman (London: Batsford, 1992), pp. 16–32.

15. Natalie Davis, "Women on Top," and "City Women and Religious Change," in her *Society and Culture in Early Modern France* (Stanford, CA: Stanford University Press, 1975). For a helpful review essay, see Mary Wiesner, "Beyond Women and the Family: Towards a Gender Analysis of the Reformation," *Sixteenth Century Journal* 18, no. 3 (1987): 311–21.

16. Nancy Roelker, "The Appeal of Calvinism to French Noblewomen in the Sixteenth Century," *Journal of Interdisciplinary History* 2 (1971–2): 391–418; and her "The Role of French Noblewomen in the Reformation," *Archiv für Reformationsgeschichte* 63 (1972): 168–95.

17. See the collections in the Museum of Fine Arts, Boston; the Smithsonian Institution; the British Museum London; and the Winterthur Museum.

18. *Lace Panel*, 1600–1650 (Victoria and Albert Museum, London), Museum number T.17-1909. Available online at http://images.vam.ac.uk

19. *A Declaration of the Lords and Commons Assembled in Parliament For the appeasing and quietting of all unlawfull Tumults and Insurrections... Also an Ordinance of both Houses, for the suppressing of Stage-Playes* (London: John Wright, [September 2]1642).

20. *The Actors Remonstrance*, pp. 3, 5, 8.

21. Richard Baker, *Theatrum Redivivum or the Theater Vincated* (London: T.R. for Francis Eglesfiled, 1661).

22. George Fox, *A Warning to all the merchants in London, and such as buy and sell: with an advisement to them to lay aside their superflu and with it to nouirish the poor* (London: Thomas Simmons, 1648), pp. 1–2.

23. Ibid., p. 5.

24. "Anno 21: Jacobi Regis; CAP. 20. None shall prophanely Sweare or Curse"? in *A Whip for a Drunkard, and a Curbe for Prophanesse: Being an Abstract of all the severall Statutes in force against Sabbath-breaking, Swearing, Drunkenness and unlawful Gaming* (London: Robert White, 1646).

25. "Anno 21. Jacobi Regis CAP. 20: 'None Shall Prophanely Sweare or Curse,'" in *A Whip for a Drunkard.*

26. "Anno 4. Jacobi Regis CAP. 5. 'The Penalty of a Drunkard, and of him that continueth drinking in the Ale-house,'" in *A Whip for a Drunkard.*

27. Walter, "The Impact on Society," p. 113.

28. For insights into those rituals see Alan MacFarlane, *The Family Life of Ralph Josselin, a Seventeenth-Century Clergyman* (Cambridge: Cambridge University Press, 1970).

29. N. B. Harte, "State Control of Dress and Social Change in Pre-Industrial England," in *Trade, Government, and Economy in Pre-Industrial England*, ed. D. C. Coleman and A. H. John (London: Weidenfeld and Nicolson, 1976), pp. 150–1.

30. James Durham, *The Law Unsealed: Or a Practical Exposition of the Ten Commandments* (1655), pp. 325–6.

31. Ann Rosalind Jones and Peter Stallybrass, "Fetishizing the Glove in Renaissance Europe," *Critical Inquiry* 18 (2001): 114–32.
32. Durham, *The Law Unsealed*, p. 324.
33. Ann Rosalind Jones and Peter Stallybrass, *Renaissance Clothing and the Materials of Memory* (Cambridge: Cambridge University Press, 2000), p. 67.
34. Durham, *The Law Unsealed*, pp. 325–6.
35. David Kuchta, *The Three-Piece Suit and Modern Masculinity: England, 1550–1850* (Berkeley, CA: University of California Press, 2002); Thomas King, *The Gendering of Men, 1600–1750* (Madison, WI: University of Wisconsin Press, 2004); Laura Levine, *Men in Women's Clothing: Anti-Theatricality and Effeminization, 1579–1642* (Cambridge: Cambridge University Press, 1994).
36. For these possibilities of the use of dress more broadly see Sue Vincent, *Dressing the Elite: Clothes in Early Modern England* (Oxford: Berg, 2003).
37. Mowl and Earnshaw, *Architecture without Kings*, pp. 25, 60.
38. Mark A. Kishlansky, *The Rise of the New Model Army* (New York: Cambridge University Press, 1979).
39. On this see Mark Stoyle, *Soldiers and Strangers: An Ethnic History of the English Civil War* (New Haven, CT: Yale University Press, 2005).
40. Walter, "The Impact on Society," p. 107.
41. John Morrill, "The Impact on Society: A World Turned Upside Down," in his *Impact of the English Civil War* (London: Collins and Brown, 1991), p. 120.
42. The classic essay on this is Keith Thomas, "Women and the Civil War Sects," *Past and Present* 13 (1958): 42–62.
43. Stephen Porter, *Destruction in the English Civil* Wars (Phoenix Mill, Gloucestershire and Dover, NH: Alan Sutton, 1994), pp. 65–6.
44. Charles Carlton, *Going to the Wars: The Experience of the British Civil Wars 1638–1651* (London: Routledge, 1992), p. 155.
45. Porter, *Destruction in the English Civil Wars*, pp. 65, 118–20.
46. Ibid., p. 91.
47. Robert Brenner, *Merchants and Revolution: Commercial Change, Political Conflict, and London's Overseas Traders 1550–1653* (Princeton, NJ: Princeton University Press, 1993), p. 708.
48. Kelsey, *Inventing a Republic*, p. 97.
49. Brewer, *The Pleasures of the Imagination*, p. 8.
50. Kelsey, *Inventing a Republic*, p. 90.
51. Ibid., p. 92.
52. Ibid., p. 93.
53. Ibid., pp. 90–3.
54. Ibid., p. 97.
55. Ibid., p. 85.
56. Ibid., p. 87.
57. Philippa Glanville, *Silver in Tudor and Early Stuart England* (London: Victoria and Albert Publications, 1990).

58. Kelsey, *Inventing a Republic*, p. 89.

59. Ibid., p. 54. There was even some theater: Susan Wiseman, *Drama and Politics in the English Civil War* (Cambridge: Cambridge University Press, 1998), Part II.

60. Kelsey, *Inventing a Republic*, p. 58.

61. *Silver locket*, 1600–1700 (Victoria and Albert Museum, London), museum number 827-1864; Maden, *Brass sealing wax case*, 1657 (Victoria and Albert Museum, London), museum number M. 188-1930; *Cast iron fire back*, 1649 (Victoria and Albert Museum, London), museum number M. 119-1984; *Gold and enamel miniature slide, depicting Charles I*, 1650–1660 (Victoria and Albert Museum, London), museum number M. 263-1975; Thomas Rawlins, *Lead cast plaquette depicting Charles II as Prince of Wales*, 1645 (Victoria and Albert Museum, London), museum number A.57-1926; *Embroidered miniature portrait of Charles I*, 1640–1690 (Victoria and Albert Museum, London), museum number 812-1891. All may be viewed at http://images.vam.ac.uk.

62. See for example: *Tin-glazed earthenware bottle, decorated with a crown*, 1643 (Victoria and Albert Museum, London), museum number C.114-1938.

63. *An Act Touching Marriages and the Registering thereof; and also touching Births and Burials* (London: John Field, 1653).

64. David Armitage, "Making the Empire British: Scotland in the Atlantic World 1542–1707," *Past and Present* 155 (May 1997): 34–63, at pp. 55–6.

65. Barry Coward, *The Cromwellian Protectorate* (Manchester: Manchester University Press, 2002), p. 17.

66. For a brief but very well-illustrated history of Cromwell, see Maurice Ashley, *Oliver Cromwell and his World* (London: Thames and Hudson, 1972).

67. Roy Sherwood, *Oliver Cromwell: King in All But Name, 1653–1658* (New York: St. Martin's, 1997).

68. Roy Sherwood, *The Court of Oliver Cromwell* (London: Croom Helm, 1977), p. 25.

69. There is even a beautifully decorated harpsichord from this period in the collections of the Victoria and Albert Museum – a clear transgression of the usual interdiction on decoration.

70. Coward, *The Cromwellian Protectorate*, p. 33.

71. Sherwood, *The Court of Oliver Cromwell*, pp. 154–5.

72. *The Order of My Lord Mayor, the Aldermen, and the Sheriffes, for their meetings and wearing of their apparrel throughout the year* (Flesher, 1656), pp. 16–17.

73. *The Order of My Lord Mayor, the Aldermen, and the Sheriffes, for their meetings and wearing of their apparrel throughout the year* (London: Samuel Roycroft, Printer to the Honorable City of London, 1692).

74. Oliver Cromwell, *A Catalogue and collection of all those ordinances, proclamations, declarations, etc.* (London: William Du-Gard and Henry Hills, 1654), p. 165.

75. Walter, "The Impact on Society," p. 114.
76. Sherwood, *The Court of Oliver Cromwell*, p. 154.
77. Laura Lunger Knoppers, *Constructing Cromwell: Ceremony, Portrait, and Print 1645–1661* (Cambridge: Cambridge University Press, 2000).
78. Kevin Sharpe, "'An Image Doting Rabble': The Failure of Republican Culture in Seventeenth-Century England," in *Refiguring Revolutions*, ed. Kevin Sharpe (Berkeley, CA: University of California Press, 1998), p. 56.
79. Ibid.
80. Paul Hammond, "The King's Two Bodies: Representations of Charles II," in *Culture, Politics and Society in Britain, 1660–1800*, ed. Jeremy Black and Jeremy Gregory (Manchester: Manchester University Press, 1991), pp. 13–48.
81. On the politics of the theater in the Restoration: Nancy Klein Maguire, *Regicide and Restoration: English Tragicomedy, 1660–1671* (Cambridge: Cambridge University Press, 1992); Paula R. Backscheider, *Spectacular Politics: Theatrical Power and Mass Culture in Early Modern England* (Baltimore, MD: The Johns Hopkins University Press, 1993).
82. Gerard Reedy, "Mystical Politics: The Imagery of Charles II's Coronation," in *Studies in Change and Revolution: Aspects of English Intellectual History 1640–1800*, ed. Paul Korshin (Menston, Yorkshire: Scholar Press, 1972), pp. 19–42.
83. See Gerald Maclean, "Literature, Culture, and Society in Restoration England," in his *Culture and Society in the Stuart Restoration* (Cambridge: Cambridge University Press, 1995), pp. 3–31, especially p. 27.
84. John Spurr, *England in the 1670s: 'This Masquerading Age'* (Oxford: Blackwell Publishers, 2000).
85. Brewer, "The most polite age and the most vicious," pp. 341–61; Brewer, *The Pleasures of the Imagination*, passim.

Chapter 4   The Politics of Silk and Homespun: Contesting National Identity in Revolutionary America

1. T. H. Breen, "Narrative of Commercial Life: Consumption, Ideology, and Community on the Eve of the American Revolution," *The William and Mary Quarterly* L, no. 3 (July 1993): 486; idem, *The Marketplace of Revolution: How Consumer Politics Shaped American Independence* (New York: Oxford University Press, 2004); Simon P. Newman, *Parades and the Politics of the Street: Festive Culture in the Early American Republic* (Philadelphia: University of Pennsylvania Press, 1997), Chapter 1.
2. Michael Zakim, *Ready-made Democracy: A History of Dress in the Early American Republic, 1760–1860* (Chicago: University of Chicago Press, 2003), p. 17.

3. The term "boycott" is an anachronism here, which I am using for convenience and because the meaning applies. The term was coined in 1880: see Monroe Friedman, *Consumer Boycotts: Effecting Change through the Marketplace and the Media* (New York: Routledge, 1990), pp. 5–7.

4. Breen, *The Marketplace of Revolution*, p. 210.

5. Breen, "Narrative of Commercial Life."

6. Ibid., p. 486.

7. *Journal of the First Congress of the American Colonies, in Opposition to the Tyrannical Acts of the British Parliament. Held at New York, October 7, 1765* (New York: E. Winchester, 1845), pp. 27–9.

8. This flag may be seen at: http://www.jagriffin.net/revflag.htm.

9. See references in Chapter 2.

10. *Journal of the First Congress of the American Colonies*, pp. 27–9.

11. Henry Steele Commager (ed.), *Documents of American History* (New York: Prentice-Hall, 1973), p. 85.

12. Charles M. Andrews, "The Boston Merchants and the Non-Importation Movement," *Publications of the Colonial Society of Massachusetts* 19 (January 1917): 165–9.

13. John Dickinson, *The Late Regulations, Respecting the British Colonies on the Continent of America Considered, in a Letter from a Gentleman in Philadelphia to his Friend in London* (Philadelphia, 1765), pp. 6–7, 27.

14. Washington to Mason, April 5, 1769 in *Mason Papers* I, ed. Robert A. Rutland, pp. 97–8, cited in Rhys Isaac, *The Transformation of Virginia 1740–1790* (Chapel Hill, NC: University of North Carolina Press, 1982), p. 251.

15. Cited in John E. Crowley, "The Sensibility of Comfort," *American Historical Review* 104, no. 3 (June 1999): 771, fn. 39.

16. Ibid.

17. Cited in Linda Baumgarten, *What Clothes Reveal: The Language of Clothing in Colonial and Federal America: The Colonial Williamsburg Collection* (Williamsburg, VA: The Colonial Williamsburg Foundation, 2002), pp. 95–6.

18. For other examples see the beautifully illustrated volume by Linda Baumgarten, *Eighteenth-Century Clothing at Williamsburg* (Williamsburg, VA: The Colonial Williamsburg Foundation, 1986). Very full descriptions (and a few patterns) may be found in Elisabeth McClellan, *History of American Costume, 1607–1870* (New York: Tudor Publishing, 1937).

19. Zakim, *Ready-made Democracy*; Linda Kerber, *Women of the Republic: Intellect and Ideology in Revolutionary America* (Chapel Hill, NC: University of North Carolina Press, 1980); Mary Beth Norton, *Liberty's Daughters: The Revolutionary Experience of American Women, 1750–1800* (Boston: Little, Brown and Co., 1980); Joan R. Gundersen, *To Be Useful to the World: Women in Revolutionary America* (New York: Twayne, 1996); Laurel Thatcher Ulrich, *Good Wives: Image and Reality in the Lives of Women in Northern New*

England, 1650–1750 (New York: Knopf, 1982) and her *The Age of Homespun: Objects and Stories in the Creation of an American Myth* (New York: Knopf, 2001). For working people's dress in this period see Peter F. Copeland, *Working Dress in Colonial and Revolutionary America* (Westport, CT: Greenwood Press, 1977). Of course not all slaves were clothed in imported fabric; some wove their own. See Barbara M. Starke *et al.*, *African American Dress and Adornment: A Cultural Perspective* (Dubuque, IA: Kendall Hunt Publishing, 1990), Part II: "African American Slave Clothing."

20. Zakim, *Ready-made Democracy*, pp. 13, 17.

21. Baumgarten, *What Clothes Reveal*, pp. 95–6.

22. Breen, *The Marketplace of Revolution*; Ulrich, *Homespun*; Gundersen, *To Be Useful to the World*.

23. The differing domestication of politics in the American and French cases is particularly interesting in the light of the debate sparked by Mona Ozouf's *Women's Words: Essay on French Singularity*, trans. Jean Marie Todd (Chicago: Chicago University Press, 1997). See the superb analysis of the book and the debates by Eric Fassin, "The Purloined Gender: American Feminism in a French Mirror," *French Historical Studies* 22, no. 1 (Winter 1999): 113–38. I agree with Fassin that the key issue is not strong differences between French and American feminism, but I do think that there are more significant differences between French and American constructions of gender difference than Fassin is inclined to see.

24. Kerber, *Women of the Republic*; Norton, *Liberty's Daughters*, pp. 160ff.

25. Breen sees a greater transference of power from the home to the public world of politics than does Norton. See Breen, *The Marketplace* and Norton, *Liberty's Daughters*.

26. Peter Shaw, *American Patriots and the Rituals of Revolution* (Cambridge, MA: Harvard University Press, 1981), p. 7.

27. Ibid., Chapter 1.

28. Isaac, *Transformation of Virginia*, p. 255.

29. Commager (ed.), *Documents of American History*, p. 70.

30. Lester C. Olson, *Emblems of American Community in the Revolutionary Era: A Study in Rhetorical Iconology* (Washington, DC: Smithsonian Institution Press, 1991), Chapter 2.

31. Ibid., pp. 99–100.

32. Philip J. Deloria, *Playing Indian* (New Haven, CT: Yale University Press, 1998), pp. 21–2.

33. Ann M. Little, "'Shoot that Rogue, For He Hath an Englishman's Coat On!': Cultural Cross-Dressing on the New England Frontier, 1620–1760," *The New England Quarterly* 74, no. 2 (June 2001): 238–73. The theoretical argument draws heavily from Jones and Stallybrass.

34. Deloria, *Playing Indian*, p. 36.

35. Ibid., pp. 34–5.

36. Benjamin Franklin, first published in *The Pennsylvania Journal*, December 27, 1775. Reprinted in *A Benjamin Franklin Reader*, ed. Walter Isaacson (New York: Simon and Schuster, 2003), p. 263.

37. Benjamin Franklin, "Join or Die," *Pennsylvania Gazette* [Philadelphia], May 9, 1754, Newspaper Serial and Government Publications Division Library of Congress, available online at http://www.loc.gov/exhibits/us.capitol/one.jpg

38. Rodris Roth, "Tea Drinking in Eighteenth-Century America: Its Etiquette and Equippage," *U.S. National Museum Bulletin* 225 (Washington, DC, 1961): 61–91.

39. Commager (ed.), *Documents of American History*, p. 86.

40. Isaac, *Transformation of Virginia*, p. 246.

41. Elizabeth Louise Roark, *Artists of Colonial America* (New York: Greenwood Publishing, 2003), p. 58; Ann Fairfax Withington, *Toward A More Perfect Union: Virtue and the Formation of American Republics* (New York: Oxford University Press, 1991), p. 98. On the elaborations of mourning dress see Alice Morse Earle, *Two Centuries of Costume in America*, Vol. II (New York: Macmillan, 1903), Chapter 26.

42. Isaac, *Transformation of Virginia*, p. 255, fn. 28.

43. Ibid., p. 247.

44. Jack P. Greene, *Imperatives, Behaviors, and Identities: Essays in Early American Cultural History* (Charlottesville, VA: University Press of Virginia, 1992), Chapter 6.

45. Ann Fairfax Withington, "Manufacturing and Selling the American Revolution," in *Everyday Life in the Early Republic,* ed. Catherine Hutchins (Winterthur, DE: H. F. du Pont Winterthur Museum, 1994), p. 286.

46. Robert Morris to the President of Congress, January 15, 1782. Reprinted in Francis Whatron, *The Revolutionary Diplomatic Correspondence of the United States under Direction of Congress* Vol. 5 (Washington, DC: Government Printing Office, 1889), p. 104.

47. *The Book of Abigail and John: Selected Letters of the Adams Family, 1762– 1784*, ed. L. H. Butterfield *et al.* (Cambridge, MA: Harvard University Press, 1975), p. 210.

48. Samuel Adams, *The Writings of Samuel Adams*, Vol. 4, ed. Harry Alanzo Cushing (New York: G. P. Putnam's Sons, 1908), pp. 123–5.

49. Massachusetts Historical Society, "Warren–Adams Letters, being chiefly a correspondence among John Adams, Samuel Adams, and James Warren … 1743–1814," *Massachusetts Historical Society Collections* 73 (Boston: The Massachusetts Historical Society, 1925), p. 187.

50. *The Book of Abigail and John*, p. 217.

51. *Warren–Adams Letters*, p. 249.

52. "On American Manufactures," *American Museum* 1 (February, 1787): 119.

53. "A Confident Republican," *The Independent Chronicle and the Universal Advertiser* [Boston], 7 July 1785.

54. "'Z' For the American Herald," *American Herald* [Boston], 16 May 1785.

55. *Sans Souci, alias Free and Easy, or an Evening's Peep into a Polite Circle: An Intire New Entertainment in Three Acts* (Boston: Warden and Russell, 1785), p. 12.

56. *Sans Souci*, pp. 12, 4.

57. Royall Tyler, *The Contrast: A Comedy in Five Acts* (Boston: Houghton Mifflin, 1920), pp. 114–15.

58. Ibid., p. 48.

59. Ibid., pp. 38–9.

60. Ibid., p. 43.

61. Ibid., p. 51.

62. Ibid., p. 79.

63. Ibid., pp. 79–80.

64. Neil Harris, *The Artist in American Society: The Formative Years, 1790–1860* (Chicago: University of Chicago Press, 1982), p. 23.

65. Harris, *The Artist in American Society*, p. 16.

66. See the plates in *George Washington: A National Treasure* (Washington, DC: National Portrait Gallery, Smithsonian Institution; Seattle, WA: in association with the University of Washington Press, 2002).

67. Noble E. Cunningham, Jr, "Political Dimensions of Everyday Life in the New Republic," in *Everyday Life in the Early Republic*, ed. Catherine E. Hutchins (Winterthur, DE: H. F. du Pont Winterthur Museum, 1994), pp. 3–33; Withington, "Manufacturing and Selling the American Revolution."

68. Embroidery of Mt. Vernon, *c.*1807 by Caroline Stebbins Sheldon (1789–1865). Available online at http://www.memorialhall.mass.edu/collection/browse/results.jsp?subcategoryid=38

69. Amelia Simmons, *American Cookery, Or the Art of Dressing, Viands, Fish, Poultry and Vegetables, and the Best Modes of Making, Pastes, Puffs, Pies, Tarts Puddings, Custards and Preserves, and all kind of Cakes, from the imperial Plum to plain Cake, adapted to this Country, and all grades of life, By Amelia Simmons, an American Orphan* (Hartford, CT: Hudson and Goodwin, 1796); Mary Tolford Wilson, "Amelia Simmons Fills a Need: American Cookery, 1796," *The William and Mary Quarterly* 14, no. 1 (January 1957): 16–30; Glydis Ridley, "The First American Cookbook," *Eighteenth-Century Life* 23 (May 1999), 114–23.

70. Carol Fisher, *The American Cookbook: A History* (Jefferson, NC: MacFarland, 2006); Trudy Eden, *Cooking in America, 1590–1800* (New York: Greenwood Publishing, 2005).

71. Button bearing George Washington's portrait, produced after his inauguration, *c.*1789, available online at http://www.concise.britannica.com; the china plate

is marked "Silesia." George Washington Sulphide Portrait, 1800, diameter 8 cm, length 11.1 cm (Baccarat, France); Louis Jean Desprez, Circular clear glass plaque with faceted edges, enclosing a sulphide profile portrait of George Washington, gilded metal ring and collar (Illinois State Museum).

72. Withington, "Manufacturing and Selling the American Revolution," pp. 301, 304.

73. Timothy Dwight, *Greenfield Hill: A Poem in Seven Parts* (New York: Dwight and Swain, 1794), pp. 514–15.

74. William Howard Adams (ed.), *The Eye of Thomas Jefferson* (Washington, DC: National Gallery of Art, 1976).

75. David Waldstreicher, *In the Midst of Perpetual Fetes: The Making of American Nationalism, 1776–1820* (Chapel Hill, NC: University of North Carolina Press, 1997); Newman, *Parades and Politics of the Street.*

76. Cunningham, "Political Dimensions," pp. 3–33.

77. See, among others, Mary P. Ryan, *Women in Public: Between Banners and Ballots, 1825–1990* (Baltimore, MD: Johns Hopkins University Press, 1990).

78. This is compatible with Linda Kerber's argument in Chapter 9 of *Women of the Republic* and with Nancy Cott's *The Bonds of Womanhood: Woman's Sphere in New England, 1780–1835* (New Haven, CT: Yale University Press, 1977), p. 156 and Chapter 5, and her *The Grounding of Modern Feminism* (New Haven, CT: Yale University Press, 1987).

79. The earliest studies include: Karen Blair, *The Clubwoman as Feminist: True Womanhood Redefined, 1868–1914* (New York: Holmes and Meier, 1980); Deborah Epstein, *The Politics of Domesticity: Women, Evangelism and Temperance in Nineteenth-Century America* (Middletown, CT: Wesleyan University Press, 1981); Anne Firor Scott, *Natural Allies: Women's Associations in American History* (Urbana, IL: University of Illinois Press, 1991); Anne M. Boylan, *The Origins of Women's Activism: New York and Boston, 1797–1840* (Chapel Hill, NC: University of North Carolina Press, 2002).

80. Ellen Dubois, *Feminism and Suffrage: The Emergence of an Independent Women's Movement in America* (Ithaca, NY: Cornell University Press, 1978); Michael D. Pierson, *Free Hearts and Free Homes: Gender and American Antislavery Politics* (Chapel Hill, NC: University of North Carolina Press, 2003).

Chapter 5 Making French Republicans: Revolutionary Transformation of the Everyday

1. Henri Grégoire, "Système de dénominations topographiques Pour les places, rues, quais, etc de toutes les communes de la République," in *La Culture des Sans-Culottes,* ed. Bernard Deloche and Jean-Michel Leniaud (Paris: Editions de Paris, 1989), p. 120.

2. D. A. F. de Sade, *Philosophy in the Bedroom* (New York: Grove Press, 1990). My thanks to Lauren Silvers for calling this text to my attention.

3. The classic general works on this theme include: Lynn Hunt, *Politics, Culture, and Class in the French Revolution* (Berkeley, CA and Los Angeles: University of California Press, 1990); Roger Chartier, *The Cultural Origins of the French Revolution*, trans. Lydia Cochrane (Durham, NC: Duke University Press, 1991); Mona Ozouf, *Festivals and the French Revolution*, trans. Alan Sheridan (Cambridge, MA: Harvard University Press, 1988); Serge Bianchi, *La Révolution culturelle de l'an II: Elites et peuple 1789–1799* (Paris: Aubier, 1982); Special Issue on the French Revolution, *Eighteenth Century Studies* 22, no. 3 (Spring 1989); George Levitine (ed.), *Culture and Revolution: Cultural Ramifications of the French Revolution* (College Park, MD: University of Maryland, Department of Art History, 1989). For the question of embodied culture in the French Revolution, see Sara Melzer and Kathryn Norberg (eds), *From the Royal to the Republican Body* (Berkeley, CA: University of California Press, 1998); Antoine de Baecque, *The Body Politic: Corporeal Metaphor in Revolutionary France, 1770–1800*, trans. Charlotte Mandell (Stanford, CA: Stanford University Press, 1997); Dorinda Outram, *The Body and the French Revolution: Sex, Class and Political Culture* (New Haven, CT: Yale University Press, 1989).

4. Ozouf, *Festivals and the French Revolution*, p. 9.

5. *Opinion de Gastin sur le projet de résolution relatif à la Cocarde nationale, 29 floréal VII* (Paris: Imprimerie Nationale, 1799).

6. Daniela del Pesco, "Entre projet et utopie: les écrits et la théorie architecturale, 1789–1799," in *Les Architectes de la liberté, 1789–1799: Ecole nationale supérieure des Beaux-Arts Paris, 4 octobre 1989–7 janvier 1990* (Paris: Ministère de la culture et de la communication, des grands travaux et du bicentennaire, 1989), pp. 329–33.

7. Louis Réau, *L'histoire du vandalisme: les monuments détruits de l'art français* (Paris: Laffont, 1994); Françoise Choay, *The Invention of the Historic Monument*, trans. Lauren O'Connell (New York: Cambridge University Press, 2001).

8. Del Pesco, "Entre projet et utopie."

9. Société populaire et républicaine des arts, *Considérations sur les avantages de changer le costume français* (Paris: De l'imprimerie de Fantelin, 1790).

10. Eschassériaux, jeune, *Sur le projet de résolution relatif à la cocarde nationale* (Paris: Imprimerie National, 1799), pp. 5, 7.

11. Société populaire, *Considérations sur les avantages*, p. 3.

12. *Pensées sur les coupeurs de tresses* (Paris: 1794), p. 5.

13. I am grateful to Lynn Hunt for bringing this to my attention.

14. The one exception is Paul Avril, *L'ameublement parisien avant, pendant, et après la révolution* (Paris: A. Sinjon, 1929) but Avril is unable to bring much evidence to bear for his argument.

15. See references in Chapters 1 and 2.

16. Patrick Laurens, "La figure officielle de la république française: monnaies et timbres," in *La France déomocratique: Mélanges en l'honneur de M. Agulhon* (Paris: Publications de la Sorbonne, 1998), p. 421.

17. Jennifer Harris, "The Red Cap of Liberty: A Study of Dress Worn by French Revolutionary Partisans, 1789–95," *Eighteenth-Century French Studies* 14, no. 3 (Spring 1981): 283–312.

18. Avril, *L'Ameublement*, pp. 8–10; Jean-François Barrielle, *Le style empire* (Paris: Flammarion, 1982), pp. 15–16.

19. Spire Blondel, *L'art pendant la révolution, beaux-arts, arts décoratifs* (Paris: Laurens, 1887), pp. 302–3. See also Barry George Bergdoll, "Historical Reasoning and Architectural Politics: Léon Vaudoyer and the Development of French Historicist Architecture" (PhD diss., Columbia University, 1986), pp. 28–9.

20. Yvonne Korshak, "The Liberty Cap as a Revolutionary Symbol in America and France," *Smithsonian Studies in American Art* 1, no. 2 (Autumn 1987): 52–69; Harris, "The Red Cap of Liberty," p. 286; Richard Wrigley, *The Politics of Appearance: Representations of Dress in the French Revolution* (Oxford: Berg, 2002), Chapter 4.

21. This paragraph is based on M. Elizabeth C. Bartlet, "The New Repertory at the Opéra during the Reign of Terror: Revolutionary Rhetoric and Operatic Consequences," *Music and the French Revolution*, ed. Malcolm Boyd (Cambridge: Cambridge University Press, 1992), pp. 107–56.

22. Wrigley, *The Politics of Appearance*, Chapter 5.

23. Daniel Roche, *The People of Paris: An Essay in Popular Culture in the Eighteenth Century*, trans. Marie Evans with Gywnne Lewis (Berkeley, CA: University of California Press, 1987), Chapter 6.

24. See Chapters 2 and 4. For French servants' dress see Cissie F. Fairchilds, *Domestic Enemies: Servants and their Masters in Old Regime France* (Baltimore, MD: Johns Hopkins University Press, 2004) and Sarah C. Maza, *Servants and Masters in Eighteenth-Century France: The Use of Loyalty* (Princeton, NJ: Princeton University Press, 1983).

25. For details see below and the following essay (although my interpretations have changed somewhat since its publication): Leora Auslander, "Regeneration through the Everyday? Furniture in Revolutionary Paris," *Art History* 28, no. 2 (April 2005): 227–47.

26. Claudine de Vaulchier, "Iconographie des décors révolutionnaires," in *Les architectes de la liberté, 1789–1799* (Paris: Ecole nationale supérieure des Beaux Arts, 1989), pp. 255–67; Hans-Jürgen Lüsebrink and Rolf Reichhardt, *The Bastille: A History of Symbol of Despotism and Freedom*, trans. Norbert Schürer (Durham, NC: Duke University Press, 1997).

27. François-Antoine Davy de Chavigné, *Projet d'un monument sur l'emplacement de la Bastille* (Paris, 1789), p. 8.

28. Aileen Ribeiro, *Fashion in the French Revolution* (New York: Holmes and Meier, 1988), p. 101.

29. Annie Jourdan, *Les monuments de la révolution, 1770–1804: Une histoire de représentation* (Paris: Champion, 1997).

30. See, for example, A.-R. Chevalier de Mopinot de la Chapotte, *Proposition d'un monument à élever dans la capitale de la France, pour transmetter aux races futures l'époque de l'heureuse révolution qui l'a revivifiée sous le règne de Louis XVI* (Paris, 1790), p. 8.

31. See Chevalier, illustration 48 on p. 45; Lüsebrink and Reichhardt, *The Bastille*.

32. Béatrice Fink, "Cènes civiques, repas révolutionnaires," *The French Review* 62, no. 6 (May 1989): 957–66.

33. For examples of these objects see Marie-Hélène Parinaud's introduction to Jean Tulard, *The French Revolution in Paris seen through the Collections of the Carnavalet Museum* (Paris: Paris-Musées, 1989); *Modes et révolutions, 1789–1804: Exposition faite au Musée de la Mode et du Costume, Palais Galliera, 8 février–7 mai 1989* (Paris: Editions Paris-Musées, 1989), pp. 170–1.

34. Colin Jones, "Bourgeois Revolution Revivified: 1789 and Social Change," in *Re-writing the French Revolution*, ed. Colin Lucas (Oxford: Oxford University Press, 1991), pp. 69–70.

35. See Avril's introduction to *L'Ameublement*.

36. On this building see James A. Leith, *Space and Revolution: Projects for Monuments, Squares and Public Buildings in France, 1789–1799* (Montréal: McGill University Press, 1991), pp. 79–85; Philippe Madec, *Boullée* (Paris: F. Hazan, 1986), pp. 64–71.

37. Pierre Arizzoli-Clémentel, "Les Arts du décor," in *Aux Armes et aux arts! Les Arts de la Révolution, 1789–1799*, ed. Philippe Bordes and Régis Michel (Paris: A. Biro, 1988), p. 283.

38. For a complete listing of Georges Jacob's revolutionary era production see Hector Lefuel, *Georges Jacob: Ébéniste du XVIIIè siècle* (Paris: A. Morancé, 1923). For Bernard Molitor, see Ulrich Leben, *Molitor: Ébéniste from the Ancien Régime to the Bourbon Restoration*, trans. William Wheeler (London: P. Wilson, 1992). For Adam Weisweiler, see Patricia Lemonnier, *Weisweiler* (Paris: Editions d'art Monelle Hayot, 1983).

39. Ronald Paulson, *Representations of Revolution: 1789–1820* (New Haven, CT: Yale University Press, 1983), Chapter 1; Guillaume Janneau, *Les Ateliers parisiens d'ébénistes et de menuisiers aux XVIIe et XVIIIe siècles* (Paris, S.E.R.G, 1975), p. 41.

40. See Leben, *Molitor*, pp. 125ff.

41. Leith, *Space and Revolution*, Chapters 2, 3 and 4.

42. Chavigné, *Projet d'un monument sur l'emplacement de la Bastille*, p. 14.

43. On this issue see Cissie Fairchilds, "Fashion and Freedom in the French Revolution," *Continuity and Change* 15, no. 3 (2000): 419–33.

44. Annemarie Kleinert, "La Mode – Miroir de la Révolution Française," *Francia* 16 (1989): 91, 78, 79, 81; and Daniel Roche, "Apparences révolutionnaires ou

révolution des apparences," in *Modes et Révolutions, 1780–1804*, pp. 105–28 and the excellent illustrations throughout the volume.

45. This paragraph is drawn from Laura Mason, *Singing the French Revolution: Popular Culture and Politics, 1787–1799* (Ithaca, NY: Cornell University Press, 1996), Chapter 2; the quotation may be found on p. 60.

46. André Bendjebbar, "Le théâtre angevin pendant la Révolution (1789–1799)," *Revue de la Société d'histoire du théâtre* 169 (1991): 141; James H. Johnson, "Revolutionary Audiences and the Impossible Imperatives of Fraternity," in *Re-creating Authority in Revolutionary France,* ed. Bryant T. Ragan, Jr. and Elizabeth A. Williams (New Brunswick, NJ: Rutgers University Press, 1992), p. 60.

47. On women's political participation in this period, see Dominique Godineau, *Citoyennes tricoteuses: Les femmes du peuple à Paris pendant la Révolution française* (Aix-en-Provence: Alinéa, 1988).

48. See *Journal de la mode et du goût, ou Amusemens du salon et de la toilette* (February 25, 1790): 2, as well as (March 5, 1790): 17.

49. Kleinert, "La Mode – Miroir de la Révolution Française," pp. 79–90.

50. On the invention of melodrama as a form see Peter Brooks, *The Melodramatic Imagination Balzac, Henry James, Melodrama, and the Mode of Excess* (New Haven, CT: Yale University Press, 1976). On theater in the early days of the revolution: Jeffry Ravel, *The Contested Parterre: Public Theater and French Political Culture, 1680–1791* (Ithaca, NY: Cornell University Press, 1999).

51. H. J. Jansen, *Projet tendant à concerver les Arts en France* (Paris, 1791); Andrew McClellan, *Inventing the Louvre: Art, Politics, and the Origins of the Modern Museum in Eighteenth-Century Paris* (Cambridge: Cambridge University Press, 1994), pp. 96–7; Dominique Poulot, *Musée, Nation, Patrimoine: 1789–1815* (Paris: Gallimard, 1997).

52. Le Chapelier, cited in Johnson, "Revolutionary Audiences," in *Re-creating Authority in Revolutionary France,* p. 63; Paul Friedland, *Political Actors: Representative Bodies and Theatricality in the Age of the French Revolution* (Ithaca, NY: Cornell University Press, 2002).

53. Archives Nationales, AJ12 44, cited in Bartlet, "The New Repertory at the Opéra during the Reign of Terror," p. 109.

54. Jennifer Heuer, "Hats on for the Nation! Women, Citizens, Soldiers, and the 'Sign of the French,'" *French History* 16, no. 1 (2002): 28–52.

55. *Observations sur le calendrier républicain* (Paris: 15 floréal, year III), pp. 1–2.

56. *Rapport fait au nom du comité d'instruction publique sur la nécessité et les moyens d'introduire dans toute la République les nouveaux poids et mesures précéemment décrétés* (Paris: 11 Ventose, Year 3), p. 5.

57. Bianchi, *La révolution culturelle de l'an II*, pp. 196–7; Michel de Certeau, *Une Politique de la Langue: La Révolution française et les patois* (Paris: Editions Gallimard, 1975).

58. Ken Alder, *The Measure of All Things: The Seven-year-Odyssey that Transformed the World* (London: Little, Brown, 2002).

59. M. Bureaux de Pusy in Marquis de Bonnay, *Rapport fait au nom du Comité d'Agriculture et de Commerce, sur l'uniformité à établir dans les Poids et mesures et opinion de M. Bureaux de Pusy* (Paris, May 6, 1790), p. 20.

60. G. Romme, *Rapport sur l'ère de la République* (Paris: September 10, 1793), p. 2.

61. For fascinating and subtle work on the complexities revolutionary time see Sanja Perovic, "Epochal Breaks: A Semantics of Revolutionary Time," paper presented at the Modern France Workshop, University of Chicago, April 28, 2006.

62. Ozouf, *Festivals and the French Revolution.*

63. For an exhaustive treatment of naming during the Revolution, see the special issue of *Annales historiques de la Révolution française* 72, no. 4 (2000).

64. Laurens, "La figure officielle de la république française," in *La France démocratique*, p. 421 [421–9].

65. Roche, *The People of Paris*, p. 162.

66. J. Guillaume (ed.), "Vol. 1: Projet d'éducation nationale, par P.-P. Rabaut, Deputé de l'Aude, du 21 décembre, 1792, l'an I de la république," in *Procès-verbaux du comité d'instruction publique de la Convention Nationale* (Paris: Imprimerie Nationale, 1891), pp. 233–5, cited in Jennifer Harris, "The Red Cap of Liberty," p. 302.

67. Harris, "The Red Cap of Liberty," p. 299.

68. Lynn Hunt, "Symbolic Forms of Political Practice," in her *Politics, Culture and Class in the French Revolution* (Berkeley, CA: University of California Press, 1984), p. 76.

69. Ibid., p. 77.

70. Société Populaire et Républicaine des Arts, *Considérations sur les avantages de changer le costume français* (Paris: Imprimerie de Fontelin, 1794); Cl. Fr. X. Mercier, *Comment M'habillerai-je? Réflexions politiques et philosophiques sur l'habillement français et sur la nécessité d'un costume national* (Paris: Printed by the author, 1793).

71. On conditions of production see Claire Crowston, *Fabricating Women: The Seamstresses of Old Regime France, 1675–1791* (Durham, NC: Duke University Press, 2001).

72. Cited in del Pesco, "Entre projet et utopie: les écrits et la théorie architecturale, 1789–1799," p. 334.

73. See Verhelst, *Plan allégorique d'un jardin de la Révolution Française et des vertus Républicaines* (Paris: De l'Imprimerie d' Emmanuel Brosselard, 1794); Jean-Pierre-Louis-Laurent Houël, *Projet d'un Monument Public* (Paris: 1799–1800); Antoine Voinier, *Projet d'un monument triomphal en l'honneur des quatorze Armées de la République* (Paris: 1794); Nicolas Letemple Goulet,

Le Temples des lois et de la liberté: Projet présenté au Comité d'Instruction publique de la Convention nationale, par le Citoyen Goulet, Architecte Expert du Département pour l'estimation des Domaines nationaux (Paris: s.d.); François-Antoine Davy de Chavigné, *Projet d'un monument sur l'emplacement de la Bastille* (Paris: 1789); Auguste Hubert, *Rapport sur l'embellissement du Palais et du Jardin National, du Pont et de la Place de la Révolution; présenté au Comité de Salut public par Hubert, Architecte* (Paris: 1794); A.-R. Chevalier de Mopinot de la Chapotte, *Proposition d'un monument à élever dans la capitale de la France, pour transmetter aux races futures l'époque de l'heureuse révolution qui l'a revivifiée sous le règne de Louis XVI* (Paris: 1790). The most helpful secondary texts on this issue are James A. Leith, *Space and Revolution: Projects for Monuments, Squares and Public Buildings in France 1789–1799* (Montreal: Queen University Press, 1991), and Werner Szambien, *Les Projets de l'an II: Concours d'Architecture de la période révolutionnaire* (Paris: Ecole nationale supérieure des beaux-arts, 1986).

74. Staatliche Kunsthalle Baden-Baden, *Revolutionsarchitektur: Boullée, Ledoux, Lequeu* (Stuttgart-Bad Cannstatt: 1970). Although as Leith points out, they were not themselves necessarily convinced republicans: Leith, *Space and Revolution*, p. 34.

75. Lefuel, *Georges Jacob: Ébéniste du XVIIIè siècle*; Arizzoli-Clémentel, "Les Arts du décor," p. 299.

76. Lefuel, *Georges Jacob*, pp. 144ff; Michel Beurdeley, *Georges Jacob (1739–1814) et son temps* (Saint-Rémy-en-l'Eau: Monelle Hayot, 2002), Chapter 10.

77. Marie-Noëlle De Grandry, *Le Mobilier Français: Directoire, Consulat, Empire* (Paris: Editions Massin, 1996), p. 32.

78. Laurie Dahlberg, "France Between the Revolutions, 1789–1848," in *The Sèvres Porcelain Manufactory: Alexandre Brongniart and the Triumph of Art and Industry, 1800–1847*, ed. Tamara Préaud (New Haven, CT: Yale University Press, published for The Bard Graduate Center for Studies in the Decorative Arts, New York, 1997), p. 16.

79. For a fuller elaboration of this argument see Leora Auslander, *Taste and Power: Furnishing Modern France* (Berkeley, CA: University of California Press, 1996).

80. Auslander, *Taste and Power*, Parts II and III.

81. Gayle V. Fischer, *Pantaloons and Power: Nineteenth-Century Dress Reform in the United States* (Kent, OH: Kent State University Press, 2001); Carol Mattingly, *Appropriate(ing) Dress: Women's Rhetorical Style in Nineteenth-Century America* (Carbondale, IL: Southern Illinois University Press, 2002).

82. Suzanne Desan, *The Family on Trial in Revolutionary France* (Berkeley, CA: University of California Press, 2004).

83. Some appear even earlier. See the "Avis" in *Le journal des dames et des modes*, XIIIeme cahier (25 June 1790): 5 in which it is stated that Le sieur Boucher is now carrying revolutionary furniture, including patriotic beds.

84. *Table de chevet à trois tiroirs*, late 18ᵗʰ century (Musée Carnavalet, Paris), inventory number MB 199.

85. *Meuble à deux corps* (Musée Carnavalet, Paris), inventory number MB 200.

86. *Coiffeuse emblèmes révolutionnaires* (Musée Carnavalet, Paris), inventory number MB211.

87. *Manufacture de Sèvres*, about 1795 (Alfred Duane Pell Collection, National Museum of American History, Smithsonian Institution, Washington, DC), Figure 2 in Catherine Arminjon, *L'art de vivre: Decorative Arts and Design in France, 1789–1989* (London: Thames and Hudson, 1989).

88. Bordeaux, Musée des arts décoratifs, inv. 5376. "Illustration 93" in *La vie en France autour de 1789: Images et représentation 1785–1795*. Exhibition catalogue (Dordogne: Le Château; Nancy: Le Musée, 1989), p. 9.

89. Musée Gadagne, Lyon, "Illustration 96," in Michel Beurdeley, *La France à l'encan 1789–1799: Exode des objets d'art sous la Révolution* (Paris: Librairie Jules Tallandier, 1981), p. 91.

90. James H. Johnson, *Listening in Paris: A Cultural History* (Berkeley, CA: University of California Press, 1995), p. 116.

91. Johnson, "Revolutionary Audiences and the Impossible Imperatives of Fraternity," p. 59.

92. Ibid., p. 69.

93. Ibid., p. 121.

94. Mason, *Singing the French Revolution*; the paragraph is drawn from Chapter 2, the quotation from p. 60.

95. Johnson, *Listening in Paris*, p. 135; Mason, *Singing the French Revolution*, Chapter 4.

96. Johnson, *Listening in Paris*, pp. 126–7.

97. Ibid., p. 8. See also the contributions to Malcolm Boyd (ed.), *Music and the French Revolution* (Cambridge: Cambridge University Press, 1992).

98. Bartlet, "The new Repertory at the Opéra during the Reign of Terror," pp. 107–56.

99. Johnson, *Listening in Paris*, pp. 152–3.

100. I am following – and expanding – James Johnson's argument.

101. Jean-Marc Devocelle, "La cocarde directoriale dérivée d'un symbole révolutionnaire," *Annales Historiques de la Révolution Française* no. 3 (July–September 1992): 355.

102. Heuer, "Hats on for the Nation!" pp. 28–52.

103. Jacques-Paul Fronton Duplantier, *Opinion sur le projet relatif à la cocarde nationale, Séance du 3 floréal, An 7* (Paris: Imprimerie Nationale, 1799).

104. Dumesnil Charles Desplanques, *Opinion de Desplanques, sur le projet de résolution relative à la cocarde nationale, séance du 7 nivose An 7* (Paris: Imprimerie nationale, 1799), cited in Heuer, "Hats on for the Nation!"

105. Eschasseriaux, jeune, *Sur le projet de résolution relatif à la cocarde nationale, 3 floréal, an 7* (Paris: Imprimerie Nationale, 1799), p. 1.

106. Ibid., p. 2.

107. Ibid., p. 8.

108. Ibid., p. 7.

109. Ibid.

110. Devocelle, "La cocarde directoriale dérivée d'un symbole révolutionnaire," p. 362.

111. Mason, *Singing the French Revolution*, Chapter 5.

112. Johnson, "Revolutionary Audiences and the Impossible Imperatives of Fraternity," p. 78; Johnson, *Listening in Paris*, p. 159.

113. Ribeiro, *Fashion in the French Revolution*, pp. 124–9.

114. Mason, *Singing the French Revolution*, Chapter 6.

115. Johnson, *Listening in Paris*, p. 159.

116. Henri Grégoire, "Rapport et Projet de Décret sur les costumes des législateurs et des autres fonctionnaires publics (28 fructidor, an III)," in *La culture des sans culottes*, ed. Bernard Deloche and Jean-Michel Leniaud (Paris: Les éditions de Paris, 1989), pp. 295–303.

117. Hunt, "Symbolic Forms of Political Practice," p. 78.

118. Herbert Josephs, "Opera during the Revolution: Lyric Drama in a Political Theater," *The French Review* 62, no. 6 (May 1989): 979.

Chapter 6   Legacies: Culture in the Modern Nation-state

1. In the interests of economy and parallelism, this chapter will not address changes in Britain in the eighteenth century, but rather discuss the nineteenth century in all three cases.

2. Nancy F. Cott, *The Bonds of Womanhood: "Woman's Sphere" in New England, 1780–1835* (New Haven, CT: Yale University Press, 1977); Bonnie G. Smith, *Ladies of the Leisure Class: The Bourgeoises of Northern France in the Nineteenth Century* (Princeton, NJ: Princeton University Press, 1981); Leonore Davidoff and Catherine Hall, *Family Fortunes: Men and Women of the English Middle Class, 1780–1850* (Chicago: University of Chicago Press, 1987).

3. T. J. Lears, *Fables of Abundance: A Cultural History of Advertising in America* (New York: Basic Books, 1994); Marc Martin, *Trois siècles de publicité en France* (Paris: Editions Odile Jacob, 1992); Richard Thomas, *The Commodity Culture of Victorian England: Advertising and Spectacle, 1851–1914* (Stanford, CA: Stanford University Press, 1980).

4. Lisa Tiersten, *Marianne in the Market: Envisioning Consumer Society in fin-de-siècle France* (Berkeley, CA: University of California Press, 2001).

5. Georges de Landemer, *Le carnet de fiançailles* (Paris: Féderlé, *c.*1910), no pagination; see also Henri de Noussane, *Le goût dans l'ameublement* (Paris: Firmin-Didot, 1896), p. 191.

6. Jules Michelet, *Le Peuple* (Paris: Libraire Marcel Didier, 1946 [1846]), p. 231, Note 2, p. 233.

7. Charles Fonsegrive, *La crise sociale* (Paris: Librairie Victor Lecoffre, 1901), p. 57.

8. Pascal Ory, *Les Expositions Universelles de Paris: panorama raisonné, avec des aperçus nouveaux et des illustrations par les meilleurs auteurs* (Paris: Ramsay, 1982), p. 26.

9. Robert W. Rydell, "The Culture of Imperial Abundance: World's Fairs in the Making of American Culture," in *Consuming Visions: Accumulation and Display of Goods in America, 1880–1920*, ed. Simon J. Bronner (New York: W. W. Norton, 1989), pp. 191–216.

10. Paul Greenhalgh, *Ephemeral Vistas: The Expositions Universelles, Great Exhibitions and World's Fairs, 1851–1939* (Manchester: Manchester University Press, 1988).

11. Ibid.

12. Charles Rearick, *Pleasures of the Belle Epoque: Entertainment and Festivity in Turn-of-the-Century France* (New Haven, CT: Yale University Press, 1985), p. 119. For a rather different interpretation, see Werner Plum, *Les expositions universelles au 19è siècle, spectacles du changement socio-culturel,* trans. Pierre Gallissaires (Bonn: Friedrich-Ebert-Stiftung, 1977), p. 63; Richard D. Mandell, *Paris 1900: The Great World's Fair* (Toronto: University of Toronto Press, 1967), p. 4.

13. Paula Findlen, "The Museum: Its Classical Etymology and Renaissance Genealogy," *Journal of the History of Collections* 1, no. 1 (1989): 59–78.

14. Archives Départementales de la Seine VR 219, unidentified clipping (12 April 1895).

15. *Rapport au nom de la 4e Commission sur l'ouverture d'un musée du soir au Petit-Palais.* Presenté par M. Henri Turot et Quentin-Bauchart, p. 6. ADS VR 219.

16. For the paragraph as whole see Neil Harris, Introduction to *The Land of Contrasts, 1880–1901* (New York: George Braziller, 1970), pp. 1–28; the quotation is on p. 24.

17. Barry D. Karl and Stanley N. Katz, "The American Private Philanthropic Foundation and the Public Sphere 1890–1930," *Minerva* 29, no. 2 (Summer 1981): 236–270.

18. For gender argument, see Jane Przybysz, "Quilts, Old Kitchens, and the Social Geography of Gender at Nineteenth Century Sanitary Fairs," in *The Material Culture of Gender, The Gender of Material Culture,* ed. Katharine Martinez and Kenneth L. Ames (Hanover, NH: University Press of New England, 1997).

Bibliography

Visual Sources

Balvay, Charles Clément. *Portrait of Louis XVI*, 1790. Online at http://commons. wikimedia.org.

*Button bearing George Washington's portrait, produced after his inauguration, c.*1789. Tatler & Lawson, Trenton. No. 522-1. Online at http://www.concise. britannica.com.

Callet, Antoine-François. *Louis XVI*, oil on canvas, 1789. Collection du musée d'art Roger-Quilliot, Ville de Clermont-Ferrand, photo by Musée Roger-Quilliot, Clermont-Ferrand. Online at http://www.royalacademy.org.uk/exhibitions/ citizensandkings/portraits-of-sovereigns-and-heads-of-state,318,AR.html.

Cast iron fire back, 1649. Victoria and Albert Museum, London. Museum number M. 119-1984.

Coiffeuse emblèmes révolutionnaires. Musée Carnavalet, Paris. Inventory number MB211. ©Photo copyright Musées de la Ville, Paris/Cliché Andreani.

Cup and cover. Victoria and Albert Museum, London. Museum number REPRO.1888B/1,2-635. Online at http://images.vam.ac.uk.

Desprez, Louis Jean. *Circular clear glass plaque with faceted edges, enclosing a sulphide profile portrait of George Washington*, gilded metal ring and collar. Illinois State Museum.

Embroidered miniature portrait of Charles I, 1640–1690. Victoria and Albert Museum, London. Museum number 812-1891.

Embroidery Collection. Museum of Fine Arts, Boston.

Embroidery Collection. Smithsonian Institution, Washington, DC.

Embroidery Collection. British Museum, London.

Embroidery Collection. Winterthur Museum, Winterthur, DE.

Furniture Collection. The Louvre, Paris.

Furniture Collection. Musée des Arts Décoratifs, Paris.

Furniture Collection. Château de Versailles, Versailles.

Gheeraerts, Marcus. *Portrait of Margaret Laton*, 1620. Victoria and Albert Museum, London. Museum number E. 214-1994. Online at http://images.vam.ac.uk.

George Washington: A National Treasure. Washington, DC: National Portrait Gallery, Smithsonian Institution Press; Seattle, WA: in association with the University of Washington Press, 2002.

George Washington Sulphide Portrait, 1800. Baccarat, France.

Gerbier, Sr. Balthazar. *Portrait miniature of Charles I*, 1618–1620. Victoria and Albert Museum, London. Museum number P.47.1935. Online at http://images.vam.ac.uk.

Gold and enamel miniature slide, depicting Charles I, 1650–1660. Victoria and Albert Museum, London. Museum number M. 263-1975.

Govaers [Gouvers], Daniel and Massé, Jean-Baptiste. *Gold enameled snuff box depicting Louis XV and Maria Leckzinska*. The Louvre, Paris. Museum number 1725l. Online at http://www.louvre.fr/llv/oeuvres.

Lace Panel, 1600–1650. Victoria and Albert Museum, London. Museum number T.17-1909. Online at http://images.vam.ac.uk

Lord Keeper's seal cup, The, 1626–1627. Victoria and Albert Museum, London. Museum number M.59:1,2-1993. Online at http://images.vam.ac.uk.

Maden. *Brass sealing wax case*, 1657. Victoria and Albert Museum, London. Museum number M. 188-1930.

Manufacture de Sèvres, 1795. Alfred Duane Pell Collection, National Museum of American History, Smithsonian Institution, Washington, DC.

Modes et Révolutions, 1789–1804: Exposition faite au Musée de la Mode et du Costume, Palais Galliera, 8 février–7 mai 1989. Paris: Editions Paris-Musées, 1989.

Mortlake Tapestry Factory. *Tapestry from the story of Vulcan*, 1620–1625. Victoria and Albert Museum, London. Museum number T.170-1978. Online at http://images.vam.ac.uk.

Meuble à deux corps. Musée Carnavalet, Paris. Inventory number MB 200.

Oliver, Isaac. *Portrait miniature of Henry Frederick Prince of Wales*, 1612. Victoria and Albert Museum, London. Museum number P.149-1910. Online at http://images.vam.ac.uk.

Passe, Simon de. *Medallion of Charles, Prince of Wales*, 1616. Victoria and Albert Museum, London. Museum number 961-1904. Online at http://images.vam.ac.uk.

Passe, Simon de. *Medallion of King James I, Anne of Denmark, and Charles Prince of Wales*, 1616–1620. Victoria and Albert Museum, London. Museum number 062-1904. Online at http://images.vam.ac.uk.

Portrait of Captain Smart, 1639. Victoria and Albert Museum, London. Museum number 534-1892. Online at http://images.vam.ac.uk

Portrait of Dudley, Third Baron North, 1615. Victoria and Albert Museum, London. Museum number P.4&:1-1948. Online at http://images.vam.ac.uk

Ramsay, David. *Clock depicting James 1*, 1610–1615. Victoria and Albert Museum, London. Museum number A. 35-1910. Online at http://images.vam.ac.uk.

Rawlins, Thomas. *Lead cast plaquette depicting Charles II as Prince of Wales*, 1645. Victoria and Albert Museum, London. Museum number A.57-1926.

Sheldon, Caroline Stebbins. *Embroidery of Mt. Vernon*, 1807. Online at http://www.memorialhall.mass.edu/collection.

Silver locket, 1600–1700. Victoria and Albert Museum, London. Museum number 827-1864.

Sueur, Hubert le. *Bust of Charles I,* marble, 1631. Victoria and Albert Museum, London. Museum number M.7-1931. Online at http://images.vam.ac.uk.

Table de chevet à trois tiroirs, late 18ᵗʰ century. Musée Carnavalet, Paris. Inventory number MB 199.

Tin-glazed earthenware bottle, decorated with a crown, 1643. Victoria and Albert Museum, London. Museum number C.114-1938.

Vie en France autour de 1789: Images et représentation 1785–1795, La. Exhibition catalogue for the Bordeaux Musée des Arts Décoratifs, inv. 5376. Paris, 1989.

Primary Printed Sources

An Act Touching Marriages and the Registering thereof; and also touching Births and Burials. London: John Field, 1653.

The Actors Remonstrance or Complaint. London: Eward Nickson, 1643.

Adams, Samuel. *The Writings of Samuel Adams*, ed. Harry Alanzo Cushing. New York: G. P. Putnam's Sons, 1908.

Avalon Project at Yale Law School. http://www.yale.edu/lawweb/avalon.

Baker, Richard. *Theatrum Redivivum or the Theater Vincated.* London: T. R. for Francis Eglesfiled, 1661.

Blondel, Spire. *L'art pendant la révolution, beaux-arts, arts décoratifs.* Paris: Laurens, 1887.

Bonnay, Charles-François, marquis de. *Rapport fait au nom du Comité d'Agriculture et de Commerce, sur l'uniformité à établir dans les Poids et mesures et opinion de M. Bureaux de Pusy sur le même sujet.* Paris: De l'Imprimerie nationale, 1790.

Butterfield, L. H., *et al.* (eds). *The Book of Abigail and John: Selected Letters of the Adams Family, 1762–1784.* Cambridge, MA: Harvard University Press, 1975.

By the King a proclamation concerning the execution of the lawes against recusants. London: Bonham Norton and Iohn Bill, Printers to the Kings most Excellent Maiestie, 1626–1627.

By the King: A proclamation concerning the trade of Ginney, and Binney, in the parts of Africa. London: Robert Barker, printer to the Kings most excellent Maiestie and by the assignes of Iohn Bill, 1631.

Chapotte, A.-R. Chevalier de Mopinot de la. *Proposition d'un monument à élever dans la capitale de la France, pour transmetter aux races futures l'époque de l'heureuse révolution qui l'a revivifiée sous le règne de Louis XVI.* Paris, 1790.

Chavigné, François-Antoine Davy de. *Projet d'un monument sur l'emplacement de la Bastille.* Paris, 1789.

Commager, Henry Steele (ed.). *Documents of American History.* New York: F. S. Crofts & Co., 1943.

"Confident Republican, A." *The Independent Chronicle and the Universal Advertiser* [Boston], July 7, 1785.

Cresswell, Nicholas. *The Journal of Nicholas Cresswell, 1774–1777.* Port Washington, NY: Kennikat Press, 1968.

Cromwell, Oliver. *A Catalogue and Collection of All Those Ordinances, Proclamations, Declarations, etc.* London: William Du-Gard and Henry Hills, 1654.

A Declaration of the Lords and Commons Assembled in Parliament For the Appeasing and Quietting of All Unlawfull Tumults and Insurrections... Also an Ordinance of Both Houses, for the Suppressing of Stage-Playes. London: John Wright, September 2, 1642.

"Déclaration portant règlement pour les habits, et défenses de porter aucuns passemens d'or et d'argent: Paris, 31 mai 1644." In *Receuil générale des anciennes lois françaises*, vol. 17. Paris: Belin-leprieur, 1829.

Desplanques, Dumesnil Charles. *Opinion de Desplanques, sur le projet de résolution relative à la cocarde nationale, séance du 7 nivose an 7.* Paris: Imprimerie nationale, An 7.

Dickinson, John. *The Late Regulations, Respecting the British Colonies on the Continent of America Considered, in a Letter from a Gentleman in Philadelphia to his Friend in London.* Philadelphia, 1765.

Duplantier, Jacques-Paul Fronton. *Opinion sur le projet relatif à la cocarde nationale.* Séance du 3 floréal, year 7. Paris: Imprimerie Nationale, 1799. Newberry 2.12056. FRC.

Durham, James. *The Law Unsealed: Or a Practical Exposition of the Ten Commandments.* 1655.

Dwight, Timothy. *Greenfield Hill: A Poem in Seven Parts.* New York: Childs and Swaine, 1794.

"Edit sur la réforme des habits, (1): Paris, 12 juillet, 1549." In *Recueil générale des anciennes lois françaises*, vol. 13. Paris: Belin-leprieur, 1828.

Eschasseriaux, jeune. *Sur le projet de résolution relatif à la cocarde nationale*, Séance du 3 floréal. Paris: Imprimerie Nationale, 1799. Newberry 2.12812 FRC.

Fox, George. *A Warning to all the merchants in London, and such as buy and sell: with an advisement to them to lay aside their superflu and with it to nouirish the poor.* London: Thomas Simmons, 1648.

Gastin. *Sur le projet de résolution relatif à la Cocarde nationale*, Séance du 29 floréal, year 7. Paris: Imprimerie Nationale, 1799. Newberry 2.14372 FRC.

Goulet, Nicolas Letemple. *Le Temples des lois et de la liberté: Projet présenté au Comité d'Instruction publique de la Convention nationale, par le Citoyen Goulet, Architecte Expert du Département pour l'estimation des Domaines nationaux.* Paris, no date.

Grégoire, H. "Rapport et Projet de Décret sur les costumes des législateurs et des autres fonctionnaires publics, 28 fructidor, an III," in *La Culture des Sans-*

Culottes, ed. Bernard Deloche and Jean-Michel Leniaud. Paris: Editions de Paris, 1989.

Grégoire, H. "Système de dénominations topographiques Pour les places, rues, quais, etc de toutes les communes de la République," in *La Culture des Sans-Culottes*, ed. Bernard Deloche and Jean-Michel Leniaud. Paris: Editions de Paris, 1989.

Guillaume, J. (ed.). *Procès-verbaux du comité d'instruction publique de la Convention Nationale*. Paris: Imprimerie nationale, 1891.

Houël, Jean-Pierre-Louis-Laurent. *Projet d'un Monument Public*. Paris: 1799–1800.

Hubert, Auguste. *Rapport sur l'embellissement du Palais et du Jardin National, du Pont et de la Place de la Révolution; présenté au Comité de Salut public par Hubert, Architecte*. Paris: 1794.

Journal de la mode et du goût, ou Amusemens du salon et de la toilette, February 25, 1790.

Journal de la mode et du goût, ou Amusemens du salon et de la toilette, March 5, 1790.

Le journal des dames et des modes, XIIIeme cahier June 25, 1790.

Journal of the First Congress of the American Colonies, in Opposition to the Tyrannical Acts of the British Parliament; Held at New York, October 7, 1765. New York: E. Winchester, 1845.

Landemer, Georges de. *Le carnet de fiançailles*. Paris: Féderlé, *c*.1910.

Mather, Cotton. *India Christiana*. Boston: B. Green, 1721.

Mercier, Cr. Fr. X. *Comment M'habillerai-je? Reflexions politiques et philosophiques sur l'habillement français et sur la nécessité d'un costume national*. Paris: printed by the author, 1793.

Milton, John. *The Doctrine and Discipline of Divorce: Restord to the Good of Both Sexes*. London: T. P. and M. S., 1643.

Morris, Robert. "Robert Morris to the President of Congress, January 15, 1782." Reprinted in Francis Whatron, *The Revolutionary Diplomatic Correspondence of the United States under Direction of Congress*, Vol. 5. Washington, DC: Government Printing Office, 1889.

Noussane, Henri de. *Le goût dans l'ameublement*. Paris: Firmin-Didot, 1896.

Observations sur le calendrier républicain, 15 Floréal. Paris: 1795.

"On American Manufactures." *American Museum* 1 (February 1787): 119.

The Order of My Lord Mayor, the Aldermen, and the Sheriffes, for their meetings and wearing of their apparrel throughout the year. London: Flesher, 1656.

The Order of My Lord Mayor, the Aldermen, and the Sheriffes, for their meetings and wearing of their apparrel throughout the year. London: Samuel Roycroft, 1692.

Pensées sur les coupeurs de tresses. Paris: 1794.

Rapport au nom de la IVe Commission sur l'ouverture d'un musée du soir au Petit-Palais, presenté par M. Henri Turot et Quentin-Bauchart. Archives Départementales de la Seine VR 219.

Rapport fait au nom du comité d'instruction publique sur la nécessité et les moyens d'introduire dans toute la République les nouveaux poids et mesures précéemment décrétés. Paris: 1795.

Romme, G. *Rapport sur l'ere de la République.* Paris: September 10, 1793.

Sade, D.A.F. de. *Philosophy in the Bedroom.* New York: Grove Press, 1990.

Saint-Simon, Louis de Rouvroy de. *The Memoirs of the Duke de Saint-Simon: Volume V,* trans. Francis Arkwright. New York: Brentano's, 1915.

Sans Souci, alias Free and Easy, or an Evening's Peep into a Polite Circle: An Intire New Entertainment in Three Acts. Boston: Warden and Russell, 1785.

Simmons, Amelia. *American Cookery, Or the Art of Dressing, Viands, Fish, Poultry and Vegetables, and the Best Modes of Making, Pastes, Puffs, Pies, Tarts Puddings, Custards and Preserves, and all kind of Cakes, from the imperial Plum to plain Cake, adapted to this Country, and all grades of life, By Amelia Simmons, an American Orphan.* Hartford, CT: Hudson and Goodwin, 1796.

Smyth, J. F. D. *A Tour of the United States of America.* London: G. Robinson, 1784.

Société populaire et républicaine des arts. *Considérations sur les avantages de changer le costume français.* Paris: De l'imprimerie de Fantelin, 1790.

Two Broad-Sides Against Tobacco: The First by King James of Famous Memory; his Counterblast to tobacco and the Second transcribed out of that learned Physician Dr. Everard Maynwaringe. London: John Hancock, 1672.

Tyler, Royall. *The Contrast: A Comedy in Five Acts.* Boston: Houghton Mifflin, 1920.

"Unidentified Clipping of 12 April 1795." Archives Départementales de la Seine. VR 219.

Verhelst. *Plan allégorique d'un jardin de la Révolution Française et des vertus Républicaines.* Paris: De l'Imprimerie d'Emmanuel Brosselard, 1794.

Voinier, Antoine. *Projet d'un monument triomphal en l'honneur des quatorze Armées de la République.* Paris: 1794.

"Warren–Adams Letters, being chiefly a correspondence among John Adams, Samuel Adams, and James Warren, 1743–1814." *Massachusetts Historical Society Collections* 73 (1925): 187.

Washington, George. "Washington to Mason, April 5, 1769," in *Papers of George Mason,* 1752–1792, ed. Robert A. Rutland. Chapel Hill, NC: University of North Carolina Press, 1970.

A Whip for a Drunkard, and a Curbe for Prophanesse: Being an Abstract of all the severall Statutes in force against Sabbath-breaking, Swearing, Drunkenness and unlawful Gaming. London: Robert White, 1646.

"'Z' For the American Herald." *American Herald* [Boston], May 16, 1785.

Secondary Sources

Abrahams, Roger D. "Antick Dispositions and the Perilous Politics of Culture: Costume and Culture in Jacobean England and America." *The Journal of American Folklore* 111, No. 440 (Spring 1998): 115–32.

Achinstein, Sharon. "Women on Top in the Pamphlet Literature of the English Revolution." *Women's Studies* 1 (1994): 131–63.

Adams, William Howard (ed.). *The Eye of Thomas Jefferson.* Washington, DC: National Gallery of Art, 1976.

Agnew, Jean-Christophe. *Worlds Apart: The Market and the Theater in Anglo-American Thought, 1550–1750.* Cambridge: Cambridge University Press, 1986.

Alder, Ken. *The Measure of All Things.* London: Little Brown, 2002.

Anderson, Benedict. *Imagined Communities: Reflections on the Origin and Spread of Nationalism.* London: Verso, 1983.

Anderson, Jenny and Sauer, Elizabeth (eds). *Books and Readers in Early Modern England: Material Studies.* Philadelphia: University of Pennsylvania Press, 2002.

Andrews, Charles M. "The Boston Merchants and the Non-Importation Movement." *Publications of the Colonial Society of Massachusetts* 19 (January 1917): 165–9.

Arizzoli-Clémentel, Pierre. "Les Arts du décor." In *Aux Armes et aux arts! Les Arts de la Révolution, 1789–1799*, ed. Philippe Bordes and Régis Michel. Paris: A. Biro, 1988.

Arminjon, Catherine. *L'art de vivre: Decorative Arts and Design in France, 1789–1989.* London: Thames and Hudson, 1989.

Armitage, David. "Making the Empire British: Scotland in the Atlantic World 1542–1707." *Past and Present* 155 (May 1997): 34–63.

Ashley, Maurice. *Oliver Cromwell and his World.* London: Thames and Hudson, 1972.

Auslander, Leora. *Taste and Power: Furnishing Modern France.* Berkeley, CA: University of California Press, 1996.

Auslander, Leora. "Women's Suffrage, Citizenship Law and National Identity: Gendering the Nation-State in France and Germany, 1871–1918," in *Women's Rights and Human Rights: International Historical Perspectives*, ed. Patricia Grimshaw, Katie Holmes and Marilyn Lake. London: Macmillan, 2001, pp. 138–52.

Auslander, Leora. "Regeneration through the Everyday? Furniture in Revolutionary Paris." *Art History* 28, No. 2 (April 2005): 227–47.

Auslander, Leora. "Beyond Words." *American Historical Review* 110 (October 2005): 1015–45.

Avril, Paul. *L'ameublement parisien avant, pendant, et après la revolution.* Paris: A. Sinjon, 1929.

Axtell, James. "The White Indians of Colonial America." *The William and Mary Quarterly* 32, No. 1 (Jan. 1975): 55–88.

Axtell, James. *The Invasion Within: The Contest of Cultures in Colonial North America.* New York: Oxford University Press, 1985.

Axtell, James. "Colonial America without the Indians: Counterfactual Reflections." *Journal of American History* 73, No. 4 (Mar. 1987): 981–96.

Axtell, James. *Natives and Newcomers: The Cultural Origins of North America.* New York: Oxford University Press, 2001.

Axtell, James and Sturtevant, William C. "The Unkindest Cut, or Who Invented Scalping?" *William and Mary Quarterly* 37, no. 3 (July 1980): 451–72.

Backscheider, Paula R. *Spectacular Politics: Theatrical Power and Mass Culture in Early Modern England.* Baltimore, MD: Johns Hopkins University Press, 1993.

Baden-Baden, Staatliche Kunsthalle. *Revolutionsarchitektur: Boullée, Ledoux, Lequeu.* Stuttgart-Bad Cannstatt, 1970.

Baecque, Antoine de. *La caricature révolutionnaire.* Paris: Editions du CNRS, 1988.

Baecque, Antoine de. *The Body Politic: Corporeal Metaphor in Revolutionary France, 1770–1800*, trans. Charlotte Mandell. Stanford, CA: Stanford University Press, 1997.

Baker, Keith Michel. *Inventing the French Revolution: Essays on French Political Culture in the Eighteenth Century.* Cambridge: Cambridge University Press, 1990.

Baker, Keith Michel *et al. The French Revolution and the Creation of Modern Political Culture.* Oxford: Pergamon Press, 1987–94.

Barrielle, Jean-François. *Le style empire.* Paris: Flammarion, 1982.

Bartlet, M. Elizabeth C. "The New Repertory at the Opéra during the Reign of Terror: Revolutionary Rhetoric and Operatic Consequences," in *Music and the French Revolution*, ed. Malcolm Boyd. Cambridge: Cambridge University Press, 1992, pp. 107–56.

Bauman, Zygmunt. *Modernity and the Holocaust.* Ithaca, NY: Cornell University Press, 1989.

Baumgarten, Linda. *Eighteenth-Century Clothing at Williamsburg.* Williamsburg: The Colonial Williamsburg Foundation, 1986.

Baumgarten, Linda. *What Clothes Reveal: The Language of Clothing in Colonial and Federal America: The Colonial Williamsburg Collection.* Williamsburg, VA: The Colonial Williamsburg Foundation, 2002.

Beaune, Colette. *The Birth of an Ideology: Myths and Symbols of Nation in Late-medieval France*, trans. Susan Ross Huston. Berkeley: University of California Press, 1991.

Bedini, Silvio A. "The Mace and the Gavel: Symbols of Government in America." *Transactions of the American Philosophical Society* 87, No. 4 (1997): 1–84.

Beeman, Richard R. "Deference, Republicanism, and the Emergence of Popular Politics in Eighteenth-Century America." *The William and Mary Quarterly* 49, No. 3 (July 1992): 401–30.

Beik, William. *Absolutism and Society in Seventeenth-Century France: State Power and Provincial Aristocracy in Languedoc*. Cambridge: Cambridge University Press, 1988.

Bell, David. *The Cult of the Nation in France: Inventing Nationalism, 1680–1800*. Cambridge, MA: Harvard University Press, 2001.

Bendjebbar, André. "Le théâtre angevin pendant la Révolution." *Revue de la Société d'histoire du théâtre* 169 (1991): 136–46.

Bercé, Jean-Yves. *Revolt and Revolution in Early Modern Europe: An Essay on the History of Political Violence*, trans. Joseph Bergin. New York: St. Martins, 1987.

Bergdoll, Barry George. "Historical Reasoning and Architectural Politics: Léon Vaudoyer and the Development of French Historicist Architecture." Ph.D. dissertation, Columbia University, 1986.

Bergeron, David. *English Civic Pageantry 1558–1642*. London: Edward Arnold, 1971.

Berlant, Lauren. *The Anatomy of National Fantasy: Hawthorne, Utopia, and Everyday Life*. Chicago: Chicago University Press, 1991.

Berlant, Lauren (ed.). *Intimacy*. Chicago: Chicago University Press, 2000.

Berlin, Ira. *Many Thousands Gone: The First Two Centuries of Slavery in America*. Cambridge, MA: Belknap, 1998.

Beurdeley, Michel. *La France à l'encan 1789–1799: Exode des objets d'art sous la Revolution*. Paris: Librairie Jules Tallandier, 1981.

Beurdeley, Michel. *Georges Jacob (1739–1814) et son temps*. Paris: Monelle Hayot, 2002.

Bianchi, Serge. *La révolution culturelle de l'an II: Elites et peuple 1789–1799*. Paris: Aubier, 1982.

Blackburn, Roderic H. and Ruth Piwonka. *Remembrance of Patria: Dutch Arts and Culture in Colonial America, 1609–1776*. New York: Albany Institute of History and Art, 1988.

Blair, Karen. *The Clubwoman as Feminist: True Womanhood Redefined, 1868–1914*. New York: Holmes and Meier, 1980.

Blank, Paula. *Broken English: Dialects and the Politics of Language in Renaissance Writings*. New York: Routledge, 1996.

Blanning, T. C. W. *The Culture of Power and the Power of Culture: Old Regime Europe 1660–1789*. Oxford: Oxford University Press, 2002.

Bloch, Ruth. *Gender and Morality in Anglo-American Culture*. Berkeley, CA: University of California Press, 2001.

Bonney, Richard. "What's New about the New French Fiscal History." *Journal of Modern History* 70, No. 3 (Sept. 1998): 639–67.

Bourdieu, Pierre. *Distinction: A Social Critique of the Judgment of Taste*, trans. Richard Nice. Cambridge, MA: Harvard University Press, 1984.

Boyd, Malcolm. *Music and the French Revolution*. Cambridge: Cambridge University Press, 1992.

Boylan, Anne M. *The Origins of Women's Activism: New York and Boston, 1797–1840*. Chapel Hill, NC: University of North Carolina Press, 2002.

Breen, T. H. "English Origins and New World Development: The Case of the Covenanted Militia in Seventeenth-Century Massachusetts." *Past and Present* 57 (November 1972): 74–96.

Breen, T. H. "An Empire of Goods: The Anglicization of Colonial America, 1690–1776." *Journal of British Studies* 25 (Oct. 1986): 467–99.

Breen, T. H. "Narrative of Commercial Life: Consumption, Ideology, and Community on the Eve of the American Revolution." *The William and Mary Quarterly*, No. 3 (July 1993): 471–501.

Breen, T. H. *The Marketplace of Revolution: How Consumer Politics Shaped American Independence*. New York: Oxford University Press, 2004.

Brenner, Robert. *Merchants and Revolution: Commercial Change, Political Conflict, and London's Overseas Traders 1550–1653*. Princeton, NJ: Princeton University Press, 1993.

Brewer, John. "'The Most Polite Age and the Most Vicious': Attitudes towards Culture as Commodity 1600–1800," in *The Consumption of Culture, 1600–1800*, ed. Ann Bermingham and John Brewer. London: Routledge, 1995, pp. 341–61.

Brewer, John. *The Pleasures of the Imagination: English Culture in the Eighteenth Century*. New York: Farrar, Straus, Giroux, 1997.

Brooks, Peter. *The Melodramatic Imagination: Balzac, Henry James, Melodrama, and the Mode of Excess*. New Haven, CT: Yale University Press, 1976.

Brown, Jonathan. *Kings and Connoisseurs: Collecting Art in Seventeenth-century Europe*. Princeton, NJ: Princeton University Press, 1995.

Brown, Keith M. "The Scottish Aristocracy, Anglicization and the Court, 1603–38." *The Historical Journal* 36, No. 3 (Sept. 1993): 543–76.

Burgess, Glenn. *Absolute Monarchy and the Stuart Constitution*. New Haven, CT: Yale University Press, 1996.

Burgess, Glenn. "Was the English Civil War a War of Religion? The Evidence of Political Propaganda." *The Huntington Library Quarterly* 61, No. 2 (1998): 173–201.

Burt, Richard A. "'Licensed by Authority': Ben Jonson and the Politics of Early Stuart Theater." *English Literary History* 54, No. 3 (Autumn 1987): 529–60.

Bushman, Richard L. *The Refinement of America: Persons, Houses, Cities*. New York: Vintage, 1992.

Butler, Jon. *Becoming America: The Revolution before 1776*. Cambridge, MA: Harvard University Press, 2000.

Butler, Jon. "Enthusiasms Described and Decried: The Great Awakening as Interpretive Fiction." *Journal of American History* 69, No. 2 (Sept. 1982): 305–25.

Butler, Martin. "Early Court Culture: Compliment or Criticism?" *The Historical Journal* 32, No. 2 (June 1989): 425–35.

Calloway, Colin G. *New Worlds for Old: Indians, Europeans and the Remaking of Early America.* Baltimore, MD: Johns Hopkins University Press, 1988.

Campbell, Peter R. "Review: New Light on Old Regime Politics." *The Historical Journal* 40, No. 3 (Sept. 1997): 835–43.

Canny, Nicholas. "The British Atlantic World: Working Towards a Definition." *The Historical Journal* 33, No. 2 (June 1990): 479–97.

Canny, Nicholas and Padgen, Anthony (eds). *Colonial Identity in the Atlantic World, 1500–1800.* Princeton, NJ: Princeton University Press, 1987.

Carlton, Charles. *Going to the Wars: The Experience of the British Civil Wars 1638–1651.* London: Routledge, 1992.

Castelot, André. *Queen of France.* New York: Harper & Brothers, 1957.

Certeau, Michel de *et al. Une Politique de la Langue: La Révolution française et les patois.* Paris: Editions Gallimard, 1975.

Chapman, Sara E. *Private Ambition and Political Alliances: The Phélypeaux de Pontchartrain Family and Louis XIV's Government, 1650–1715.* Rochester, NY and Woodbridge, Suffolk, UK: University of Rochester Press, 2004.

Chartier, Roger. *The Cultural Uses of Print in Early Modern France*, trans. Lydia G. Cochrane. Princeton, NJ: Princeton University Press, 1987.

Chartier, Roger. "Introduction to Part II." In *A History of Private Life III: Passions of the Renaissance*, ed. Roger Chartier, trans. Arthur Goldhammer. Cambridge, MA: Harvard, 1989, pp. 163–6.

Chartier, Roger. *The Cultural Origins of the French Revolution*, trans. Lydia Cochrane. Durham, NC: Duke University Press, 1991.

Chase, Judith Wragg. *Afro-American Art and Craft.* New York: Van Nostrand Reinhold, 1971.

Choay, Françoise. *The Invention of the Historic Monument*, trans. Lauren O'Connell. New York: Cambridge University Press, 2001.

Clark, Katerina. *Petersburg, Crucible of Cultural Revolution.* Cambridge, MA: Harvard University Press, 1995.

Cobban, Alfred. *Social Interpretation of the French Revolution.* Cambridge: Cambridge University Press, 1964.

Cohen, Deborah and O'Connor, M. (eds). *Comparison and History.* New York: Routledge, 2004.

Cohn, Barney. "Cloth, Clothes and Colonialism: India in the nineteenth century," in *Cloth and the Human Experience*, ed. Annette B. Weiner and Jane Schneider. Washington, DC: Smithsonian Institution Press, 1989.

Collinson, Patrick. "Protestant Culture and the Cultural Revolution," in *Reformation to Revolution: Politics and Religion in Early Modern England*, ed. Margo Todd. London and New York: Routledge, 1995, pp. 33–52.

Conway, Cecelia. *African Banjo Echoes in Appalachia: A Study of Folk Traditions.* Knoxville, TN: University of Tennessee Press, 1995.

Copeland, Peter F. *Working Dress in Colonial and Revolutionary America*. Westport, CT: Greenwood Press, 1977.

Coquery, Natacha. *L'espace de pouvoir: de la demeure privé à l'edifice public, Paris 1700–1790*. Paris: Seli Arslan, 2000.

Corns, Thomas N. (ed.). *The Royal Image: Representations of Charles I*. Cambridge: Cambridge University Press, 1999.

Corrigan, Philip and Sayer, Derek. *The Great Arch: English State Formation as Cultural Revolution*. Oxford: Basil Blackwell, 1985.

Cott, Nancy F. *The Grounding of Modern Feminism*. New Haven, CT: Yale University Press, 1987.

Cott, Nancy F. *The Bonds of Womanhood: "Woman's Sphere" in New England, 1780–1835*. New Haven, CT: Yale University Press, 1977.

Coward, Barry. *The Cromwellian Protectorate*. Manchester: Manchester University Press, 2002.

Crawford, Katherine. *Perilous Performances: Gender and Regency in Early Modern France*. Cambridge, MA: Harvard University Press, 2004.

Crawford, Patricia. "The Challenges to Patriarchalism: How Did the Revolution Affect Women?", in *Revolution and Restoration*, ed. John Morrill. London: Collins and Brown, 1992, pp. 112–28.

Cressy, David. *Agnes Bowker's Cat: Travesties and Transgressions in Tudor and Stuart England*. Oxford: Oxford University Press, 2000.

Cressy, David. *Bonfires and Bells: National Memory and the Protestant Calendar in Elizabethan and Stuart England*. Stroud: Sutton, 2004.

Cronon, William. *Changes in the Land: Indians, Colonists, and the Ecology of New England*. New York: Hill and Wang, 1983.

Crowley, John E. "The Sensibility of Comfort." *The American Historical Review* 104, No. 3 (June 1999): 749–82.

Crowston, Claire. *Fabricating Women: The Seamstresses of Old Regime France, 1675–1791*. Durham, NC: Duke University Press, 2001.

Cruickshanks, Eveline (ed.). *The Stuart Courts*. Stroud: Sutton, 2000.

Csikszentmihalyi, Mihaly and Eugene Rochberg-Halton. *The Meaning of Things: Domestic Symbols and the Self*. Cambridge: Cambridge University Press, 1981.

Cumming, Valerie. *Royal Dress: The Image and Reality 1580 to the Present Day*. New York: Holmes and Meier, 1989.

Cunningham, Noble E., Jr. "Political Dimensions of Everyday Life in the New Republic," in *Everyday Life in the Early Republic*, ed. Catherine E. Hutchins. Winterthur, DE: H. F. du Pont Winterthur Museum, 1994, pp. 3–34.

Curtin, Michael. "A Question of Manners: Status and Gender in Etiquette and Courtesy." *Journal of Modern History* 57, No. 3 (Sept. 1985): 395–423.

Dahlberg, Laurie. "France Between the Revolutions, 1789–1848," in *The Sèvres Porcelain Manufactory: Alexandre Brongniart and the Triumph of Art and Industry, 1800–1847*, ed. Tamara Préaud. New Haven, CT: Yale University Press, published for The Bard Graduate Center for Studies in the Decorative Arts, New York, 1997, pp. 15–24.

Darnton, Robert. *The Literary Underground of the Old Regime*. Cambridge, MA: Harvard University Press, 1982.

Darnton, Robert. *The Forbidden Best-Sellers of Pre-Revolutionary France*. New York: W. W. Norton, 1995.

Daufresne, Jean-Claude. *Le Louvre et les Tuileries: Architectures de fêtes et d'apparat: Architectures ephémères*. Paris: Mengès, 1994.

Davidoff, Leonore and Catherine Hall. *Family Fortunes: Men and Women of the English Middle Class, 1780–1850*. Chicago: University of Chicago Press, 1987.

Davis, Natalie. *Society and Culture in Early Modern France*. Stanford, CA: Stanford University Press, 1975.

Deloche, Bernard and Jean-Michel Leniaud (eds). *La culture des sans culottes*. Paris: Les éditions de Paris, 1989.

Deloria, Philip J. *Playing Indian*. New Haven, CT: Yale University Press, 1998.

Desan, Suzanne. *The Family on Trial in Revolutionary France*. Berkeley, CA: University of California Press, 2004.

Desrochers, Robert E. "'Not Fade Away': The Narrative of Venture Smith, an African American in the Early Republic." *The Journal of American History* 84, No. 1 (June 1997): 40–66.

Detienne, Marcel. *Comparer l'incomparable*. Paris: Editions du Seuil, 2000.

Devocelle, Jean-Marc. "La cocarde directoriale dérives d'un symbole révolution-naire." *Annales Historiques de la Révolution Française* No. 3 (July–Sept. 1992): 355–66.

Downs, Joseph. "The de Forest Collection of Work by Pennsylvania German Craftsmen." *The Metropolitan Museum of Art Bulletin* 29, No. 10 (1934): 161, 163–9.

Doyle, William. *Venality: The Sale of Offices in Eighteenth-Century France*. Oxford: Clarendon Press, 1996.

Dubois, Ellen. *Feminism and Suffrage: The Emergence of an Independent Women's Movement in America*. Ithaca, NY: Cornell University Press, 1978.

Dunn, Elizabeth E. "'Grasping at the Shadow': The Massachusetts Currency Debate, 1690–1751." *The New England Quarterly* 71, No. 1 (Mar. 1998): 54–76.

Durston, Christopher. *Charles I*. London: Routledge, 1998.

Earle, Alice Morse. *Two Centuries of Costume in America*, Vol. II. New York: Macmillan, 1903.

Eden, Trudy. *Cooking in America, 1590–1800*. New York: Greenwood, 2005.

Edwards, Jay D. "The Origins of Creole Architecture." *Winterthur Portfolio* 29, No. 2/3 (1994): 155–89.

Eley, Geoff and William Hunt (eds). *Reviving the English Revolution: Reflections and Elaborations on the Work of Christopher Hill*. London and New York: Verso, 1988.

Elias, Norbert. *The Court Society*, trans. Edmund Jephcott. New York: Pantheon, 1983.

Elkins, Stanley. *Slavery: A Problem in American Institutional and Intellectual Life.* Chicago: University of Chicago Press, 1959.

Ellis, Geoffrey. "The 'Marxist Interpretation' of the French Revolution." *English Historical Review* 93, No. 367 (April 1978): 353–76.

Epstein, Deborah. *The Politics of Domesticity: Women, Evangelism and Temperance in Nineteenth-Century America.* Middletown, CT: Wesleyan University Press, 1981.

Fairchilds, Cissie. "The Production and Marketing of Populuxe Goods in Eighteenth-century Paris," in *Consumption and the World of Goods*, ed. John Brewer and Roy Porter. London: Routledge, 1993, pp. 228–48.

Fairchilds, Cissie. "Fashion and Freedom in the French Revolution." *Continuity and Change* 18, No. 3 (2000): 419–33.

Fairchilds, Cissie. *Domestic Enemies: Servants and their Masters in Old Regime France.* Baltimore, MD: Johns Hopkins University Press, 2004.

Fassin, Eric. "Fearful Symmetry: Culturalism and Cultural Comparison after Tocqueville." *French Historical* Studies 19, No. 2 (Autumn 1995): 451–60.

Fassin, Eric. "The Purloined Gender: American Feminism in a French Mirror." *French Historical Studies* 22, No. 1 (Winter 1999): 113–38.

Ferguson, Leland. *Uncommon Ground: Archaeology and Early African America, 1650–1800.* Washington, DC: Smithsonian Institution Press, 1992.

Findlen, Paula. "The Museum: Its Classical Etymology and Renaissance Genealogy." *Journal of the History of Collections* 1, No. 1 (1989): 59–78.

Fink, Béatrice. "Cènes civiques, repas révolutionnaires." *The French Review* 62, No. 6 (1989): 957–66.

Fischer, David Hackett. *Albion's Seed: Four British Folkways in America.* New York: Oxford University Press, 1989.

Fischer, Gayle V. *Pantaloons and Power: Nineteenth-Century Dress Reform in the United States.* Kent, OH: Kent State University Press, 2001.

Fisher, Carol. *The American Cookbook: A History.* Jefferson, NC: MacFarland, 2006.

Fitzpatrick, Sheila (ed.). *Cultural Revolution in Russia, 1928–1931.* Bloomington, IN: Indiana University Press, 1977.

Fitzpatrick, Sheila (ed.). *The Cultural Front: Power and Culture in Revolutionary Russia.* Ithaca, NY: Cornell University Press, 1992.

Fleming, E. McClung. "Early American Decorative Arts as Social Documents." *The Mississippi Historical Review* 45, No. 2 (Sept. 1958): 276–84.

Fonsegrive, Charles. *La crise sociale.* Paris: Librairie Victor Lecoffre, 1901.

Forrest, Alan. *Paris, the Provinces, and the French Revolution.* London: Arnold, 2004.

Forster, Robert. *Merchants, Landlords, Magistrates: The Depont Family in the Eighteenth Century.* Baltimore, MD: Johns Hopkins University Press, 1980.

Fox, Adam. "Rumour, News and Popular Political Opinion in Elizabethan and Early Stuart England." *The Historical Journal* 40, No. 3 (Sept. 1997): 597–620.

Fraisse, Geneviève. *Reason's Muse: Sexual Difference and the Birth of Democracy*, trans. Jean Marie Todd. Chicago: University of Chicago Press, 1994.

Friedland, Paul. *Political Actors: Representative Bodies and Theatricality in the Age of the French Revolution.* Ithaca, NY: Cornell University Press, 2002.

Friedman, Monroe. *Consumer Boycotts: Effecting Change through the Marketplace and the Media.* New York: Routledge, 1990.

Furet, François. *Interpreting the French Revolution*, trans. Elborg Forster. Cambridge: Cambridge University Press, 1981.

Gadoury, Victor. *Les monnaies royales françaises de Louis XIII à Louis XVI: 1610–1792.* Monte Carlo: V. Gadoury, 1978.

Garrioch, David. *The Formation of the Parisian Bourgeoisie, 1690–1830.* Cambridge, MA: Harvard University Press, 1996.

Geggus, David. *The Impact of the Haitian Revolution in the Atlantic World.* Columbia, SC: University of South Carolina Press, 2001.

Giesey, Ralph. *Rulership in France 15ᵗʰ–17ᵗʰ centuries.* Aldershot: Ashgate, 2004.

Gillespie, Kate. *Domesticity and Dissent in the Seventeenth Century: English Women Writers and the Public Sphere.* Cambridge: Cambridge University Press, 2006.

Glanville, Philippa. *Silver in Tudor and Early Stuart England.* London: Victoria and Albert Publications, 1990.

Glassie, Henry. *Pattern in the Material Folk Culture of the Eastern United States.* Philadelphia: University of Pennsylvania Press, 1968.

Godineau, Dominique. *Citoyennes tricoteuses: Les femmes du peuple à Paris pendant la Révolution française.* Aix-en-Provence: Alinéa, 1988.

Goldstein, Jan. *The Post-Revolutionary Self: Politics and Psyche in France, 1750–1850.* Cambridge, MA: Harvard University Press, 2005.

Goodfriend, Joyce D. *Before the Melting Pot: Society and Culture in Colonial New York City, 1664–1730.* Princeton, NJ: Princeton University Press, 1992.

Goodman, Dena. *The Republic of Letters: A Cultural History of the Enlightenment.* Ithaca, NY: Cornell University Press, 2004.

Goodwin, Jeff and Jasper, James (eds). *Rethinking Social Movements: Structure, Meaning, and Emotion.* Lanham, MD: Rowman & Littlefield, 2003.

Goodwin, Jeff, Jasper, James and Polletta, Francesca (eds). *Passionate Politics: Emotions and Social Movements.* Chicago: University of Chicago Press, 2001.

Gordon, Daniel. *Citizens without Sovereignty: Equality and Sociability in French Thought, 1670–1789.* Princeton, NJ: Princeton University Press, 1994.

Gould, Deborah. *Feeling Activism: Emotions and Reason in ACT UP's Fight Against AIDS.* Chicago: University of Chicago Press, 2007.

Gould, Eliga H. *The Persistence of Empire: British Political Culture in the Age of Revolution.* Chapel Hill, NC: University of North Carolina Press, 2000.

Grandry, Marie-Noelle de. *Le Mobilier Français: Directoire, Consulat, Empire.* Paris: Editions Massin, 1996.

Greene, Jack P. "Political Mimesis: A Consideration of the Historical and Cultural Roots of Legislative Behavior in the British Colonies in the Eighteenth Century." *American Historical Review* 75, No. 2 (Dec. 1969): 337–60.

Greene, Jack P. *Peripheries and Center: Constitutional Development in the Extended Polities of the British Empire and the United States, 1607–1788.* Athens, GA: University of Georgia Press, 1986.

Greene, Jack P. *Imperatives, Behaviors, and Identities: Essays in Early American Cultural History.* Charlottesville, VA: University Press of Virginia, 1992.

Greene, Jack P. *et al.* "Albion's Seed: Four British Folkways in America – A Symposium." *William and Mary Quarterly* 48, No. 2 (Apr. 1991): 224–308.

Greenhalgh, Paul. *Ephemeral Vistas: The Expositions Universelles, Great Exhibitions and World's Fairs, 1851–1939.* Manchester: Manchester University Press, 1988.

Grégoire, Henri. "Système de dénominations topographiques Pour les places, rues, quais, etc de toutes les communes de la République," in *La Culture des Sans-Culottes*, ed. Bernard Deloche and Jean-Michel Leniaud. Paris: Editions de Paris, 1989, pp. 119–33.

Gullickson, Gay L. *Spinners and Weavers of Auffay: Rural Industry and the Sexual Division of Labor in a French Village, 1750–1850.* Cambridge: Cambridge University Press, 1986.

Gundersen, Joan R. *To Be Useful to the World: Women in Revolutionary America.* New York: Twayne Publishers, 1996.

Habermas, Jürgen. *The Structural Transformation of the Public Sphere: An Inquiry into a Category of Bourgeois Society*, trans. Thomas Burger. Cambridge, MA: MIT Press, 1989.

Hall, Timothy D. *Contested Boundaries: Itinerancy and the Shaping of the Colonial American Religious World.* Durham, NC: Duke University Press, 1994.

Hammond, Paul. "The King's Two Bodies: Representations of Charles II," in *Culture, Politics and Society in Britain, 1660–1800*, ed. Jeremy Black and Jeremy Gregory. Manchester: Manchester University Press, 1991, pp. 13–48.

Hancock, David. "The British Atlantic World: Coordination, Complexity, and the Emergence of the Atlantic Market Economy, 1651–1815." *Itinerario* (Autumn 1999): 107–26.

Hanley, Sarah. *The Lit de Justice of the Kings of France: Constitutional Ideology in Legend, Ritual and Discourse.* Princeton, NJ: Princeton University Press, 1983.

Harris, Jennifer. "The Red Cap of Liberty: A Study of Dress Worn by French Revolutionary Partisans, 1789–95." *Eighteenth-Century French Studies* 14, No. 3 (1981): 283–312.

Harris, Neil. *The Land of Contrasts, 1880–1901.* New York: Braziller, 1970.

Harris, Neil. *The Artist in American Society: The Formative Years, 1790–1860.* Chicago: University of Chicago Press, 1982.

Harris, Tim. "Propaganda and Public Opinion in Seventeenth-Century England," in *Media and Revolution*, ed. Jeremy D. Popkin. Lexington, KY: University Press of Kentucky, 1995, pp. 48–72.

Harte, N. B. "State Control of Dress and Social Change in Pre-Industrial England," in *Trade, Government, and Economy in Pre-Industrial England*, ed. D. C. Coleman and A. H. John. London: Weidenfeld and Nicolson, 1976, pp. 132–65.

Henshall, Nicholas. *The Myth of Absolutism: Change and Continuity in Early Modern European Monarchy*. London: Longman, 1992.

Heuer, Jennifer. "Hats on for the Nation! Women, Citizens, Soldiers, and the 'Sign of the French.'" *French History* 16, No. 1 (2002): 28–52.

Higgins, Patricia. "The Reactions of Women," in *Politics, Religion and the English Civil War*, ed. Brian Manning. London: Edward Arnold, 1973, pp. 179–224.

Hill, Christopher (ed.). *The English Revolution of 1640: Three Essays*. London: Lawrence & Wishart, 1940.

Hill, Christopher. The World Turned Upside Down*: Radical Ideas in the English Revolution*. New York: Viking, 1972.

Hill, Sarah H. "Weaving History: Cherokee Baskets from the Springplace Mission." *The William and Mary Quarterly* 53, No. 1 (Jan. 1996): 115–36.

Hobby, Elaine. "'Discourse So Unsavoury': Women's Published Writings of the 1650s," in *Women, Writing, History: 1640–1740*, ed. Isobel Grundy and Susan Wiseman. London: Batsford, 1992, pp. 16–32.

Hoffmann, H. *Les monnaies royales de France depuis Hugues Capet jusqu'à Louis XVI*. Paris: H. Hoffmann, 1878.

Holifield, E. Brooks. "Peace, Conflict, and Ritual in Puritan Congregations." *Journal of Interdisciplinary History* 23 (Winter 1993): 551–70.

Holstun, James. *Ehud's Dagger: Class Struggle in the English Revolution*. London: Verso, 2000.

Howarth, David. *Images of Rule: Art and Politics in the English Renaissance, 1485–1640*. Berkeley, CA: University of California Press, 1997.

Hulsebosch, Daniel J. "*Imperia in Imperio:* The Multiple Constitutions of Empire in New York, 1750–1777." *Law and History Review* 16, No. 2 (1998): 319–79.

Hunt, Alan. *Governance of the Consuming Passions: A History of Sumptuary Law*. New York: St. Martin's Press, 1996.

Hunt, Lynn. "Introduction: The French Revolution in Culture: New Approaches and Perspectives." *Eighteenth Century Studies* 22, No. 3 (Spring 1989): 293–301.

Hunt, Lynn. *Politics, Culture, and Class in the French Revolution*. Berkeley, CA: University of California Press, 1990.

Hunt, Lynn. *The Family Romance of the French Revolution*. Berkeley, CA: University of California Press, 1992.

Hutton, Ronald. *Debates in Stuart History*. London: Palgrave, 2004.

Hyde, Elizabeth. *Cultivated Power: Flowers, Culture and Politics in the Age of Louis XIV*. Philadelphia: University of Pennsylvania Press, 2005.

Isaac, Rhys. *The Transformation of Virginia 1740–1790*. Chapel Hill, NC: University of North Carolina Press, 1982.

Israel, Jonathan, I. *The Dutch Republic: Its Rise, Greatness and Fall 1477–1806*. New York: Oxford University Press, 1995.

Janneau, Guillaume. *Les Ateliers parisiens d'ébénistes et de menuisiers aux XVIIe et XVIIIe siècles*. Paris: SERG, 1975.

Jansen, H. J. *Projet tendant à concerver les Arts en France*. Paris, 1791.

Jobe, Brock. "The Boston Furniture Industry, 1720–1740," in *Boston Furniture of the Eighteenth Century*, ed. Walter Muir Whitehill. Boston: Colonial Society of Massachusetts, 1974, pp. 191–204.

Johnson, James H. "Musical Experience and the Formation of a French Musical Public." *Journal of Modern History* 64, No. 2 (June 1992): 191–226.

Johnson, James H. "Revolutionary Audiences and the Impossible Imperatives of Fraternity," in *Re-creating Authority in Revolutionary France*, ed. by Bryant T. Ragan Jr. and Elizabeth A. Williams. New Brunswick, NJ: Rutgers University Press, 1992, pp. 57–98.

Johnson, James H. *Listening in Paris: A Cultural History*. Berkeley, CA: University of California Press, 1995.

Johnson, Richard R. "The Search for a Usable Indian: An Aspect of the Defense of Colonial New England." *The Journal of American History* 64, No. 3 (Dec. 1977): 623–51.

Jones, Ann and Peter Stallybrass. *Renaissance Clothing and the Materials of Memory*. Cambridge: Cambridge University Press, 2000.

Jones, Ann and Peter Stallybrass. "Fetishizing the Glove in Renaissance Europe," *Critical Inquiry* 18 (2001): 114–32.

Jones, Colin. "Bourgeois Revolution Revivified: 1789 and Social Change," in *Re-writing the French Revolution*, ed. Colin Lucas. Oxford: Clarendon Press, 1991, pp. 69–118.

Jones, Colin. "The Great Chain of Buying: Medical Advertisement, The Bourgeois Public Sphere, and the Origins of the French Revolution." *American Historical Review* 101 (Feb. 1996): 13–40.

Jones, Colin. "Political Styles and Power in *Ancien Régime* France." *The Historical Journal* 41, No. 4 (Dec. 1998): 1173–82.

Jones, Jennifer M. *Sexing La Mode: Gender, Fashion and Commercial Culture in Old Regime France*. Oxford and New York: Berg, 2004.

Josephs, Herbert. "Opera during the Revolution: Lyric Drama in a Political Theater." *The French Review* 62, No. 6 (May 1989): 975–84.

Jourdan, Annie. *Les monuments de la révolution, 1770–1804: une histoire de representation*. Paris: Champion, 1997.

Kamil, Neil D. "Hidden in Plain Sight: Disappearance and Material Life in Colonial New York," in *American Furniture 1995*, ed. Luke Becherdite and William Hosley. Hanover, NH: University Press of New England, 1995, pp. 191–249.

Kamil, Neil D. *Fortress of the Soul: Violence, Metaphysics, and Material Life in the New World, 1517–1751*. Baltimore, MD: Johns Hopkins University Press, 2005.

Kaplan, Steven L. *Bread, Politics and Political Economy in the Reign of Louis XV: Vol. 1*. The Hague: Martinus Nijhoff, 1976.

Karl, Barry D. and Stanley N. Katz. "The American Private Philanthropic Foundation and the Public Sphere 1890–1930." *Minerva* 29, No. 2 (1981): 236–70.

Kelsey, Sean. *Inventing a Republic: The Political Culture of the English Commonwealth, 1649–1653*. Stanford, CA: Stanford University Press, 1997.

Kerber, Linda. *Women of the Republic: Intellect and Ideology in Revolutionary America*. Chapel Hill, NC: University of North Carolina Press, 1980.

Kerber, Linda. *No Constitutional Right to be Ladies: Women and the Obligations of Citizenship*. New York: Hill and Wang, 1998.

Kettering, Sharon. *Patrons, Brokers, and Clients in Seventeenth-century France*. New York: Oxford University Press, 1986.

King, Thomas. *The Gendering of Men, 1600–1750*. Madison, WI: University of Wisconsin Press, 2004.

Kishlansky, Mark A. *The Rise of the New Model Army*. New York: Cambridge University Press, 1979.

Kleinert, Annemarie. "La Mode – Miroir de la Révolution Française." *Francia* 16 (1989): 78–91.

Knoppers, Laura Lunger. *Constructing Cromwell: Ceremony, Portrait, and Print 1645–1661*. Cambridge: Cambridge University Press, 2000.

Korshak, Yvonne. "The Liberty Cap as a Revolutionary Symbol in America and France." *Smithsonian Studies in American Art* 1, No. 2 (Autumn 1987): 52–69

Kuchta, David. *The Three-Piece Suit and Modern Masculinity: England, 1550–1850*. Berkeley, CA: University of California Press, 2002.

Kwass, Michel. *Privilege and the Politics of Taxation: Liberté, Égalité, Fiscalité*. Cambridge: Cambridge University Press, 2000.

Labrousse, Ernest. *La crise de l'économie française à la fin de l'ancien régime et au début de la Révolution*. Paris: Presses Universitaires de France, 1944.

Landes, Joan B. *Women and the Public Sphere in the Age of the French Revolution*. Ithaca, NY: Cornell University Press, 1988.

Landsmark, Theodore C. "Comments on African American Contributions to American Material Life." *Winterthur Portfolio* 33, No. 4 (Winter 1998): 261–82.

Laurens, Patrick. "La figure officielle de la république française: monnaies et timbres," in *La France démocratique: Mélanges en l'honneur de M. Agulhon*. Paris: Publications de la Sorbonne, 1998, pp. 421–30.

Lears, T. J. *Fables of Abundance: A Cultural History of Advertising in America*. New York: Basic Books, 1994.

Leben, Ulrich. *Molitor: Ébéniste from the Ancien Régime to the Bourbon Restoration*, trans. William Wheeler. London: P. Wilson, 1992.

Lecoq, Anne-Marie. "La symbolique de l'Etat: Les images de la monarchie des premiers Valois à Louis XIV," in *Les lieux de mémoire Vol 2: La Nation*, ed. Pierre Nora. Paris: Gallimard, 1986, pp. 145–92.

Lefebvre, Georges. *Quatre-vingt-neuf*. Paris: Maison du Livre Français, 1939.

Lefuel, Hector. *Georges Jacob: Ébéniste du XVIIIè siècle*. Paris: A. Morancé, 1923.

Leith, James. *Space and Revolution: Projects for Monuments, Squares, and Public Buildings in France, 1789–1799*. Montreal: McGill-Queen's Press, 1991.

Lemire, Beverly. "'A Good Stock of Cloaths': The Changing Market for Cotton Clothing in Britain, 1750–1800." *Textile History* 22, No. 2 (1991): 311–28.

Lemonnier, Patricia. *Weisweiler*. Paris: Editions d'art Monelle Hayot, 1983.

Lepore, Jill. *The Name of War: King Philip's War and the Origins of American Identity*. New York: Knopf, 1998.

Levine, Laura. *Men in Women's Clothing: Anti-Theatricality and Effeminization, 1579–1642*. Cambridge: Cambridge University Press, 1994.

Lichten, Frances. "Pennsylvania-German Folk Art," in *The Concise Encyclopedia of American Antiquities*, ed. Helen Comstock. New York: Hawthorn Books, 1965.

Lindley, David. "Courtly Play: The Politics of Chapman's *The Memorable Masque*," in *The Stuart Courts*, ed. Eveline Cruickshanks. Stroud: Sutton, 2000, pp. 42–58.

Linebaugh, Peter and Marcus Rediker. *The Many-Headed Hydra: Sailors, Slaves and Commoners, and the Hidden History of the Revolutionary Atlantic*. Boston: Beacon Press, 2000.

Little, Ann M. "'Shoot that Rogue, For He Hath an Englishman's Coat on!': Cultural Cross-Dressing on the New England Frontier, 1620–1760." *The New England Quarterly* 74, No. 2 (June 2001): 238–73.

Lougee, Carolyn. *Le Paradis des Femmes: Women, the Salon and Social Stratification in Seventeenth-Century France*. Princeton, NJ: Princeton University Press, 1976.

Lüsebrink, Hans-Jürgen and Rolf Reichhardt. *The Bastille: A History of a Symbol of Despotism and Freedom*, trans. Norbert Schürer. Durham, NC: Duke University Press, 1997.

MacFarlane, Alan. *The Family Life of Ralph Josselin, a Seventeenth-Century Clergyman*. Cambridge: Cambridge University Press, 1970.

Mack, Phyllis. *Visionary Women: Ecstatic Prophecy in Seventeenth-Century England*. Los Angeles: University of California Press, 1992.

Maclean, Gerald. "Literature, Culture, and Society in Restoration England," in *Culture and Society in the Stuart Restoration*, ed. Gerald Maclean. Cambridge: Cambridge University Press, 1995, pp. 3–30.

Madec, Philippe. *Boullée*. Paris: F. Hazan, 1986.

Maguire, Nancy Klein. *Regicide and Restoration: English Tragicomedy, 1660–1671*. Cambridge: Cambridge University Press, 1992.

Mandell, Richard D. *Paris 1900: The Great World's Fair*. Toronto: University of Toronto Press, 1967.

Mansell, Philip. *Dressed to Rule: Royal and Court Costume from Louis XIV to Elizabeth II*. New Haven, CT: Yale University Press, 2005.

Maroteaux, Vincent. *Versailles: Le Roi et son Domaine*. Paris: Picard, 2000.

Martin, Marc. *Trois siècles de publicité en France*. Paris: Editions Odile Jacob, 1992.

Mason, Laura. *Singing the French Revolution: Popular Culture and Politics, 1787–1799*. Ithaca, NY: Cornell University Press, 1996.

Mattingly, Carol. *Appropriate(ing) Dress: Women's Rhetorical Style in Nineteenth-Century America*. Carbondale, IL: Southern Illinois Press, 2002.

Mayes, Charles R. "The Sale of Peerages in Early Stuart England." *Journal of Modern History* 29, No. 1 (March 1957): 21–37.

Maza, Sarah. *Servants and Masters in Eighteenth Century France: The Uses of Loyalty*. Princeton, NJ: Princeton University Press, 1983.

Maza, Sarah. *The Myth of the French Bourgeoisie: An Essay on the Social Imaginary, 1750–1850*. Cambridge, MA: Harvard University Press, 2003.

McClellan, Andrew. *Inventing the Louvre: Art, Politics, and the Origins of the Modern Museum in Eighteenth-Century Paris*. Cambridge: Cambridge University Press, 1994.

McClellan, Elisabeth. *History of American Costume, 1607–1870*. New York: Tudor Publishing, 1937.

McKendrick, Neil, Brewer, John and Plumb, J. H. (eds). *The Birth of a Consumer Society: The Commercialization of Eighteenth-Century England*. London: Europa Publications, 1982.

Melzer, Sara and Norberg, Kathryn (eds). *From the Royal to the Republican Body*. Berkeley, CA: University of California Press, 1998.

Merrell, James H. "Some Thoughts on Colonial Historians and American Indians." *William and Mary Quarterly* 46, No. 1 (Jan. 1989): 94–119.

Merrick, Jeffrey. *The Desacralization of the French Monarchy in the Eighteenth Century*. Baton Rouge, LA: Louisiana State University Press, 1990.

Merrick, Jeffrey. "The Body Politics of French Absolutism," in *From the Royal to the Republican Body: Incorporating the Political in Seventeenth and Eighteenth-century France*, ed. Sara E. Melzer and Kathryn Norberg. Berkeley, CA: University of California Press, 1998, pp. 11–31.

Merrick, Jeffrey. *Order and Disorder under the Ancien Régime*. Newcastle-on-Tyne: Cambridge Scholars Publishing, 2007.

Michelet, Jules. *Le Peuple*. Paris: Librairie Marcel Didier, 1946 [1846].

Modes et Révolutions, 1789–1804: Exposition faite au Musée de la Mode et du Costume, Palais Galliera, 8 février–7 mai 1989. Paris: Editions Paris-Musées, 1989.

Montrose, Louis A. *The Subject of Elizabeth: Authority, Gender, and Representation*. Chicago: University of Chicago Press, 2006.

Morrill, John. "The Impact on Society: A World Turned Upside Down," in *Impact of the English Civil War*, ed. John Morrill. London: Collins and Brown, 1991, pp. 8–16.

Morrill, John. "The British Problem, *c.*1534–1707," in *The British Problem c.1534–1707: State Formation in the Atlantic Archipelago*, ed. Brandan Bradshaw and John Morrill. New York: Palgrave, 1996, pp. 1–38.

Mousnier, Roland E. *The Institutions of France under the Absolute Monarchy 1598–1789: Society and the State,* trans. Brian Pearce. Chicago: University of Chicago, 1979.

Mowl, Timothy and Brian Earnshaw. *Architecture without Kings: The Rise of Puritan Classicism under Cromwell.* Manchester: Manchester University Press, 1995.

Mukerji, Chandra. *Territorial Ambition and the Gardens of Versailles.* Cambridge: Cambridge University Press, 1997.

Mullen, Harryette. "African Signs and Spirit Writing." *Callaloo* 19, No. 3 (Summer 1995): 670–89.

Negroni, Barbara de. *Lectures interdites: Le travail des censures au XVIIIe siècle, 1723–1774.* Paris: Albin Michel, 1995.

Newman, J. "Inigo Jones and the Politics of Architecture," in *Culture and Politics in Early Stuart England,* ed. Kevin Sharpe and Peter Lake. Stanford, CA: Stanford University Press, 1993, pp. 229–57.

Newman, Simon P. *Parades and Politics of the Street: Festive Culture In the Early American Republic.* Philadelphia: University of Pennsylvania Press, 1997.

Norton, Mary Beth. *Liberty's Daughters: The Revolutionary Experience of American Women, 1750–1800.* Boston: Little, Brown and Co., 1980.

Ollard, Richard. *The Image of the King: Charles I and Charles II.* New York: Atheneum, 1979.

Olson, Lester C. *Emblems of American Community in the Revolutionary Era: A Study in Rhetorical Iconology.* Washington, DC: Smithsonian Institution Press, 1991.

O'Neal, John C. *The Authority of Experience: Sensationalist Theory in the French Enlightenment.* University Park, PA: Pennsylvania State University Press, 1996.

Ortiz, Fernando. *Cuban Counterpoint: Tobacco and Sugar.* New York: Knopf, 1947.

Ory, Pascal. *Les Expositions Universelles de Paris: panorama raisonné, avec des aperçus nouveaux et des illustrations par les meilleurs auteurs.* Paris: Ramsay, 1982.

Outram, Dorinda. *The Body and the French Revolution: Sex, Class and Political Culture.* New Haven, CT: Yale University Press, 1988.

Ozouf, Mona. *Festivals and the French Revolution,* trans. Alan Sheridan. Cambridge, MA: Harvard University Press, 1988.

Ozouf, Mona. *Women's Words: Essay on French Singularity,* trans. Jean Marie Todd. Chicago: Chicago University Press, 1997.

Parinaud, Marie-Hélène. Introduction to *The French Revolution in Paris seen through the Collections of the Carnavalet Museum,* ed. Jean Tulard. Paris: Paris-Musées, 1989, pp. 11–14.

Pateman, Carole. *The Sexual Contract.* Stanford, CA: Stanford University Press, 1988.

Paulson, Ronald. *Representations of Revolution: 1789–1820.* New Haven, CT: Yale University Press, 1983.

Peck, Linda Levy. *Court Patronage and Corruption in Early Stuart England*. London and Boston: Unwin Hyman, 1990.

Peck, Linda Levy. "The Language of Patronage: A Discourse of Connection," in *Court Patronage and Corruption in Early Stuart England*, ed. Linda Levy Peck. London: Unwin Hyman, 1990, pp. 12–29.

Peck, Linda Levy. *Consuming Splendour: Society and Culture in Seventeenth-Century England*. Cambridge: Cambridge University Press, 2005.

Perovic, Sanja. "Epochal Breaks: A Semantics of Revolutionary Time." Paper presented at the Modern France Workshop, University of Chicago, April 28, 2006.

Pesco, Daniela del. "Entre projet et utopie: les écrits et la théorie architecturale, 1789–1799," in *Les architectes de la liberté, 1789–1799*. Paris: Ecole nationale supérieure des Beaux Arts, 1989.

Pestana, Carla. *The English Atlantic in an Age of Revolution, 1640–1661*. Cambridge, MA: Harvard University Press, 2004.

Pierson, Michael D. *Free Hearts and Free Homes: Gender and American Anti-slavery Politics*. Chapel Hill, NC: University of North Carolina Press, 2003.

Plum, Werner. *Les expositions universelles au XIXe siècle, spectacles du change-ment socio-culturel*, trans. Pierre Gallissaires. Bonn: Friedrich-Ebert-Stiftung, 1977.

Pommier, Edouard. "Versailles, l'image du souverain," in *Les lieux de mémoire Vol 2: La Nation*, ed. Pierre Nora. Paris: Gallimard, 1986, pp. 451–96.

Porter, Stephen. *Destruction in the English Civil* Wars. Phoenix Mill and Dover, NH: Alan Sutton, 1994.

Poulot, Dominique. *Musée, Nation, Patrimoine: 1789–1815*. Paris: Gallimard, 1997.

Pradère, Alexandre. *French Furniture Makers: The Art of the Ebéniste from Louis XIV to the Revolution*, trans. Perran Wood. London: Sothebys, 1989.

Przybysz, Jane. "Quilts, Old Kitchens, and the Social Geography of Gender at Nineteenth Century Sanitary Fairs," in *The Material Culture of Gender, The Gender of Material Culture*, ed. Katharine Martinez and Kenneth L. Ames. Hanover, NH: University Press of New England, 1997, pp. 411–42.

Quitt, Martin H. "Immigrant Origins of the Virginia Gentry: A Study of Cultural Transmission and Innovation." *The William and Mary Quarterly* 45, No. 4 (Oct. 1988): 630–55.

Ranum, Orest. *Paris in the Age of Absolutism*. Bloomington, IN: Indiana University Press, 1979.

Ravel, Jeffry. *The Contested Parterre: Public Theater and French Political Culture, 1680–1791*. Ithaca, NY: Cornell University Press, 1999.

Rearick, Charles. *Pleasures of the Belle Epoque: Entertainment and Festivity in Turn-of-the-Century France*. New Haven, CT: Yale University Press, 1985.

Réau, Louis. *L'histoire du vandalisme: les monuments détruits de l'art française*. Paris: Laffont, 1994.

Reddy, William M. *The Navigation of Feelings: A Framework for the History of Emotions*. New York: Cambridge University Press, 2001.

Reedy, Gerard. "Mystical Politics: The Imagery of Charles II's Coronation," in *Studies in Change and Revolution: Aspects of English Intellectual History 1640–1800*, ed. Paul Korshin. Menston: Scolar Press, 1972, pp. 19–42.

Renan, Ernest. "What is a Nation?" in *Nations and Identities*, ed. Vincent P. Pecora. Oxford: Blackwell, 2001, pp. 162–77.

Ribeiro, Aileen. *Fashion in the French Revolution*. New York: Holmes and Meier, 1988.

Ridley, Glynis. "The First American Cookbook." *Eighteenth-century Life* 23 (May 1999): 114–22.

Rigogne, Thierry. *Between State and Market: Printing and Bookselling in Eighteenth-Century France*. Oxford: Voltaire Foundation, 2007.

Roark, Elizabeth Louise. *Artists of Colonial America*. New York: Greenwood Publishing, 2003.

Roche, Daniel. *The People of Paris*, trans. Marie Evans. Berkeley, CA: University of California Press, 1987.

Roche, Daniel. "Apparences révolutionnaires ou révolution des apparences," in *Modes et Révolutions, 1780–1804*. Paris: Editions Paris-Musées, 1989, pp. 105–28.

Roelker, Nancy. "The Appeal of Calvinism to French Noblewomen in the Sixteenth Century." *Journal of Interdisciplinary History* 2 (1971–1972): 391–418.

Roelker, Nancy. "The Role of French Noblewomen in the Reformation." *Archiv für Reformationsgeschichte* 63 (1972): 168–95.

Root, Hilton. *The Fountain of Privilege: Political Foundations of Markets in Old Regime France and England*. Berkeley, CA: University of California, 1994.

Rosengarten, Dale. *Row upon Row: Sea Grass Baskets of the South Carolina Lowcountry*. Columbia, SC: University of South Carolina, 1986.

Roth, Rodris. "Tea Drinking in Eighteenth-Century America," in *Material Life in America, 1600–1860*, ed. Robert Blair St. George. Boston: Northeastern University Press, 1988, pp. 439–62.

Ryan, Mary P. *Women in Public: Between Banners and Ballots, 1825–1990*. Baltimore, MD: Johns Hopkins University Press, 1990.

Rydell, Robert W. "The Culture of Imperial Abundance: World's Fairs in the Making of American Culture," in *Consuming Visions: Accumulation and Display of Goods in America, 1880–1920*, ed. Simon J. Bronner. New York: W. W. Norton, 1989, pp. 191–204.

Sabatier, Gérard. *Versailles ou la figure du roi*. Paris: Albin Michel, 1999.

Sahlins, Peter. *Unnaturally French: Foreign Citizens in the Old Regime and After.* Ithaca, NY: Cornell University Press, 2004.

St. George, Robert Blair. *Conversing by Signs: Poetics of Implication in Colonial New England Culture*. Chapel Hill, NC: University of North Carolina Press, 1998.

Samford, Patricia. "The Archaeology of African-American Slavery and Material Culture." *The William and Mary Quarterly* 53, No. 1 (Jan. 1996): 87–114.

Schama, Simon. *The Embarrassment of Riches: An Interpretation of Dutch Culture in the Golden Age.* Berkeley: University of California Press, 1988.

Scott, Anne Firor. *Natural Allies: Women's Associations in American History.* Urbana, IL: University of Illinois Press, 1991.

Scott, Joan Wallach. *Only Paradoxes to Offer: French Feminists and the Rights of Man.* Cambridge, MA: Harvard University Press, 1996.

Scott, Katie. *The Rococo Interior: Decoration and Social Spaces in Early Eighteenth-century Paris.* New Haven: Yale University Press, 1995.

Sear, Louis Martin. "The Puritan and His Indian Ward." *American Journal of Sociology* 22 (July 1916): 80–93.

Sewell, William H. "The Concept(s) of Culture," in *Beyond the Cultural Turn: New Directions in the Study of Society and Culture.* Berkeley, CA: University of California Press, 1999, pp. 35–61.

Shammas, Carole. *The Pre-Industrial Consumer in England and America.* Oxford: Oxford University Press, 1991.

Shammas, Carole. "Changes in English and Anglo-American Consumption from 1550 to 1800," in *Consumption and the World of Goods*, ed. John Brewer and Roy Porter. London: Routledge, 1993, pp. 177–205.

Sharpe, Kevin. "'An Image Doting Rabble': The Failure of Republican Culture in Seventeenth-Century England," in *Refiguring Revolutions*, ed. Kevin Sharpe. Berkeley, CA: University of California Press, 1998, pp. 25–6.

Sharpe, Kevin and Zwicker, Steven (eds). *Refiguring Revolutions: Aesthetics and Politics from the English Revolution to the Romantic Revolution.* Berkeley, CA and Los Angeles: University of California Press, 1998.

Shaw, Peter. *American Patriots and the Rituals of Revolution.* Cambridge, MA: Harvard University Press, 1981.

Sherwood, Roy. *The Court of Oliver Cromwell.* London: Croom Helm, 1977.

Sherwood, Roy. *Oliver Cromwell: King in All But Name, 1653–1658.* New York: St. Martin's 1997.

Shovlin, John. *The Political Economy of Virtue: Luxury, Patriotism, and the Origins of the French Revolution.* Ithaca, NY: Cornell University Press, 2006.

Shute, Michael N. "Furniture, the American Revolution and the Modern Antique," in *American Material Culture: The Shape of Things Around Us*, ed. Edith Mayo. Bowling Green, OH: Bowling Green State University Press, 1984, pp. 182–207.

Siebert, Frederick. *Freedom of the Press in England 1476–1776.* Urbana, IL: University of Illinois Press, 1952.

Slotkin, Richard. *Regeneration through Violence: The Mythology of the American Frontier, 1600–1800.* Middletown, CT: Wesleyan University Press, 1973.

Smith, Bonnie G. *Ladies of the Leisure Class: The Bourgeoises of Northern France in the Nineteenth Century.* Princeton, NJ: Princeton University Press, 1981.

Smith, David L. "The Impact on Government," in *The Impact of the English Civil War*, ed. John Morrill. London: Collins and Brown, 1991, pp. 32–49.

Smith, Jay M. *The Culture of Merit: Nobility, Royal Service and the Making of Absolute Monarchy in France*. Ann Arbor, MI: University of Michigan Press, 1996.

Smith, Jay M. (ed.). *The French Nobility in the Eighteenth Century: Reassessments and Reinterpretations*. University Park, PA: Pennsylvania State University Press, 2006.

Smith, Mark M. "Culture, Commerce, and Calendar Reform in Colonial America." *The William and Mary Quarterly* 55, No. 4 (Oct. 1998): 557–84.

Smuts, R. Malcolm. *Court Culture and the Origins of a Royalist Tradition in Early Stuart England*. Philadelphia: University of Pennsylvania Press, 1987.

Smuts, R. Malcolm. "The Court and Its Neighborhood: Royal Policy and Urban Growth in the Early Stuart West End." *Journal of British Studies* 30 (April 1991): 117–49.

Smuts, R. Malcolm. "Art and the Material Culture of Majesty in Early Stuart England," in *The Stuart Court and Europe*, ed. R. Malcolm Smuts. New York: Cambridge University Press, 1996, pp. 86–112.

Sobel, Mechal. *The World They Made Together: Black and White Values in Eighteenth-Century Virginia*. Princeton, NJ: Princeton University Press, 1987.

Sobel, Mechal. *Teach Me Dreams: The Search for Self in the Revolutionary Era*. Princeton, NJ: Princeton University Press, 2000.

Soboul, Albert. *Les Sans-culottes parisiens en l'an II*. Paris: Librairie Clavreuil, 1958.

Special issue of *Annales historiques de la Révolution française* 72, No. 4 (2000).

Spraggon, Julie. *Puritan Iconoclasm during the English Civil War*. Rochester, NY: Boydell Press, 2003.

Spufford, Margaret. *The Great Reclothing of Rural England: Petty Chapmen and their Wares in Seventeenth-Century England*. London: Hambledon Press, 1984.

Spurr, John. *England in the 1670s: This Masquerading Age*. Oxford: Blackwell, 2000.

Starke, Barbara M., *et al*. *African American Dress and Adornment: A Cultural Perspective*. Dubuque, IA: Kendall Hunt, 1990.

Starkey, David. "Representation through Intimacy," in *Symbols and Sentiments: Cross-cultural Studies in Symbolism*, Joan Lewis, ed. London: Academic Press, 1977.

Stearns, Peter N. "Stages of Consumerism: Recent Work on the Issues of Periodization." *Journal of Modern History* 69 (March 1997): 102–17.

Stites, Richard. *Revolutionary Dreams: Utopian Vision and Experimental Life in the Russian Revolution*. Oxford: Oxford University Press, 1989.

Stites, Richard. "Russian Revolutionary Culture: Its Place in the History of Cultural Revolutions," in *Culture and Revolution*, ed. Paul Dukes and John Dunkley. London: Pinter Publishers, 1990, pp. 132–41.

Stone, Lawrence. "The Bourgeois Revolution of Seventeenth-Century England Revisited." *Past and Present* 109 (Nov. 1985): 44–54.

Stoyle, Mark. *Soldiers and Strangers: An Ethnic History of the English Civil War.* New Haven, CT and London: Yale University Press, 2005.

Strong, Roy C. *The Renaissance Garden in England.* London: Thames and Hudson, 1979.

Strong, Roy C. *Tudor and Stuart Monarchy: Painting, Pageantry, Iconography*, Vol. 3. Woodbridge and Rochester, NY: Boydell Press, 1997.

Strong, Roy C. *Coronation: A History of Kingship and the English Monarchy.* London: HarperCollins, 2005.

Sussman, Charlotte. "Lismahago's Captivity: Transculturation in *Humphrey Clinker*," *ELH* 61, No. 3 (Autumn 1994): 597–618.

Szambien, Werner. *Les Projets de l'an II: Concours d'Architecture de la période révolutionnaire.* Paris: Ecole nationale supérieure des beaux-arts, 1986.

Tawney, R. H. "The Rise of the Gentry." *Economic History Review* 11, No. 1 (1941): 1–38.

Tayacke, Nicolas. *Anti-Calvinists: The Rise of English Arminianism 1590–1640.* Oxford: Clarendon Press, 1987.

Taylor, George. "Non-Capitalist Wealth and the Origins of the French Revolution." *American Historical Review* 72 (1967): 469–96.

Thirsk, Joan. *Economic Policy and Projects: The Development of a Consumer Society in Early Modern England.* Oxford: Clarendon Press, 1978.

Thomas, Keith. "Women and the Civil War Sects," in *Crisis in Europe, 1560–1660*, ed. Trevor Aston. New York: Basic Books, 1965, pp. 332–57.

Thomas, Richard. *The Commodity Culture of Victorian England: Advertising and Spectacle, 1851–1914.* Stanford, CA: Stanford University Press, 1980.

Thurley, Simon. *Whitehall Palace: An Architectural History of the Royal Apartments, 1240–1698.* New Haven, CT: Yale University Press, 1999.

Tiersten, Lisa. *Marianne in the Market: Envisioning Consumer Society in fin-de-siècle France.* Berkeley, CA: University of California Press, 2001.

Tisseron, Serge. *Comment l'esprit vient aux objets.* Paris: Aubier, 1999.

Underdown, David. "Puritanism, Revolution, and Christopher Hill." *The History Teacher* 22, No. 1 (1988): 67–75.

Ulrich, Laurel Thatcher. *Good Wives: Image and Reality in the Lives of Women in Northern New England, 1650–1750.* New York: Knopf, 1982.

Ulrich, Laurel Thatcher. *The Age of Homespun: Objects and Stories in the Creation of an American Myth.* New York: Knopf, 2001.

Vaughn, Hart. "On Inigo Jones and the Stuart Legal Body: Justice and Equity … and Proportions Appertaining," in *Body and Building: Essays on the Changing Relation of Body and Architecture*, ed. George Dodds and Robert Tavernor. Cambridge, MA: MIT Press, 2002, pp. 138–49.

Vaulchier, Claudine de. "Iconographie des décors révolutionnaires," in *Les architectes de la liberté, 1789–1799*. Paris: Ecole nationale supérieure des Beaux Arts, 1989.

Vincent, Sue. *Dressing the Elite: Clothes in Early Modern England*. Oxford: Berg, 2003.

Vlach, John Michael. "Afro-American Domestic Artifacts in Eighteenth-Century Virginia." *Material Culture* 19 (1987): 3–23.

Vlach, John Michael. *The Afro-American Tradition in Decorative Design*. Athens, GA: University of Georgia Press, 1990.

Vlach, John. *Back of the Big House: The Architecture of Plantation Slavery*. Chapel Hill, NC: University of North Carolina Press, 1993.

Vonglis, Bernard. *L'Etat c'était bien lui: essai sur la monarchie absolue*. Paris: Cujas, 1997.

Wahrman, Dror and Jones, Colin (eds). *The Age of Cultural Revolutions: Britain and France, 1750–1820*. Berkeley, CA: University of California Press, 2002.

Waldstreicher, David. *In the Midst of Perpetual Fetes: The Making of American Nationalism, 1776–1820*. Chapel Hill, NC: University of North Carolina Press, 1997.

Walter, John. "The Impact on Society: A World Turned Upside Down?" in *The Impact of the English Civil War*, ed. John Morrill. London: Collins and Brown, 1991, pp. 104–22.

Walton, Guy. *Louis XIV's Versailles*. Chicago: University of Chicago Press, 1986.

Walzer, Michael. *The Revolution of the Saints: A Study in the Origins of Radical Politics*. New York: Atheneum, 1965.

Warnke, Martin. *The Court Artist: On the Ancestry of the Modern Artist*, trans. David McLintock. Cambridge: Cambridge University Press, 1993.

Watt, Tessa. *Cheap Print and Popular Piety 1550–1640*. Cambridge: Cambridge University Press, 1991.

Weber, Caroline. *Queen of Fashion: What Marie Antoinette Wore to the Revolution*. New York: H. Holt, 2006.

Weber, William. "*La musique ancienne* in the Waning of the Ancien Régime." *Journal of Modern History* 56, No. 1 (March 1984): 58–88.

Weber, William. La musique ancienne *in the Waning of the Ancien Regime*. Chicago: University of Chicago Press, 1984.

Werner, Michael and Zimmermann, Bénédicte. "Penser l'histoire croisée: entre empirie et réflexivité." *Annales: HSS* 1 (Jan–Feb 2003): 7–36.

Wheaton, Thomas R. *et al. Yaughan and Curriboo Plantations: Studies in Afro-American Archaeology*. Atlanta, GA: National Park Service, 1983.

White, Shane. "A Question of Style: Blacks in and around New York City in the Late 18th Century." *The Journal of American Folklore* 102, No. 403 (Jan.–Mar. 1989): 23–44.

White, Shane. *Somewhat More Independent: The End of Slavery in New York City, 1770–1810*. Athens, GA: University of Georgia Press, 1991.

Wiesner, Mary. "Beyond Women and The Family: Towards a Gender Analysis of the Reformation." *Sixteenth Century Journal* 18, No. 3 (1987): 311–21.

Wilson, Mary Tolford. "Amelia Simmons Fills a Need: American Cookery, 1796." *The William and Mary Quarterly* 14, No. 1 (Jan. 1957): 16–30.

Wiseman, Susan. *Drama and Politics in the English Civil War*. Cambridge: Cambridge University Press, 1998.

Withington, Ann Fairfax. *Toward a More Perfect Union: Virtue and the Formation of American Republics*. New York: Oxford University Press, 1991, pp. 285–316.

Withington, Ann Fairfax. "Manufacturing and Selling the American Revolution," in *Everyday Life in the Early Republic*, ed. Catherine Hutchins. Winterthur, DE: H. F. du Pont Winterthur Museum, 1994.

Wood, Gordon S. *The Creation of the American Republic, 1776–1787*. Chapel Hill, NC: University of North Carolina Press, 1969.

Wood, Peter H. "The Changing Population of the Colonial South: An Overview by Race and Region 1685–1790," in *Powhatan's Mantle: Indians in the Colonial Southeast*, ed. Peter H. Wood *et al*. Lincoln, NB: University of Nebraska Press, 1989, pp. 61–6.

Woodward, Jennifer. *The Theater of Death: The Ritual Management of Royal Funerals in Renaissance England, 1570–1625*. Rochester, NY: Boydell Press, 1997.

Wrigley, Richard. *The Politics of Appearances: Representations of Dress in Revolutionary France*. Oxford: Berg, 2002.

Yungblut, Laura Hunt. *Strangers Settled Here Amongst Us – Policies, Perceptions and the Presence of Aliens in Elizabethan England*. London: Routledge, 1996.

Zakim, Michael. *Ready-made Democracy: A History of Dress in the Early American Republic, 1760–1860*. Chicago: University of Chicago Press, 2003.

Zaller, Robert. "Breaking the Vessels: The Desacralization of the Monarchy in Early Modern England." *Sixteenth Century Journal* 29, No. 3 (1998): 757–78.

Zaret, David. *Origins of Democratic Culture: Printing, Petitions and the Public Sphere in Seventeenth-century England*. Princeton, NJ: Princeton University Press, 2000.

Zink, Clifford. "Dutch Framed Houses in New York and New Jersey." *Winterthur Portfolio* 22 (1987): 265–94.

Zupko, Ronald Edward. *British Weights & Measures: A History from Antiquity to 17th Century*. Madison, WI: University of Wisconsin Press, 1977.

Zupko, Ronald Edward. *French Weights and Measures before the Revolution: A Dictionary of Provincial and Local Units*. Bloomington, IN: Indiana University Press, 1978.

Index

Note: *Italicized* page numbers indicate illustrations